Navigating *through* Discrete Mathematics *in* Grades 6–12

Eric W. Hart
Margaret J. Kenney
Valerie A. DeBellis
Joseph G. Rosenstein

Eric W. Hart
Volume Editor

Peggy A. House
Navigations Series Editor

NATIONAL COUNCIL OF
TEACHERS OF MATHEMATICS

Copyright © 2008 by
The National Council of Teachers of Mathematics, Inc.
1906 Association Drive, Reston, VA 20191-1502
(703) 620-9840; (800) 235-7566; www.nctm.org

Library of Congress Cataloging-in-Publication Data

Navigating through discrete mathematics in grades 6–12 / Eric W. Hart ... [et al.],
editors ; Peggy A. House, Navigations series editor.
    p. cm. — (Navigations series)
  Includes bibliographical references.
  ISBN 978-0-87353-586-1
1. Mathematics—Study and teaching (Middle school) 2. Mathematics—
Study and teaching (Secondary) I. Hart, Eric W.
QA11.2.N38 2007
510.71'2—dc22

                                2007044153

The National Council of Teachers of Mathematics is a public voice of mathematics education, providing vision, leadership, and professional development to support teachers in ensuring equitable mathematics learning of the highest quality for all students.

Printed in the United States of America

NAVIGATIONS **S**ERIES

GRADES 6–12

TABLE OF CONTENTS

CONTENTS OF THE CD-ROM

Introduction

Recommendations for Discrete Mathematics, Pre-K–Grade 12

Applets

Coloring Pascal's Triangle
Tower of Hanoi
Trout Pond

Blackline Masters and Templates

All blackline titles listed above, plus the following:
Geodot Paper
Centimeter Grid Paper

Readings from Publications of the National Council of Teachers of Mathematics

Figurate Numbers
Stanley J. Bezuszka, S.J.
NCTM Student Math Notes

Massive Graphs, Power Laws, and the World Wide Web
L. Charles Biehl
Mathematics Teacher

Benoit Mandelbrot: The Euclid of Fractal Geometry
Dane R. Camp
Mathematics Teacher

A Bibliography of Print Resources for Discrete Mathematics

About This Book

Navigating through Discrete Mathematics in Grades 6–12 and the companion book for prekindergarten through grade 5 (DeBellis et al. forthcoming) elaborate on the vision of discrete mathematics presented in NCTM's *Principles and Standards for School Mathematics* (NCTM 2000). These books answer an important question: What discrete mathematical content and processes should students understand and apply in prekindergarten through twelfth grade? The intended audience is primarily classroom teachers but also includes curriculum coordinators, supervisors, mathematics educators at the college level, and others who are interested in the school mathematics curriculum. An important feature of the books is the inclusion of many rich student activities that are ready for use in the classroom.

Principles and Standards for School Mathematics integrates recommendations for discrete mathematics throughout the Content and Process Standards at all grade levels. In keeping with this integration—and to help navigate through and explain the recommendations—we present specific grade-level guidelines with examples. These guidelines outline a scope and sequence for the study of discrete mathematics in prekindergarten through grade 12, while furnishing a framework for integrating discrete mathematics into a Standards-based curriculum.

The first question for many readers is likely to be a very basic one: What is discrete mathematics? The introduction, which presents an overview of discrete mathematics in prekindergarten through grade 12, answers this question. The chapters of the book then focus on implementing these ideas in grades 6–12. *Principles and Standards* recommends that the curriculum for grades 6–12 include three main discrete mathematics topics: systematic listing and counting, vertex-edge graphs, and iteration and recursion. This volume includes two chapters on each of these topics, one for middle school and one for high school.

Each chapter presents a comprehensive set of grade-level recommendations, along with several classroom-ready student activities. Although each recommendation is discussed at least briefly, it is not possible to address all of them fully in the activities or text of the book. Thus, the specific goals for the activities are less comprehensive than the full set of recommendations. References given throughout provide additional information on all recommendations.

Since discrete mathematics content may not be familiar to all readers, the discussion of each activity includes a section that briefly summarizes the relevant mathematics. To accommodate readers who may focus on chapters at one grade level, the mathematical summaries in one chapter may slightly overlap those in others.

The activity sheets for students appear as reproducible blackline masters in the appendix, along with solutions to the problems. Readers will find that working through an activity before reading the discussion and solutions is helpful. The students should use copies of the activity pages. However, the pages do not allow enough space for complete solutions, so students will need additional sheets of paper to record their work.

Many of the activities that this book presents for grades 6–8 also support core topics suggested for emphasis in NCTM's Curriculum Focal Points for Prekindergarten through Grade 8 Mathematics: A Quest for Coherence *(2006). This publication specifies by grade level essential content and processes that* Principles and Standards for School Mathematics *(NCTM 2000) discusses in depth by grade band.*

Key to Icons

Blackline Master

CD-ROM

Principles and Standards

Three different icons appear in the book, as shown in the key. One signals the activity pages and indicates their locations in the appendix, another points readers to supplementary materials on the CD-ROM that accompanies the book, and a third alerts readers to references to *Principles and Standards for School Mathematics*.

The CD-ROM that accompanies the book includes all blackline masters, selected readings for the professional development of teachers, and special computer applets that complement ideas in the text and activities. Teachers can allow students to use the applets in conjunction with particular activities or apart from them, to extend or deepen understanding.

Margin notes throughout the book highlight teaching tips, additional references, suggestions about related materials on the CD-ROM, and pertinent references to *Principles and Standards for School Mathematics.*

The organization of the companion book, *Navigating through Discrete Mathematics in Prekindergarten–Grade 5*, parallels that of this volume. Although all four authors planned and reviewed drafts of both books, Hart and Kenney wrote the materials for grades 6–12, and DeBellis and Rosenstein wrote the materials for pre-K–grade 5. Hart also served as organizer and coordinator for the whole project. We wish to thank our reviewers—Jim Sandefur, Peggy House, and Dave Thronson—who provided many thoughtful and useful comments, and we also thank the always professional, friendly, and efficient publication staff at NCTM.

NAVIGATING *through* DISCRETE MATHEMATICS

Introduction

"Discrete mathematics should be an integral part of the school mathematics curriculum." (NCTM 2000, p. 31)

Discrete mathematics is an important branch of contemporary mathematics that is widely used in business and industry. Elements of discrete mathematics have been around as long as mathematics itself. However, discrete mathematics emerged as a distinct branch of mathematics only in the middle of the twentieth century, when it began expanding rapidly, primarily because of the computer revolution, but also because of the need for mathematical techniques to help plan and implement such monumental logistical projects as landing a man on the moon. Discrete mathematics has grown to be even more important and pervasive today.

Principles and Standards for School Mathematics (NCTM 2000) recommends that discrete mathematics be "an integral part of the school mathematics curriculum" (p. 31). In the area of discrete mathematics, *Principles and Standards* features two major changes from NCTM's 1989 *Curriculum and Evaluation Standards for School Mathematics*, which included a Discrete Mathematics Standard for grades 9–12. First, *Principles and Standards* recommends including discrete mathematics in the curriculum for all grades, from prekindergarten through grade 12. Second, *Principles and Standards* does not include a separate standard for discrete mathematics. Rather, it recommends that the main topics of discrete mathematics be distributed across all the Standards, since "these topics naturally occur throughout the other strands of mathematics" (p. 31).

The goal of this book is to elaborate on the vision of discrete mathematics presented in *Principles and Standards*. In this introduction, we give an overview of discrete mathematics and guidelines for integrating discrete mathematics topics into a curriculum that is based on the NCTM Standards. Because discrete mathematics may be unfamiliar to many readers, we begin by considering a fundamental question: What is discrete mathematics?

What Is Discrete Mathematics?

Descriptions of discrete mathematics often list the topics that it includes, such as vertex-edge graphs, systematic counting, and iteration and recursion. Other topics relevant to the school curriculum include matrices, voting methods, fair division, cryptography, coding theory, and game theory. In general, discrete mathematics deals with finite processes and whole-number phenomena. Sometimes described as the mathematical foundation of computer science, discrete mathematics has even broader application, since the social, management, and natural sciences also use it. Discrete mathematics contrasts with continuous mathematics, such as the mathematics underlying most of calculus. However, this association gives the impression that discrete mathematics is only for advanced high school students, although elements of discrete mathematics are actually accessible and important for all students in all grades.

Broad definitions of discrete mathematics identify it as "the mathematics of decision making for finite settings" (NCTM 1990, p. 1) and the mathematics for optimizing finite systems. Common themes in discrete mathematics include the following:

- Discrete mathematical modeling—using discrete mathematical tools such as vertex-edge graphs and recursion to represent and solve problems
- Algorithmic problem solving—designing, using, and analyzing step-by-step procedures to solve problems
- Optimization—finding the best solution

For further discussion of discrete mathematical modeling and algorithmic problem solving, see Hart (1997, 1998 [available on the CD-ROM]).

Kenney (1991), Maurer (1997), and Rosenstein (2007) offer more answers to the question, What is discrete mathematics?

Which Discrete Mathematics Topics Does *Principles and Standards* Include?

Principles and Standards integrates three important topics of discrete mathematics: combinatorics, iteration and recursion, and vertex-edge graphs.

- Combinatorics is the mathematics of systematic listing and counting. It facilitates solving problems such as determining the number of different orders for picking up three friends or counting the number of different computer passwords that are possible with five letters and two numbers.
- Iteration and recursion can be used to represent and solve problems related to sequential step-by-step change, such as the growth of a population or an amount of money from year to year. To iterate

means to repeat, so iteration involves repeating a procedure, process, or rule over and over. Recursion is the method of describing the current step of a process in terms of the previous steps.

- Vertex-edge graphs, like the one pictured in figure 0.1, consist of points (called *vertices*) and line segments or arcs (called *edges*) that connect some of the points. Such graphs provide models for, and lead to solutions of, problems about paths, networks, and relationships among a finite number of elements.

Principles and Standards focuses on integrating discrete mathematics with other areas of the mathematics curriculum. For example, vertex-edge graphs are an important part of geometry. Recursion occurs in all the content strands but is particularly instrumental in algebra. Concepts of systematic listing and counting appear throughout the curriculum. Matrices, which many consider to be part of discrete mathematics, are addressed throughout *Principles and Standards*.

Other discrete mathematics topics that may receive attention in the school curriculum include the mathematics of information processing (such as error-correcting codes and cryptography) and the mathematics of democratic and social decision making (for example, voting methods, apportionment, fair division, and game theory). This book focuses on the three discrete mathematics topics that *Principles and Standards* emphasizes (p. 31): combinatorics, iteration and recursion, and vertex-edge graphs. First, however, let's consider why the school curriculum should include discrete mathematics.

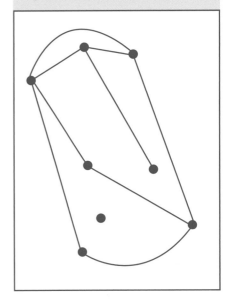

Fig. **0.1.** A vertex-edge graph

Why Should the School Curriculum Include Discrete Mathematics?

Instructional time is valuable, and the mathematics curriculum has limited space, so educators must make careful choices about what to include in the curriculum. *Principles and Standards* recommends that discrete mathematics be an integral part of the school mathematics curriculum because it is useful, contemporary, and pedagogically powerful, in addition to being a substantial and active field of mathematics.

Discrete Mathematics Is Useful Mathematics

Discrete mathematics has many uses in business, industry, and daily life. Rosenstein, Franzblau, and Roberts (1997) enumerate a variety of applications, asserting that discrete mathematics topics are "used by decision-makers in business and government; by workers in such fields as telecommunications and computing that depend upon information transmission; and by those in many rapidly changing professions involving health care, biology, chemistry, automated manufacturing, transportation, etc. Increasingly, discrete mathematics is the language of a large body of science and underlies decisions that individuals will have to make in their own lives, in their professions, and as citizens" (p. xiii–xiv).

 "As an active branch of contemporary mathematics that is widely used in business and industry, discrete mathematics should be an integral part of the school mathematics curriculum, and these topics naturally occur throughout the other strands of mathematics." NCTM 2000, p. 31)

Discrete Mathematics Is Contemporary Mathematics

Discrete mathematics is a rapidly expanding field of mathematics. It is particularly relevant in today's digital information age. For example, it underlies many aspects of the Internet, from secure encryption of consumers' credit card numbers when they make purchases online to effective compression and decompression of the music, photos, and videos that users download. Moreover, many solved and unsolved problems at the frontiers of discrete mathematics are not only relevant to today's students but also accessible to them. Students can understand the problems and some partial solutions, such as the problem of finding the shortest circuit through a network (the traveling salesman problem) or finding a more secure method for transmitting data between computers. Furthermore, since discrete mathematics has strong links to technology and today's schoolchildren are tomorrow's technological workforce, it is important for their futures, as well as for the future of our nation, that they become more familiar with the topics of discrete mathematics.

Discrete Mathematics Is Pedagogically Powerful

Not only does discrete mathematics include important mathematical content, but it is also a powerful vehicle for teaching and learning mathematical processes and engaging students in doing mathematics. Because discrete mathematics is useful and contemporary, it often motivates and interests students. Discrete mathematics topics can engage and provide success for students who have previously been unsuccessful or alienated from mathematics. Many of these topics are accessible to students in all grades, whether they are engaged in sorting different types of buttons in the early grades, counting different flag patterns in middle school, or using vertex-edge graphs and the critical path method to plan a dance in high school.

Furthermore, discrete mathematics is an effective context for addressing NCTM's Process Standards. In working with discrete mathematics, students strengthen their skills in reasoning, proof, problem solving, communication, connections, and representation in many ways. For example, they reason about paths in the visual context of vertex-edge graphs and justify whether certain circuits must exist. They argue about why a recursive formula is better than an explicit formula, or vice versa, in a particular situation. They learn new methods of proof, including proof by mathematical induction. They develop new types of reasoning, such as combinatorial reasoning, which they can use to reason about the number of different possibilities that can arise in counting situations (for example, the number of different pizzas that are possible when they choose two out of five toppings). Students exercise their problem-solving skills when they solve problems in a variety of accessible yet challenging settings. They develop new problem-solving strategies, such as algorithmic problem solving, and new ways of thinking, such as recursive thinking. Students acquire and apply new tools—including recursive formulas and vertex-edge graphs—for representing problems. Thus, students learn important mathematical content and powerful mathematical processes while they study discrete mathematics.

Discrete mathematics provides an effective context for developing the skills addressed in the Process Standards.

Recent History and Resources

Discrete mathematics surfaced as a curricular issue in the 1980s, when the Mathematical Association of America (MAA) began debating the need for more instruction in discrete mathematics during the first two years of college. This debate culminated in a report released in 1986 (MAA 1986). Although the recommendations of this report were not implemented in full, educators instituted more discrete mathematics courses, which continue to be taught in colleges around the world. In particular, discrete mathematics is now a standard course in collegiate computer science programs and a required course for many mathematics majors.

This discussion about discrete mathematics in college made its way down to the high school level a few years later, when the National Council of Teachers of Mathematics recommended a Discrete Mathematics Standard for grades 9–12 in its seminal Standards publication, *Curriculum and Evaluation Standards for School Mathematics* (NCTM 1989). As a result of these Standards, discrete mathematics expanded rapidly in the school curriculum. The National Science Foundation (NSF) funded teacher-enhancement projects to help implement the Discrete Mathematics Standard.

High schools began offering courses in discrete mathematics, and many states added discrete mathematics to their state frameworks. Discrete mathematics courses play an increasingly important role in the high school curriculum, providing essential mathematics for the technology- and information-intensive twenty-first century, particularly since more students are required to take more mathematics, and the traditional calculus-preparatory high school curriculum does not serve all students well.

Several NSF-funded Standards-based curriculum development projects have integrated discrete mathematics into new high school textbook series. These series include *Core-Plus Mathematics* (Hirsch et al. 2008), *Interactive Mathematics Program* (Alper et al. 2003), *Mathematics: Modeling Our World* (COMAP 1999), and *SIMMS Integrated Mathematics* (SIMMS 2006). In addition, several new textbooks are available for high school courses in discrete mathematics (see COMAP [2006], Crisler and Froelich [2006], and Tannenbaum [2007], for example). Some teacher education textbooks address discrete mathematics, including *Making Math Engaging: Discrete Mathematics for K–8 Teachers* (DeBellis and Rosenstein 2008). Finally, many articles about discrete mathematics and activities for teaching it are available.

Thus far, we have considered what discrete mathematics is, along with some history and resources, and we have described why discrete mathematics should be part of the curriculum. In the remainder of this introduction, we present an overview across the grades of the three main topics: combinatorics (systematic listing and counting), vertex-edge graphs, and iteration and recursion. In developing these topics across the grade levels, we have in mind two important progressions in the prekindergarten–grade 12 curriculum—from concrete to abstract and from informal to more formal reasoning.

The chapters that follow address these topics one at a time, for grades 6–8 and 9–12 in the present book, and for prekindergarten

Eric W. Hart and Harold L. Schoen worked on NSF-funded teacher enhancement projects from 1987 to 1994, Margaret J. Kenney's projects extended from 1992 to 1997, the work of Joseph G. Rosenstein and Valerie A. DeBellis extended from 1990 until 2005, and James T. Sandefur's projects extended from 1992 to 1995.

 "A Bibliography of Print Resources for Discrete Mathematics" on the accompanying CD-ROM indicates the topics and grade bands covered by the identified resources.

through grade 2 and grades 3–5 in the companion book, *Navigating through Discrete Mathematics in Prekindergarten–Grade 5* (DeBellis et al. forthcoming). In fact, we can use discrete mathematics to reason that since each book includes three topics and two grade bands, each book must include 3 × 2, or 6, chapters—which brings us to the first topic, systematic listing and counting.

Overview of Systematic Listing and Counting in Prekindergarten–Grade 12

Students at all grade levels should be able to solve counting problems. Examples of appropriate problems at different levels follow:

- In elementary school: "How many different outfits can someone put together with three shirts and two pairs of shorts?"

- In middle school: "How many different four-block towers can a person build with red and blue blocks?"

- In high school: "What is the number of possible computer passwords that use six letters and three digits?"

The key to answering such questions is to develop strategies for listing and counting, in a systematic manner, all the ways of completing the task. As students advance through the grade levels, the tasks change—the objects to be counted become abstract as well as concrete, the numbers of objects increase, the representations become more algebraic, and the reasoning becomes more formal, culminating in proof—but the common thread is that the students need to do the counting systematically. If students have enough opportunities to explore counting problems at all grade levels, then these transitions will be smooth, and they will acquire a deep understanding. In addition, knowledge of the counting strategies helps lay the necessary foundation for understanding ideas of probability.

All the NCTM Standards integrate concepts and methods of systematic listing and counting. In support of this integration, the following recommendations suggest how to develop systematic listing and counting throughout the grades.

Knowledge of counting strategies helps lay a foundation for understanding ideas of probability.

Recommendations for Systematic Listing and Counting in Prekindergarten–Grade 12

In prekindergarten–grade 2, all students should—

- sort, organize, and count small numbers of objects;

- informally use the addition principle of counting;

- list all possibilities in counting situations;

- sort, organize, and count objects by using Venn diagrams.

In grades 3–5, all students should—

- represent, analyze, and solve a variety of counting problems by using arrays, systematic lists, tree diagrams, and Venn diagrams;
- use and explain the addition principle of counting;
- informally use the multiplication principle of counting;
- understand and describe relationships among arrays, systematic lists, tree diagrams, and the multiplication principle of counting.

In grades 6–8, all students should—

- represent, analyze, and solve counting problems that do or do not involve ordering and that do or do not involve repetition;
- understand and apply the addition and multiplication principles of counting and represent these principles with algebra, including factorial notation;
- solve counting problems by using Venn diagrams and use algebra to represent the relationships shown by a Venn diagram;
- construct and describe patterns in Pascal's triangle;
- implicitly use the pigeonhole principle and the inclusion-exclusion principle.

In grades 9–12, all students should—

- understand and apply permutations and combinations;
- use reasoning and formulas to solve counting problems in which repetition is or is not allowed and ordering does or does not matter;
- understand, apply, and describe relationships among the binomial theorem, Pascal's triangle, and combinations;
- apply counting methods to probabilistic situations involving equally likely outcomes;
- use combinatorial reasoning to construct proofs as well as solve a variety of problems.

Overview of Vertex-Edge Graphs in Prekindergarten–Grade 12

Another discrete mathematics topic that *Principles and Standards* recommends for study is vertex-edge graphs. Vertex-edge graphs are mathematical models that consist of points (*vertices*), with curves or line segments (*edges*) connecting some of the points (see fig. 0.1 on p. 3). Such diagrams aid in solving problems related to paths, circuits, and networks. For example, vertex-edge graphs can help in optimizing a telecommunications network, planning the most efficient circuit through cities that a salesperson visits, finding an optimal path for plowing snow from city streets, or determining the shortest route for collecting money from neighborhood ATM machines.

More abstractly, vertex-edge graphs may be useful in analyzing situations that involve relationships among a finite number of objects. Vertices represent the objects, and the relationship among the objects is

Vertex-edge graphs aid in solving problems related to paths, circuits, and networks.

shown by edges that connect some vertices. The relationships may be very concrete, such as airline routes that connect cities in the salesman example; or they may be more abstract, as in vertex-edge graphs depicting conflicts or prerequisites. For instance, a vertex-edge graph facilitates scheduling committee meetings without conflicts (where an edge links two committees that cannot meet at the same time because of a shared member) or finding the earliest completion time for a large construction project consisting of many tasks (where directed edges are used to link a task to its prerequisite tasks).

Graph theory is the formal study of vertex-edge graphs. The term *vertex-edge graph* distinguishes these diagrams from other types of graphs, such as graphs of functions or graphs used in data analysis. Nevertheless, a commonly used term is simply *graphs*. In this volume, we employ both terms, as appropriate.

Graph theory is part of discrete mathematics, but it is also part of geometry, since graphs are geometric diagrams that consist of vertices and edges. Graphs share some characteristics with other geometric objects in school mathematics—for example, both polyhedra and graphs have vertices and edges. But in contrast with most of school geometry—which focuses on the size and shape of figures—size, shape, and position are not essential characteristics of vertex-edge graphs. In vertex-edge graphs, it does not really matter whether the graph is large or small or whether the edges are straight or curved. All that really matters are the number of vertices and edges and how the vertices are connected by edges.

The school mathematics curriculum should include several fundamental graph-theory topics. Table 0.1 summarizes these topics. Chapters 3 and 4 furnish more detail and explanation about vertex-edge graphs.

The analysis and representation of all these problems are concrete at the early grades and become more formal and abstract as a student moves upward through the grades. In this volume, chapters 3 and 4 elaborate on specific recommendations for grades 6–8 and 9–12, respectively. However, a common set of goals exists for all grades. All students should—

- use vertex-edge graphs to model and solve a variety of problems related to paths, circuits, networks, and relationships among a finite number of objects;

- understand and apply properties of graphs;

- devise, describe, and analyze algorithms to help solve problems related to graphs;

- use graphs to understand and solve optimization problems.

Important themes at all grade levels include mathematical modeling, applications, optimization, and algorithmic problem solving. Mathematical modeling is a multistep process of solving a real-world problem by using mathematics to represent the problem, finding a mathematical solution, translating that solution into the context of the original problem, and finally interpreting and judging the reasonableness of the result. Optimization problems are important throughout mathematics and in many applications. The goal is to find the best solution—for example, the shortest path, the most efficient strategy, the fewest

Size, shape, and position are not essential characteristics of vertex-edge graphs.

Table 0.1.
Fundamental Topics in Graph Theory for the School Curriculum

Optimal Paths and Circuits		
Graph Topic	Basic Problem	Sample Application
Euler paths	Find a route through a graph that uses each edge exactly once.	Determine routes for a snowplow.
Hamilton paths	Find a route through a graph that visits each vertex exactly once.	Rank players in a tournament.
Shortest paths	Find a shortest path from here to there.	Measure the degree of influence among people in a group.
Critical paths	Find a longest path or critical path.	Schedule large projects.
Traveling salesman problem (TSP)[1]	Find a circuit through a graph that visits all vertices, that starts and ends at the same location, and that has minimum total weight.	Determine the least expensive circuit through cities that a sales representative visits.

Optimal Spanning Networks		
Graph Topic	Basic Problem	Sample Application
Minimum spanning trees	Find a network within a graph that joins all vertices, has no circuits, and has minimum total weight.	Create an optimal computer or road network.

Optimal Graph Coloring		
Graph Topic	Basic Problem	Sample Application
Vertex coloring	Assign different colors to adjacent vertices, and use the minimum number of colors.	Avoid conflicts—for example, in meeting schedules or in chemical storage.

[1]When this problem was formulated, there were very few female sales representatives, so the historic name for the problem is the *traveling salesman problem*. We will often call the problem the *TSP*.

conflicts, or the earliest completion time. Algorithmic problem solving is the process of devising, using, and analyzing algorithms—step-by-step procedures—for solving problems.

When teaching these vertex-edge graph topics and themes, don't become bogged down in formal definitions and algorithms. Use the visual nature of graphs to make this material engaging, accessible, and fun. In fact, if you present vertex-edge graphs in this lively manner, many students who have previously experienced difficulty or apathy in mathematics may discover that the study of graphs is refreshing and interesting, and they may experience success in learning this topic, thereby gaining confidence about digging into other topics.

The following recommendations suggest how to develop the topic of vertex-edge graphs throughout the grades in a manner that is consistent with *Principles and Standards for School Mathematics*.

Many students who have previously experienced difficulty or apathy in mathematics may discover that the study of graphs is refreshing and interesting.

Recommendations for Vertex-Edge Graphs in Prekindergarten–Grade 12

In prekindergarten–grade 2, all students should—

- build and explore vertex-edge graphs by using concrete materials;
- explore simple properties of graphs, such as the numbers of vertices and edges, neighboring vertices and the degree of a vertex, and whole-number weights on edges;
- use graphs to solve problems related to paths, circuits, and networks in concrete settings;
- color simple pictures by using the minimum number of colors;
- follow and create simple sets of directions related to building and using graphs;
- concretely explore the notion of the shortest path between two vertices.

In grades 3–5, all students should—

- draw vertex-edge graphs to represent concrete situations;
- investigate simple properties of graphs, such as vertex degrees and edge weights, and explore ways to manipulate two graphs physically to determine whether they are the "same";
- use graphs to solve problems related to paths, circuits, and networks in concrete and abstract settings;
- color maps and color the vertices of a graph by using the minimum number of colors as an introduction to the general problem of avoiding conflicts;
- follow, devise, and describe step-by-step procedures related to working with graphs;
- analyze graph-related problems to find the "best" solution.

In grades 6–8, all students should—

- represent concrete and abstract situations by using vertex-edge graphs and represent vertex-edge graphs with adjacency matrices;
- describe and apply properties of graphs, such as vertex degrees, edge weights, directed edges, and isomorphism (whether two graphs are the "same");
- use graphs to solve problems related to paths, circuits, and networks in real-world and abstract settings, including explicit use of Euler paths, Hamilton paths, minimum spanning trees, and shortest paths;
- understand and apply vertex coloring to solve problems related to avoiding conflicts;
- use algorithmic thinking to solve problems related to vertex-edge graphs;
- use vertex-edge graphs to solve optimization problems.

In grades 9–12, all students should—

- understand and apply vertex-edge graph topics, including Euler paths, Hamilton paths, the traveling salesman problem (TSP), minimum spanning trees, critical paths, shortest paths, vertex coloring, and adjacency matrices;

- understand, analyze, and apply vertex-edge graphs to model and solve problems related to paths, circuits, networks, and relationships among a finite number of elements in real-world and abstract settings;
- devise, analyze, and apply algorithms for solving vertex-edge graph problems;
- compare and contrast topics in terms of algorithms, optimization, properties, and types of problems that can be solved;
- extend work with adjacency matrices for graphs through such activities as interpreting row sums and using the nth power of the adjacency matrix to count paths of length n in a graph.

Overview of Iteration and Recursion in Prekindergarten–Grade 12

Iteration and recursion constitute the third main discrete mathematics topic that *Principles and Standards for School Mathematics* recommends. Iteration and recursion are powerful tools for representing and analyzing regular patterns in sequential step-by-step change, such as day-by-day changes in the chlorine concentration in a swimming pool, year-by-year growth of money in a savings account, or the rising cost of postage as the number of ounces in a package increases.

As previously mentioned, to iterate means to repeat, so iteration is the process of repeating the same procedure or computation over and over again, like adding 4 each time to generate the next term in the sequence 4, 8, 12, 16, …. Recursion is the method of describing a given step in a sequential process in terms of the previous step or steps. A recursive formula provides a description of an iterative process. For example, the recursive formula NEXT = NOW + 4, or $s_{n+1} = s_n + 4$, with $n \geq 1$ and $s_1 = 4$, describes the pattern in the preceding sequence. The cluster of symbols s_n, which we read as "s sub n," provides a name for an arbitrary term, the nth term, of sequence s. Thus, s_4 is the fourth term, s_{10} is the tenth term, and so on. The equation $s_{n+1} = s_n + 4$ indicates that the $(n + 1)$st term of the sequence is 4 more than the nth term of the sequence; it has the same meaning as the equation NEXT = NOW + 4.

Iteration and recursion are two sides of the same coin. You can think of recursion as moving backward from the current step to previous steps, whereas iteration moves forward from the initial step. Both iteration and recursion are powerful tools for analyzing regular patterns of sequential change. (Computer science uses precise technical definitions for *iteration* and *recursion*, but this volume uses the terms in the more informal sense just described.)

As in the case of other topics, the students' work with iteration and recursion in the early grades is concrete and exploratory. The representation and analysis become more abstract and formal as the students progress through the grades. For example, in prekindergarten–grade 2, they should explore sequential patterns by using physical, auditory, or pictorial representations, like a pattern of handclaps that increases by two each time. In grades 3–5, students might describe a pattern of

"Mathematics topics such as recursion, iteration, and the comparison of algorithms are receiving more attention in school mathematics because of their increasing relevance and utility in a technological world." (NCTM 2000, p. 16)

adding two each time as NEXT = NOW + 2. In middle school, they can begin using subscripts in a very basic way—for example, to describe the add-2 pattern with the recursive formula $T_{n+1} = T_n + 2$. In high school, students can take a recursive view of functions, recognizing, for example, that NEXT = NOW + 2 can represent a linear function with slope 2.

In middle school and high school, students should also compare and contrast recursive formulas and explicit, or closed-form, formulas. For example, they might describe the sequence 5, 8, 11, 14, 17, … by using the recursive formula $s_{n+1} = s_n + 3$, with the initial term $s_0 = 5$, or by using the explicit formula $s_n = 5 + 3n$, for $n \geq 0$. The recursive formula describes the step-by-step change and gives a formula for the next term, s_{n+1}, in terms of the current term, s_n. In contrast, the explicit formula gives a formula for any term s_n in the sequence, without requiring knowledge of the previous term. Both representations have merit. The recursive formula more clearly shows the pattern of adding 3 each time, but the explicit formula is more efficient for computing a term far along in the sequence, such as s_{50}.

All the NCTM Standards include the ideas of iteration and recursion. In support of this integration, the following recommendations suggest how to develop iteration and recursion across the grades.

Recommendations for Iteration and Recursion in Prekindergarten–Grade 12

In prekindergarten–grade 2, all students should—

- describe, analyze, and create a variety of simple sequential patterns in diverse concrete settings;
- explore sequential patterns by using physical, auditory, and pictorial representations;
- use sequential patterns and iterative procedures to model and solve simple concrete problems;
- explore simple iterative procedures in concrete settings by using technology, such as Logo-like environments and calculators.

In grades 3–5, all students should—

- describe, analyze, and create a variety of sequential patterns, including numeric and geometric patterns, such as repeating and growing patterns, tessellations, and fractal designs;
- represent sequential patterns by using informal notation and terminology for recursion, such as NOW, NEXT, and PREVIOUS;
- use sequential patterns, iterative procedures, and informal notation for recursion to model and solve problems, including those in simple real-world contexts, such as growth situations;
- describe and create simple iterative procedures by using technology, such as Logo-like environments, spreadsheets, and calculators.

In grades 6–8, all students should—

- describe, analyze, and create simple additive and multiplicative sequential patterns (in which a constant is added or multiplied at

Both recursive and explicit representations have merit. A recursive formula gives the next term as a function of the current term. An explicit formula gives any term in the sequence without requiring knowledge of the previous term.

each step), as well as more complicated patterns, such as Pascal's triangle (in which each row of numbers, except the first two rows, is constructed from the previous row) and the Fibonacci sequence 1, 1, 2, 3, 5, 8, … (in which each term, except the first two terms, is the sum of the previous two terms);

- use iterative procedures to generate geometric patterns, including fractals like the Koch snowflake and Sierpinski's triangle;

- use informal notation such as NOW and NEXT, as well as subscript notation, to represent sequential patterns;

- find and interpret explicit (closed-form) and recursive formulas for simple additive and multiplicative sequential patterns and translate between formulas of these types;

- use iterative procedures and simple recursive formulas to model and solve problems, including those in simple real-world settings;

- describe, create, and investigate iterative procedures by using technology, such as Logo-like environments, spreadsheets, calculators, and interactive geometry software.

In grades 9–12, all students should—

- describe, analyze, and create arithmetic and geometric sequences and series;

- create and analyze iterative geometric patterns, including fractals, with an investigation of self-similarity and the areas and perimeters of successive stages;

- represent and analyze functions by using iteration and recursion;

- use subscript and function notation to represent sequential patterns;

- investigate more complicated recursive formulas, such as simple nonlinear formulas; formulas in which the added quantity is a function of n, such as $S(n) = S(n - 1) + (2n + 1)$; and formulas of the form $A(n + 1) = rA(n) + b$, recognizing that the resulting sequence is arithmetic when $r = 1$ and geometric when $b = 0$;

- use finite differences tables to find explicit (closed-form) formulas for sequences that can be represented by polynomial functions;

- understand and carry out proofs by mathematical induction, recognizing a typical situation for induction proofs, in which a recursive relationship is known and used to prove an explicit formula;

- use iteration and recursion to model and solve problems, including those in a variety of real-world contexts, particularly applied growth situations, such as population growth and compound interest;

- describe, analyze, and create iterative procedures and recursive formulas by using technology, such as computer software, graphing calculators, and programming languages.

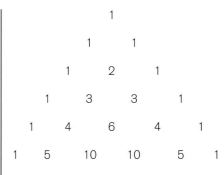

Rows 0–5 of Pascal's triangle

Stage 0   Stage 1   Stage 2

Stages 0–2 of the Koch snowflake

Stage 0   Stage 1   Stage 2

Stages 0–2 of Sierpinski's triangle

Conclusion

This introduction has presented an overview of the three topics of discrete mathematics that *Principles and Standards* recommends for study in prekindergarten–grade 12: combinatorics (systematic listing and counting), vertex-edge graphs, and iteration and recursion. It has also provided specific recommendations for developing these important topics across the grades from prekindergarten–grade 12. The chapters that follow discuss each of these topics as they might be presented in grades 6–8 and grades 9–12. The development of an understanding of discrete mathematics in the earlier years is the focus of the companion volume, *Navigating through Discrete Mathematics in Prekindergarten–Grade 5* (DeBellis et al. forthcoming).

NAVIGATIONS SERIES

GRADES 6–12

NAVIGATING *through* DISCRETE MATHEMATICS

Chapter 1
Systematic Listing and Counting in Grades 6–8

All students in grades 6–8 should—

- represent, analyze, and solve counting problems that do or do not involve ordering and that do or do not involve repetition;

- understand and apply the addition and multiplication principles of counting and represent these principles with algebra, including factorial notation;

- solve counting problems by using Venn diagrams and use algebra to represent the relationships shown by a Venn diagram;

- construct and describe patterns in Pascal's triangle;

- implicitly use the pigeonhole principle and the inclusion-exclusion principle.

The recommendations and activities described in *Navigating through Discrete Mathematics in Prekindergarten–Grade 5* (DeBellis et al. forthcoming) expose children to multiple experiences that use the addition and multiplication counting principles and help build a solid foundation for counting correctly. Children who have met the expectations of that volume will have become familiar with different representations that facilitate counting, including lists, tables, arrays, tree diagrams, and Venn diagrams. In the middle grades, students analyze counting techniques more closely and apply them to a broader range of situations. Before students proceed to more advanced ideas appropriate for the middle grades, they should understand each of the preceding representations.

Students in elementary school should use tree diagrams to solve problems such as finding the number of outfits that they can make from three shirts, two pairs of shorts, and four hats. In grades 6–8, students should learn about permutations by considering counting problems that do not allow repetition and that treat different orderings as different possibilities. They should use tree diagrams and the multiplication principle to solve counting problems. Permutations arise naturally in many situations, including, for example, the case of determining the number of routes that carpooling commuters can take to work. In such a context, teachers can introduce factorial notation to represent the number of routes. Students' understanding of tree diagrams should build from trees that are practical for them to draw (for example, one that represents 4!) to trees that are impractical for them to draw (for example, one that represents 10!).

15

When students are familiar with permutations, teachers should informally introduce them to the idea of combinations. Students should be able to understand the difference between the questions, "How many different slates of ranked officers—for example, president, vice president, and treasurer—can we select from a class of 15 students?" and, "How many different delegations of three students can we select from a class of 15 students?" Teachers do not need to emphasize the technical formulas and the formal terminology that describes the solutions for these problems—namely, *permutations* and *combinations*—at this stage.

Flag Trademarks, the first investigation in chapter 1, develops these ideas. In this investigation, students explore counting problems related to the design of flags. They consider cases in which order is relevant, as well as cases in which it is not relevant. They examine problems that allow repetition as well as problems that do not.

Students in grades 6–8 can revisit topics that they have previously explored, but these explorations should now place additional emphasis on using algebraic representation and reasoning. For example, students should use algebraic notation to represent the addition and multiplication principles of counting and the relationships shown in Venn diagrams, all of which are topics that they should have explored first in elementary school.

Venn diagrams are the primary topic of the second investigation in chapter 1, Counting the Kids. In this investigation, students examine the use of Venn diagrams as tools for solving word problems. Students who have some knowledge of linear equations and systems of linear equations should be able to make connections between the Venn-diagram approach and a solution strategy that uses a linear equation or systems of linear equations. In the students' work with Venn diagrams, they can discover that the inclusion-exclusion principle is a useful counting tool. Middle school students should use the inclusion-exclusion principle informally, and teachers should not require that students memorize the formal statement of the principle.

Another important principle that students use only informally in middle school is the pigeonhole principle. The section "Other Counting Explorations," which follows Counting the Kids, offers activities that use this principle.

Developing all these ideas with understanding takes some time. Teachers should introduce algebraic notation gradually and meaningfully. Because premature introduction of algebraic notation and formulas for combinations and permutations may impede students' efforts to understand these important topics, teachers should not introduce this notation or these formulas until high school.

Flag Trademarks

The investigation Flag Trademarks involves students in three modes of solving counting problems:

- Enumerating—in this situation, cutting and pasting all possibilities
- Using a tree diagram to exhibit the possibilities in a compact format
- Using a counting principle to determine the desired result

The problems give students a concrete context that helps them distinguish between the multiplication and addition principles of counting. The investigation includes situations that allow the repetition of objects and that do not allow such repetition and situations in which order is relevant in the counting process and situations in which it is not relevant. As students analyze and perform the tasks, half-turn symmetry also plays a role.

Goals

- Represent, analyze, and solve counting problems that do or do not involve ordering and that do or do not involve repetition
- Understand and apply the addition and multiplication principles of counting, and represent these principles with algebra, including factorial notation

Materials and Equipment

For each student—

- A copy of the activity sheet "Flag Trademarks"
- Scissors
- Paste, tape, or glue
- Poster board, newsprint, or butcher paper
- Markers

For each pair of students—

- Three copies of the template "Flag Cutouts" (one copy on red, one copy on white, and one copy on blue paper).

pp. 116–17; 118

Prior Knowledge and Activities

Before students begin middle school, they should have had numerous experiences with tree diagrams, and they should know how to solve counting problems that exemplify the addition and multiplication principles of counting, as described in figure 1.1. In middle school, students can deepen their understanding of the ideas behind these counting principles by making connections more explicitly with tree diagrams and considering the differences between the principles. Before your students attempt the investigation Flag Trademarks, review tree diagrams, targeting their connection with the addition and multiplication principles. You should also ask your students to work problems that are

Fig. **1.1.**

The two-task situation

An example of an elementary-level counting problem that exemplifies the addition and multiplication principles is the investigation Bindu Bear's Boutique in *Navigating through Discrete Mathematics in Prekindergarten–Grade 5* (DeBellis et al. forthcoming). An applet for the investigation appears on the CD-ROM that accompanies that volume.

Suppose that a counting situation consists of two tasks, the first with *m* outcomes and the second with *n* outcomes.

Addition Principle

If the two tasks have different outcomes, then the total number of outcomes is *m* + *n*.

If *p* outcomes are common to both tasks, then the total number of outcomes is *m* + *n* − *p*.

(Note that it is necessary to subtract *p* to avoid counting some outcomes twice. This application of the addition principle is also an example of the **inclusion-exclusion principle**.)

Multiplication Principle

Carrying out the first task and then carrying out the second task results in *m* × *n* possible outcomes.

similar to the following warm-up activities, which emphasize the differences between the two principles.

To strengthen students' understanding of the addition and multiplication principles, you might start by asking them to draw a tree diagram that illustrates the outcomes of the following with-replacement experiment. Tell the students to suppose that they have received a jar that contains four colored balls—a red one, a green one, a blue one, and a yellow one. Ask them to imagine that they take one ball from the container, record its color, and return it to the container. Then they take out a second ball, record its color, and return it to the container. Ask the students to make a tree diagram that systematically displays the different color pairings that can occur in this experiment and to determine the total number of different color pairings (see fig. 1.2).

Your students can create a diagram similar to that shown in the figure to investigate numerous counting situations that illustrate the addition and multiplication counting principles in the same context. For example, consider the following questions, descriptions of tasks, and answers:

1. "How many different outcomes (color pairings) are possible after drawing two balls with replacement of the balls between draws?"

   • First task: Draw the first ball, and record its color (four possible outcomes for this task).

   • Second task: Draw the second ball, and record its color (four possible outcomes for this task).

In the preceding conceptualization of the problem, students use the multiplication principle to count 4 × 4, or 16, outcomes for this situation. As in many counting situations, students can think about this problem in other ways. For example, they might consider four tasks:

   • Draw a red ball on the first draw and then a ball of any color for the second draw (four possible outcomes).

   • Draw a green ball on the first draw and then a ball of any color for the second draw (four possible outcomes).

   • Draw a blue ball on the first draw and a ball of any color on the second (four outcomes).

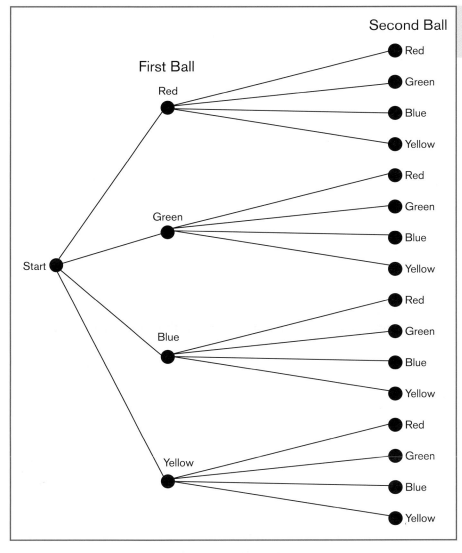

Second Ball

First Ball

Fig. **1.2.**

A "with replacement" tree diagram

- Draw a yellow ball on the first draw and a ball of any color on the second (four possible outcomes).

In this conceptualization of the problem, students use the addition principle to count 4 + 4 + 4 + 4, or 16, outcomes.

2. "How many different outcomes are possible if the goal is to draw two balls, with replacement, and have exactly one of the balls be red?"

- First task: Draw two balls so that the first ball is red and the second ball is not red (three possible outcomes).
- Second task: Draw two balls so that the first ball is not red and the second ball is red (three possible outcomes).

The two tasks have no outcomes in common. In this conceptualization of the problem, students use the addition principle to count 3 + 3, or 6, outcomes. A student might count the six outcomes differently and find a total of 3 + 1 + 1 + 1 possible outcomes in this situation. That student might have envisioned the following four tasks:

- Draw two balls so that the first ball is red and the second ball is not red.

- Draw two balls so that the first is green and the second is red.
- Draw two balls so that the first ball is blue and the second is red.
- Draw two balls so that the first is yellow and the second is red.

In this conceptualization of the problem, students use the addition principle to find the total of 3 + 1 + 1 + 1, or 6, possible outcomes.

3. "How many different outcomes are possible after drawing, with replacement, two balls that include at least one red ball?" ("At least one" means one ball or the other or both.)

- First task: Draw two balls so that the first ball is red and the second ball is any color (four possible outcomes).
- Second task: Draw two balls so that the first ball is not red and the second ball is red (three possible outcomes).

In this conceptualization of the problem, students use the addition principle to count 4 + 3, or 7, outcomes. Alternatively, a student might describe the tasks as follows:

- First task: Draw two balls so that the first ball is red and the second ball is any color (four possible outcomes).
- Second task: Draw two balls so that the first ball is any color and the second ball is red (four possible outcomes).

In this conceptualization of the problem, the first and second tasks have one pair, (red, red), in common. Students should count this pair only once and should use the addition principle to find 4 + 4 – 1, or 7, outcomes.

Allow students ample time to consider alternative interpretations of these counting problems. Students can describe each of the preceding situations by using the "task" language given in the statement of the addition and multiplication principles. This language can help students decide how to count and which counting principle to use. In some problems, the students can easily determine how to describe the distinct tasks; however, identifying the tasks in other problems may be more complex. Students should practice naming the distinct tasks in each situation. Giving sufficient attention to this detail is important preparation for generalizing the addition and multiplication counting principles.

Students should compare tree diagrams that come from experiments with replacement (similar to the preceding one) with experiments that do not allow replacement. They should discuss the effect that this condition has on the tree diagram and on the number of possible outcomes. For example, figure 1.3 shows a tree diagram for an experiment in which students draw two balls without replacement. Observe that the with-replacement diagram in figure 1.2 has four initial branches, and four more branches come from each one of those branches. The without-replacement diagram in figure 1.3 also initially displays four branches; however, three branches attach to each of those four branches. You might ask students to give responses to counting questions that are similar to the preceding questions but use a without-replacement condition. Have them analyze which questions have the same answers and which ones have different answers. After students are

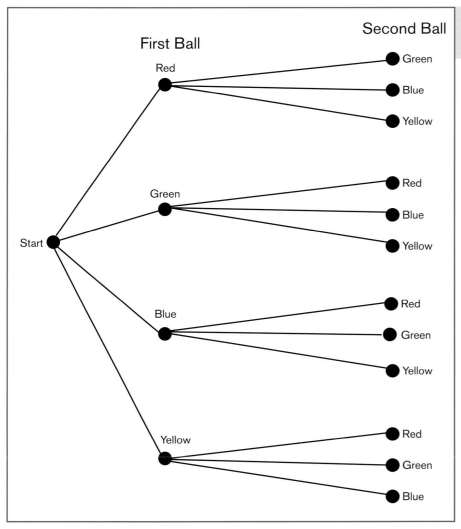

First Ball

Second Ball

Fig. **1.3.**

A "without replacement" tree diagram

comfortable with activities like the preceding, they will be ready to start the Flag Trademarks investigation.

Discussion

Read the activity pages carefully before continuing. Note that the investigation could work well in combination with an exploration of flags of various countries or with a study of signal flags. Pairs of students can work on the first problem of the investigation together to share the tasks of making and pasting flags on the paper or poster board and recording their results. Three copies of the blackline master "Flag Cutouts"—one red page, one white page, and one blue page for each pair of students—will give each pair of students more than enough pieces for forming all the different possibilities for the two flag patterns in the investigation.

The situation in Flag Trademarks is quite simple. A luggage company is considering two rectangular flag patterns, pattern A and pattern B (see fig. 1.4), with three possible colors, for use as a trademark. The company plans to use the winning pattern on one side of a certain brand of luggage in the orientation shown in the figure. Students use models that they cut from the construction paper to create a poster that represents the possibilities for patterns A and B.

Fig. **1.4.**

The two flag patterns

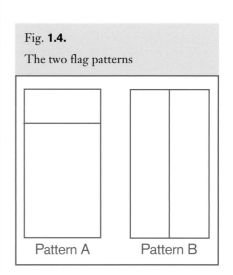

Pattern A   Pattern B

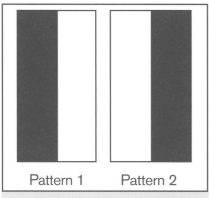

| Pattern 1 | Pattern 2 |

Fig. **1.5.**

The same or different?

Before the students begin work, you might ask them whether pattern A or pattern B will have the greater number of possibilities and why. Also make sure that the students understand when two models are the same and when they are different. In figure 1.5, for example, the two models are the same because giving either model a half-turn will make it match the other model. However, it is possible for two flag patterns that have this 180-degree rotational symmetry to differ. For example, the actual flags of Poland and Monaco both have two horizontal stripes, one red and one white. The red stripe is on top in the flag of Monaco, whereas in the Polish flag, the white stripe is on top.

The first problem in the investigation seeks the minimum number of paper models that represent all the possibilities. Pattern B needs only six, since giving three of them a half-turn produces the other three. Pattern A, however, requires nine models.

Encourage discussion among your students so that you can find out the counting principles that they use in coming up with their totals in problem 1. They will probably provide explanations similar to those described in the previous section. Be sure that the students understand the straightforward use of the multiplication or addition principles to count all the different models for pattern A. They should also see that they can count the models for pattern B by using the multiplication and addition principles, along with a mixed use of multiplication, addition, and division that results from applying the turn-symmetry property of pattern B.

Encourage your students to think about the issues of order and repetition while they solve the counting problems in the investigation. Problem 2 calls on them to investigate the possibilities with four colors, and problem 3 asks them to consider the possibilities with five colors. In particular, they should notice the following:

- Problems 1(*a*), 2(*a*), and 3(*a*) allow repetition, and order matters in these problems. Check to see whether students recognize the familiar square numbers (9, 16, and 25) in the solutions to these problems.

- Problems 1(*b*), 2(*b*), and 3(*b*) allow repetition, and order is not relevant. The triangular numbers (6, 10, and 15) appear as solutions in these problems.

- Problems 1(*c*), 2(*c*), and 3(*c*) do not allow repetition, and order is relevant.

- Problems 1(*d*), 2(*d*), and 3(*d*) do not allow repetition, and order is not relevant.

Ask your students to summarize the different approaches that they might use in doing these problems. Point out the different approaches that the directions for problems 1, 2, and 3 emphasize. Problem 1 uses a hands-on approach, problem 2 calls for making and interpreting a tree diagram, and problem 3 seeks a direct application of a counting principle.

Students should conclude that forming tree diagrams is helpful for visualizing the multiplication and addition principles; however, the diagrams become unwieldy and impractical to use when the number of outcomes for a task is large or when the experiment consists of several tasks. The students should be able to apply a counting principle directly, as in the third problem. Understanding the counting principles is a prerequisite for developing an understanding of permutations and combinations.

Problem 4, which asks the students to design their own three-color trademark pattern, affords an opportunity for some creativity, as well as a chance to review the many ways to count different patterns.

The Mathematics in the Investigation

Formalizing the addition and multiplication counting principles is appropriate during the middle school years. Students should be able to apply the principles and distinguish between them. By the end of eighth grade, students should also be skillful in extending the principles to cover more tasks than the two-task situation described in figure 1.1.

Important ideas related to the multiplication and addition principles include *factorials*, *combinations*, and *permutations*. Students in the middle grades should understand how to use factorial notation, and they should develop the conceptual underpinnings for formal study of permutations and combinations in high school.

The teacher can use the concepts of factorials, permutations, and combinations to illustrate the different types of definitions that occur in mathematics. One type of definition explains the use of a specific symbol or notation. For example, $n!$ (which is read as "n factorial") is shorthand notation for the product of the natural numbers from 1 through n. The definition of $3!$ is $1 \cdot 2 \cdot 3$, or $3 \cdot 2 \cdot 1$, or 6. The factorial symbol is a part of several counting formulas that students learn in high school. Middle school students should be able to work with expressions that involve this symbol. They should analyze factorial expressions and look for ways to simplify their calculations. For example, they should realize that it makes sense to simplify $\dfrac{10!}{7!}$ to $10 \cdot 9 \cdot 8$ before computing the answer. The next section describes extensions of the investigation Flag Trademarks that illustrate the use of factorials.

Another type of definition gives a name to an essential idea. Many counting problems, for example, deal with counting ordered arrangements of objects. *Permutation* is the term for an ordered arrangement of objects. Of particular interest is the problem of counting the number of different permutations of k objects chosen from n objects (the extensions suggested below include an example). In contrast, *combination* is the term used for a collection of objects in which order within the collection is not important.

Extensions

After students understand the multiplication principle, they can pursue extensions that involve larger numbers. Select a setting in which questions are readily accessible, and ask students to create and solve one another's questions. For example, asking the students to create flag patterns that use three, four, or more pieces of cloth can extend the investigation Flag Trademarks to include counting situations that involve more than two tasks, as shown in figure 1.6.

Students formally study combinations and permutations in high school. Chapter 2, "Systematic Listing and Counting in Grades 9–12," gives a more detailed discussion of these important ideas.

Fig. **1.6.**

Three- and four-color designs

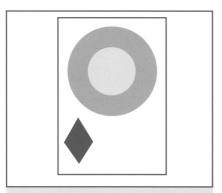

Fig. **1.7.**

A four-color design

Flag patterns can also serve as a basis for informal explorations with permutations and factorial notation. For example, you can show your students the four-color flag design in figure 1.7 and ask them such questions as the following:

- "How many flag trademark patterns are possible if you use cloth of four different colors in this pattern?" (A total of 4!, or 24, patterns are possible.)
- "How many patterns are possible if you make each flag pattern by using cloth of four different colors that you select from ten possible cloth colors?" (The number of possible patterns is 10 • 9 • 8 • 7, or 5040.)

You can select many other problems and contexts. Three representative problems follow:

1. Ask your students to consider the problem of placing items, without replacement, in boxes. Pose questions such as the following:

   a. "In how many ways can Manya Wayze place the six letters **R L S T N E**, without replacement, in six boxes so that each box contains one letter?"

   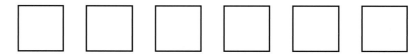

   (She can place the letters in 6!, or 720, ways.)

   b. "In how many ways can Manya Wayze place the letters if the letter in the first box must be an **R**?"

   (She can place them in 5!, or 120, ways.)

   c. "In how many ways can Manya Wayze place the letters if the letters in the last two boxes must be an **E** in the next-to-last box followed by a **T** in the last box?"

   (She can place them in 4!, or 24, ways.)

   Problems like this one serve several purposes:

   - They show the students that the multiplication principle can extend beyond two tasks. In this situation, the number of tasks is six.
   - They can help convince the students that tree diagrams have limited use, since attempting to represent all choices in problems 1(a) or 1(b) on a tree diagram would be impractical.
   - The students can see the advantage of writing 6! in place of
     $$6 \times 5 \times 4 \times 3 \times 2 \times 1.$$

   Such examples are natural lead-ins to the ordered arrangement of objects. They can help students see permutations as an application of the multiplication principle.

2. Ask your students to consider the counting involved in the well-known handshake problem. Pose the following question:

   "How many handshakes take place in a group of *n* persons if everyone shakes hands once with everyone else and if no one shakes hands with himself or herself?"

To locate further information about the handshake problem on the Internet, type "handshake problem" into a search engine. The following Web site is a good resource: http://www.wcer.wisc.edu/ NCISLA/teachers/teacher Resources.html.

The handshake problem is a rich problem-solving experience, particularly because students can use a variety of strategies to solve it. In elementary school, students should have experimented with this problem for specific values of n. Students in the middle grades who are familiar with algebraic notation should be able to express the general solution algebraically as

$$\frac{n(n-1)}{2}$$

handshakes and be able to justify this solution. If students are not familiar with this problem, ask them to work together in groups to solve it and have them explain their solution strategies to the class, so that all can view and benefit from the numerous possible approaches to the solution.

3. Ask your students to consider the counting aspect of the triangular numbers, the first five of which are shown in figure 1.8. Present the following task:

"Justify why the nth triangular number is

$$\frac{n(n+1)}{2},$$

and make a connection with the handshake problem."

In elementary school, students should have experimented with triangular numbers, and they should be able to generate them. After students are familiar with algebraic notation, they should be able to express the nth triangular number as shown above and justify this answer in several ways, including making a connection with the handshake problem. You can hint to them that triangular numbers and the handshake problem are connected with sums of consecutive natural numbers beginning with 1.

Different approaches to the handshake problem are discussed in Navigating through Mathematical Connections in Grades 9–12 *(Burke et al. 2006, pp. 1–8).*

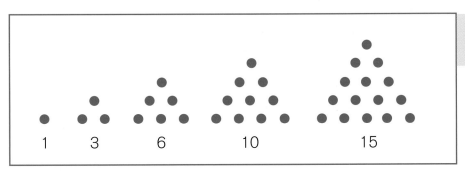

1   3   6   10   15

Fig. **1.8.**

The first five triangular numbers

For more information about the triangular numbers, see the articles "Triangular Numbers in Problem Solving" (Szetala 1999) and "Figurate Numbers" (Bezuszka 1984), both of which appear on the accompanying CD-ROM.

Counting the Kids

The investigation Counting the Kids provides students with an opportunity to explore the use of Venn diagrams to solve word problems. It includes two standard problems that give the number of elements in the intersection of all three sets and one problem where this important number is missing. Students can use several strategies to find a solution to these problems. When your students complete the investigation, allow ample class time for a discussion of the different strategies that they have discovered. This investigation can serve as a catalyst for introducing the inclusion-exclusion principle if the class has had experience with set operations.

Goals

- Solve counting problems by using Venn diagrams, and use algebra to represent the relationships shown by a Venn diagram
- Implicitly use the inclusion-exclusion principle

Materials and Equipment

For each student—
- A copy of the activity sheet "Counting the Kids"

Prior Knowledge and Activities

In prekindergarten–grade 2, students should have used Venn diagrams to sort, organize, and count small numbers of objects. In grades 3–5, they should have had more experience with Venn diagrams. Before students begin the investigation Counting the Kids, be sure that they are familiar with two- and three-set Venn diagrams.

Also be certain that your students are able to describe each region of a Venn diagram in words. You might ask them to describe the regions by using set notation, although set notation is not essential for this activity. The Venn diagram in figure 1.9 represents two sets, A and B, contained within a universal set, U, and each region, (i)–(iv), can be described in words and represented in set notation as shown in table 1.1.

Table 1.1.

Representation of Regions (i)–(iv)

Region	Contains	Set Expression
i	The elements that are in A and not in B	$A \cap B'$
ii	The elements that are in both A and B	$A \cap B$
iii	The elements that are not in A but are in B	$A' \cap B$
iv	The elements that are not in A and not in B	$A' \cap B'$

An explanation of the set notation in or related to table 1.1 follows:

- $A \cup B$ (which can be read as "A union B") is the set of elements that are in A or B or in both A and B. It consists of regions (i), (ii), and (iii).
- $A \cap B$ (which can be read as "A intersection B") is the set of elements that are in both A and B. It consists of region (ii).

pp. 119–20

An example of an investigation for students in prekindergarten through second grade that uses Venn diagrams is the investigation Bucket of Buttons in *Navigating through Discrete Mathematics in Prekindergarten–Grade 5* (DeBellis et al. forthcoming).

Fig. 1.9.

Venn diagram regions: two sets, A and B, in U

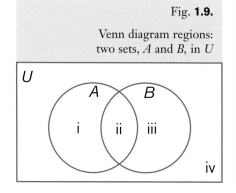

- A' (which can be read as "A complement") is the set of elements in U that are not in A. It consists of regions (iii) and (iv). Another notation for A' is $\overline{A}$.

Students should also be able to describe each of the regions in the context of specific situations. For instance, let A be the set of students who have sisters, and let B be the set of students who have brothers. Then—

- region (i) represents the set of students who have sisters only;
- region (ii) represents the set of students who have sisters and brothers;
- region (iii) represents the set of students who have brothers only;
- region (iv) represents the set of students who have neither sisters nor brothers.

Students should also be able to describe certain combinations of regions. For example, in the context of the brother-and-sister example—

- regions (i) and (iii) consist of the set of students who have either all brothers or all sisters;
- regions (i), (ii), and (iii) consist of the set of students who have siblings—all brothers, all sisters, or brothers and sisters;
- regions (iii) and (iv) consist of the set of students who do not have sisters.

Make sure that students understand the meaning of *or* and *and* in the context of Venn diagrams. The elements in A or B are elements that are in A, in B, or in both. The elements in A and B are the elements that are in both A and B.

Students should realize that they can use Venn diagrams to model a variety of circumstances. In some problems, they place the elements under discussion in certain regions. In other problems, they place the count of elements in the various regions. Students should become familiar with the notation used to count elements in Venn diagram regions. Consider examples like the one in figure 1.10, where each number displayed is the count of elements found within the corresponding region. According to the information in the figure, if A is the set of students who received an A in history and $n(A)$ is the number of elements in A, then $n(A) = 33$, since $33 = 23 + 10$. If B is the set of students who received an A in mathematics, $n(B) = 21$, since $21 = 10 + 11$. The number of students who received an A in both history and mathematics is $n(A \cap B) = 10$. The number of students who received an A in history, mathematics, or both subjects is $n(A \cup B)$, or 44. The number who received an A in neither history nor mathematics is 9.

Similarly, you can present other examples so that your students can identify the eight distinct regions formed by three sets, as shown in figure 1.11. You might choose three attributes—say, brown hair, blue eyes, and glasses—and ask your students to describe the attributes of the members of each region. Also, encourage your students to choose three characteristics to represent the sets, assign numbers to each of the eight regions, and then interpret their meaning. In the course of these discussions, emphasize vocabulary so that students understand clearly the

The complement of A is sometimes represented by $\overline{A}$ as well as by A'.

Region (iv), which represents the intersection of the complements of A and B ($A' \cap B'$), is also the complement of the union of A and B, which can be written as $(A \cup B)'$ or $\overline{A \cup B}$.

Fig. **1.10.**

Representing element counts in the regions of a Venn diagram

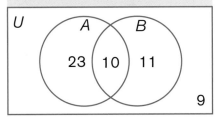

Fig. **1.11.**

Venn diagram regions: three sets—A, B, and C—in U

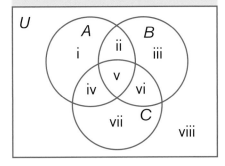

Student Count	Choices
48*	Hot dogs
36*	Chicken wings
60*	Hamburgers
12*	Hot dogs and chicken wings
20*	Chicken wings and hamburgers
16*	Hot dogs and hamburgers
5	All three items
19	None of the items

The totals marked with an asterisk (*) are *inclusive* totals.

Seventh Graders' Play

All the seventh-grade students at Pythagoras Middle School participated in a three-act play at the school. Acts I, II, and III included 31, 38, and 35 students, respectively. A total of 9 students appeared in acts I and II, 10 students appeared in acts I and III, and 15 students were in acts II and III. A total of 8 students were in all three acts, and 23 students worked on the production in other ways.

Eighth Graders' Contests

All 100 eighth-grade students at Pythagoras Middle School participated in at least one of three contests. The history, mathematics, and science contests had 44, 45, and 46 participants, respectively. A total of 12 students participated in the history and mathematics contests, 13 were in the mathematics and science contests, and 14 participated in the history and science contests.

mathematical meaning of the words *and, or, all, both, not, either ... or, neither ... nor, exactly, only, at least, at most, union, intersection,* and *complement.*

Discussion

Read the blackline master "Counting the Kids" carefully. The investigation presents three counting problems that students can represent by using three-set Venn diagrams. In problem 1, the sixth graders at fictitious Pythagoras Middle School have indicated the various foods that they are willing to eat at the class picnic. In problem 2, the seventh graders at Pythagoras have staged a three-act play, taking different roles in the production. In problem 3, the eighth graders have participated in various academic contests at Pythagoras. A breakdown of the data for each problem appears in the margin.

Problems 1 and 2 provide the key number—that is, the number of elements in the intersection of all three sets. When you discuss the problems with your students, be sure to highlight the role of this number in the Venn diagrams. The students should figure out how to use it to determine the numbers of elements in all the other regions. Because problem 3 does not provide this central number, it is considerably more challenging than the other two problems. In approaching each problem, students should begin by appropriately labeling the universal set and the other sets. The next step is entering the data in the regions.

Despite the previously suggested warm-up activities, some students may place the 12, 20, and 16 incorrectly in the Venn diagram for problem 1. In terms of the numbering system in figure 1.11, they might, for example, place 12 in region (ii) instead of distributing 12 over region (ii) and region (v). Move around the classroom while the students are doing the investigation to correct this error before students make a similar mistake in the next problem. Also verify that the students understand the difference between region (i), which is the hot-dogs-only region, and the hot-dogs region that includes regions (i), (ii), (iv), and (v).

During class discussions of the activities, use the data in each diagram to analyze the situation further and ask additional questions related to the problems. For example, for problem 1, you might ask how many students at Pythagoras Middle School preferred at most two kinds of food. (The answer to this question is 120 – 5, or 115.) For problem 2, you might ask students to explain whether the number of seventh graders who performed in act III only is the same as the number of students who performed in at least two acts. (The numbers are the same, since 18 = 1 + 2 + 7 + 8.)

Problem 3 will probably generate a variety of strategies that students should describe in detail. Ask them about the significance of "all 100" in the statement of the problem. Have someone who has used a guessing method start discussing his or her solution to problem 3, and ask that student to illustrate how to fill in each of the regions on the basis of his or her initial guess. Students can then analyze what happens if the guess is incorrect and discuss how they can use information gained from an incorrect guess to guide another guess.

Another strategy that students may use to solve problem 3 is one that focuses on the "repeats" within the count. Adding the number of students who participated in the contests for history (44), mathematics

(45), and science (46) results in an answer of 44 + 45 + 46, or 135, students. Since the total number of students is only 100, the number 135 implies that the count considers some students more than once. Here, the number of repeats is 35. Ask the students how these repeats occurred. Be sure that they understand that the 35 repeats must be coming from the overlapping regions (ii), (iv), (v), and (vi). Tallying the numbers corresponding to students taking part in combinations of two contests—history and mathematics (12), mathematics and science (14), and history and science (13)—results in a total of 12 + 14 + 13, or 39. This total again indicates an overlap. Because 39 – 35 = 4, the overlap is 4. But this result implies that 4 students must have participated in all three contests. The key number then is 4. After students find this number, they can work backward to determine the numbers in the other regions.

Students can also solve problem 3 by using an algebraic approach. If they call the number in the central region x, they can represent the number of elements in the other regions with appropriate expressions in terms of x, as shown in figure 1.12. They can then use the figure to write and solve a linear equation, as follows:

$$(44 - (26 - x)) + ((12 - x) + x + (14 - x) + (13 - x)) + (45 - (25 - x)) + (46 - (27 - x)) = 100$$

$$(18 + x) + (39 - 2x) + (20 + x) + (19 + x) = 100$$

$$96 + x = 100$$

$$x = 4$$

The Mathematics in the Investigation

Although students can solve counting problems that result in placing data in a Venn diagram by systematic guessing, by analyzing the "repeat" numbers, or by using equations, another strategy generally applies to a broad range of problems. This approach uses the inclusion-exclusion principle, which provides a method for counting the number of elements in the union of two or more sets.

The inclusion-exclusion principle for two sets A and B is as follows:

$$n(A \cup B) = n(A) + n(B) - n(A \cap B),$$

where $n(A \cup B)$ is the number of elements in set A or set B or both. In figure 1.9, $n(A \cup B)$ is the sum of the numbers in regions (i), (ii), and (iii). The number in region (ii) represents those elements that are in both sets and is the number that has been double-counted. That is, adding $n(A)$ to $n(B)$ on the right side of the equation counts the number in region (ii) twice. Subtracting this number makes it appear exactly once on each side of the equation.

The inclusion-exclusion principle for three sets A, B, and C is as follows:

$$n(A \cup B \cup C) = n(A) + n(B) + n(C) - n(A \cap B) - n(A \cap C) - n(B \cap C) + n(A \cap B \cap C).$$

Students need to understand why they add or subtract numbers in this formula. Ask them to describe in words the regions that each of the terms in the equation represents and why they need to add or subtract

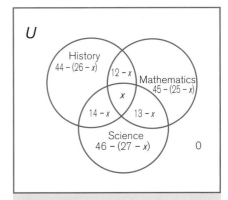

Fig. **1.12.**

An algebraic approach

the terms. The number of elements in *A*, *B*, or *C* is $n(A \cup B \cup C)$, which is the sum of the numbers in regions (i) through (vii) in figure 1.11. Adding $n(A)$, $n(B)$, and $n(C)$ on the right side of the preceding equation results in adding the numbers in the overlapping regions (ii), (iv), and (vi) twice and adding the number in the overlapping region (v) three times. Hence, to compensate for counting the same elements more than once, the students must subtract the counts that they repeated. They must therefore subtract $n(A \cap B)$, $n(A \cap C)$, and $n(B \cap C)$. However, they have added the number in region (v) three times and subtracted it three times. Thus, they must add $n(A \cap B \cap C)$ to maintain equality, with each of the regions (i) through (vii) appearing exactly once on each side of the equation.

For three sets, this principle of inclusion-exclusion yields an equation that consists of eight terms. As long as a problem gives seven of those terms, students can deduce the eighth term. Thus, you can construct a variety of counting problems for students by varying the missing region.

Other Counting Explorations

Below are additional activities related to important ideas of systematic counting. You can use these to supplement or extend your students' work on the previous investigations.

The Pigeonhole Principle

The *pigeonhole principle* is a simple yet powerful rule that middle school students can use to solve a variety of counting problems. One way to describe this principle uses an example of pigeons and pigeonholes:

> If *m* pigeons occupy *n* pigeonholes and *m* > *n*, then at least one pigeonhole has two or more pigeons roosting in it.

You can introduce the pigeonhole principle by showing your students a picture such as that in figure 1.13 and giving them the following problem: "Assume that you have four indistinguishable birds and three birdhouses, as pictured. What can you tell about the number of birds in each birdhouse?"

Fig. **1.13.**

An illustration of the pigeonhole principle

The figure shows four birds occupying three birdhouses in one particular way. Ask the students to sketch some or all of the different ways in which at least one birdhouse can contain two or more birds. They should obtain the following results:

- All four birds can be together in any one of the birdhouses, leaving two houses empty. This arrangement can occur in three different ways, since three birdhouses are available.

- Three birds can occupy any one birdhouse while one bird is in a second birdhouse and one house is empty. These arrangements can occur in six different ways, since any birdhouse can hold three birds and then any one of the two remaining houses can hold the fourth bird.

- Two birds can occupy one house and two birds can occupy another house, leaving the third house empty. Three such arrangements are possible, since there are three ways to choose two houses for the bird pairs, or equivalently, any of the three houses can be the empty house.

- Two of the houses can contain one bird each, and two birds can be in the third house. Three such arrangements are possible, since there are three ways to choose the house for the two birds.

Identify the birds as pigeons and the birdhouses as pigeonholes. In every case with four pigeons and three pigeonholes, at least one pigeonhole has two or more pigeons roosting in it. An alternative wording of the principle is the following:

If $n + 1$ or more objects occupy n boxes, then at least one box contains two or more objects.

Students should carefully explore the meaning of this principle and investigate problems that use the principle in achieving a solution. Pose questions such as the following:

- "What is the minimum number of students needed to form a group in which you can be sure that at least two persons have the same birth month?" (Thirteen students are needed for such a group.)

- "Suppose that you have a piggy bank full of pennies, nickels, dimes, and quarters, and you shake one coin at a time from the bank. What is the minimum number of coins that you must shake out to be certain that you have three coins of one kind?" (You must shake out nine coins.)

Problems that seek solutions to questions that ask about the least, most, best, worst, tallest, shortest, maximum, minimum, and so on are *optimization problems*. The two preceding problems are of this type. A helpful strategy to use is the worst-case scenario. When the goal is to seek the smallest number that satisfies a criterion, the worst-case scenario provides the largest number that does not satisfy the criterion. The smallest number that does satisfy the criterion is one more than the largest number that does not. For example, in the first problem, students determine the minimum number of people needed so that at least two of them have the same birth month. The worst-case scenario in this situation is the largest possible number that allows all the people to have different birth months. Students should conclude that twelve is the largest number of persons who could have different months of birth. Thus, the answer to the problem must be thirteen, which is the minimum number of persons for which some match of birth months is inevitable.

Another difficulty that students may need to overcome in analyzing the problems is matching the "pigeons" and "pigeonholes" with the information given in the problem. To help students apply the principle to the problem, they should identify and write down their choices of "pigeons" and "pigeonholes" when they begin to solve a problem. In the first problem, the months represent the pigeonholes and the persons represent the pigeons.

In the second problem, coin types represent the pigeonholes and the coins shaken from the bank represent the pigeons. The worst-case scenario in this problem occurs in shaking out eight coins consisting of a pair of pennies, a pair of nickels, a pair of dimes, and a pair of quarters. No matter what coin comes out ninth, its appearance will yield three coins of the same type. Thus, the optimal solution is nine coins. Notice that this problem is really an extension of the pigeonhole principle, because in this instance at least one pigeonhole must contain three (not two) or more pigeons.

Pascal's Triangle

Students may have previously met the ubiquitous *Pascal's triangle*, but there are always new patterns to explore and analyze in this triangular array of numbers. Determine what your students remember, and build on their knowledge. Even students who are unfamiliar with Pascal's triangle can try the investigation Paths, Strings, and Combinations in Pascal's Triangle, which appears in chapter 2 as an investigation for students in grades 9–12. It is actually appropriate for students from grade 6 to grade 12.

Students in grades 6–8 should know the fundamental pattern that creates Pascal's triangle: the top row consists of a single 1, each subsequent row begins and ends with a 1, and each inner entry for a row consists of the sum of the numbers that are just to its left and right in the preceding row, as shown in figure 1.14. Another basic pattern in Pascal's triangle is its vertical line of symmetry. A consequence of this symmetry is that the numbers in each row read the same from left to right as from right to left.

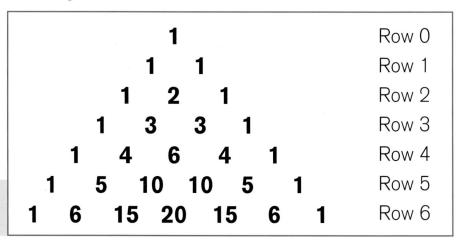

Fig. **1.14.**

Pascal's triangle

When students solve the handshake problem (see pp. 24–25), they should notice that they can also locate the solutions for two, three, four, five, and more persons on a diagonal of Pascal's triangle. By referring to the strategy of solving the handshake problem by using sums of the form

$$1 + 2 + 3 + 4 + 5 + \ldots + (n-2) + (n-1),$$

they should be able to explain why the solutions to the handshake problem appear on a diagonal.

Students can explore many other patterns in Pascal's triangle. For example, they can investigate the numbers that appear in the triangle and speculate about the number of times that a given number appears. They can also pursue the abundance of patterns that occur after they color the cells of Pascal's triangle on various grids. The applet Coloring Pascal's Triangle on the accompanying CD-ROM presents some of the possibilities.

Students can work with the applet Coloring Pascal's Triangle on the CD-ROM to explore patterns that result when they color the cells of the triangle on various grids.

Conclusion

The sampling of problems and activities in this chapter emphasizes that counting questions are everywhere. Middle school students should build a repertoire of strategies for solving counting problems with replacement of objects and without replacement and problems in which order does matter and in which it does not. In the process of their work, they should develop skill in combinatorial reasoning in addition to learning how to formulate and solve their own counting problems. After they have assimilated the basic ideas in this chapter, they will be well prepared to handle more advanced topics in grades 9–12.

For more ideas about Pascal's triangle, see the article "Pascal's Triangle—Patterns, Paths, and Plinko" (Lemon 1997) on the CD-ROM. Chapter 2, "Systematic Listing and Counting in Grades 9–12," includes additional activities that may be appropriate for your students.

NAVIGATIONS
SERIES

GRADES 6–12

NAVIGATING *through* DISCRETE MATHEMATICS

Chapter 2
Systematic Listing and Counting in Grades 9–12

All students in grades 9–12 should—

- *understand and apply permutations and combinations;*

- *use reasoning and formulas to solve counting problems in which repetition is or is not allowed and ordering does or does not matter;*

- *understand, apply, and describe relationships among the binomial theorem, Pascal's triangle, and combinations;*

- *apply counting methods to probabilistic situations involving equally likely outcomes;*

- *use combinatorial reasoning to construct proofs as well as solve a variety of problems.*

A major focus in grades 9–12 is using algebraic notation and increasingly formal reasoning to extend, explain, and connect topics discussed in previous grades. For example, high school students should explore and explain the connections among combinations, Pascal's triangle, and the binomial theorem, and they should be able to prove fundamental properties of combinations and permutations algebraically and by using combinatorial reasoning. Students should therefore also learn the formal notation for combinations and permutations, like $C(n, k)$ and $P(n, k)$, and they should meaningfully develop and use the algebraic formulas.

An important goal in grades 9–12 is for students to understand and solve four basic types of counting problems, as represented by the four cells in table 2.1. Students should understand that when repetitions are not allowed (second column of table 2.1), permutations apply when ordering matters and combinations apply when ordering does not matter. Students in elementary school and middle school have also studied such problems, but students in high school use the additional tools of algebraic formulas and formal reasoning and proof.

Students in grades 9–12 should also solve, with and without formulas, the other two types of ordering-repetition problems (first column of table 2.1)—those in which repetitions are allowed and ordering does or does not matter. They should learn that they can count selections of k objects from n objects when repetitions are allowed and ordering matters by using the expression n^k. When repetitions are allowed and ordering does not matter, they should discover that the expression $C(n + k - 1, k)$ applies.

35

Table 2.1.
Four Types of Counting Problems

Ordering ＼ Repetition	Repetitions Allowed	Repetitions Not Allowed
Ordering matters	n^k	Permutations
Ordering does not matter	$C(n + k - 1, k)$	Combinations

It is important that the more formal work in high school, especially with algebraic formulas, be always grounded in and connected with meaning, context, and multiple representations. Otherwise, solving counting problems can become a hit-or-miss process in which students try to memorize and execute formulas rather than make sense of problems and use mathematical tools to solve them.

Applications have been an important part of learning in previous grades, and they continue to be important in grades 9–12. The applications become more complex and substantive in high school. For example, students can solve counting problems related to lotteries, genetics, card games, and sports. They can count the numbers of possible computer passwords, ATM PINs, telephone numbers, or license plate numbers. In biology, systematic counting helps students understand how every person can have the same human DNA, which consists of the same four chemicals, and still be different, since the 3.1 billion letters in the DNA code can combine to form $4^{3,100,000,000}$ different human DNA chains—a number far larger than the number of atoms in the universe!

Other important applications of counting occur in probability. For example, in a situation with equally likely outcomes, the probability of an event is the ratio of the number of favorable outcomes to the total number of possible outcomes. In a situation modeled by a binomial probability distribution, students often need to count the number of "successes." High school students should be able to apply counting strategies to solve a variety of problems in probability.

The activities in this chapter focus on developing a good "counting sense" in the contexts of investigating combinations, Pascal's triangle, and the binomial theorem. Students explore and explain concepts, procedures, and connections, and they prove some fundamental properties.

For further discussion of these topics, as well as activities related to other counting topics and additional applications, see the articles on the accompanying CD-ROM.

Paths, Strings, and Combinations in Pascal's Triangle

This exploratory investigation can serve either as an informal introduction to combinations and Pascal's triangle or as a means to revisit counting ideas in new contexts. The activities are appropriate for students in grades 9–12, although some of them may be appropriate for students in seventh and eighth grades, depending on the students and the curriculum. In the process of using binary strings to analyze a hopping frog's path, students build an understanding of Pascal's triangle and discover how to use this triangle to answer a fundamental counting question: How many subsets exist? Students solve this problem, as well as other counting problems, without using formulas. Instead, they use Pascal's triangle and combinatorial reasoning. Students with different mathematics backgrounds can enjoy working together on these activities while expanding their knowledge about binary strings, combinations, and Pascal's triangle.

Goals

- Use reasoning and formulas to solve counting problems in which repetition is not allowed and ordering does not matter
- Understand, apply, and describe relationships between Pascal's triangle and combinations
- Use combinatorial reasoning

Materials and Equipment

For each student —
- A copy of each of the following activity sheets:
  ○ "Binary Strings"
  ○ "Zigzag Paths and Binary Strings"
  ○ "Combinations and Subsets"
- Markers or colored pencils

pp. 121; 122–25; 126–29

Prior Knowledge and Activities

Students should have had previous experience in thinking about and solving simple counting problems. Also, some questions in the investigation assume that students have a basic understanding of probability and symmetry.

Discussion

This investigation is exploratory and informal. It encourages students to find and explain connections among zigzag paths through a triangular array, binary strings, subsets, and Pascal's triangle. Students use the notation $C(n, k)$ to represent the number in row n at position k in Pascal's triangle. Students do not use formal definitions at this time;

Chapter 1, "Systematic Listing and Counting in Grades 6–8," includes activities that can give students background in thinking about and solving simple counting problems. Another source for such activities is *Navigating through Discrete Mathematics in Prekindergarten–Grade 5* (DeBellis et al. forthcoming).

Part 1, Problem 1

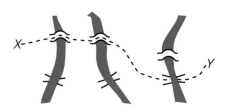

Part 1, Problem 2

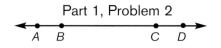

Part 2, Lily-Pad Triangle

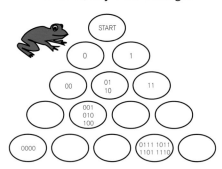

they simply explore, make connections, and give explanations. The next investigation—Combinations, Pascal's Triangle, and the Binomial Theorem—gives students an opportunity for more formal work with combinations and Pascal's triangle.

The first investigation includes three parts. Each part consists of several counting problems. You may find it helpful to work these problems before reading further.

Part 1—"Binary Strings"

"Binary Strings" gives students some warm-up activities so that they can become comfortable with the concept of a binary string before they tackle the main activities in this investigation. Problems 1 and 2 are not related, so students can do either or both, as needed. In problem 1, the students consider binary representations of various trails for Carl, who must go over or under three rivers to travel from point X to point Y (see the margin art, which shows the bridges and tunnels). In problem 2, the students examine the different line segments that four points on a line determine (see the margin), and they investigate the use of binary strings to identify them.

Part 2—"Zigzag Paths and Binary Strings"

In part 2, students explore some of the patterns of Pascal's triangle by exploring the zigzag paths of a frog hopping downward through a triangular array of lily pads (see the margin). Students represent the paths by using binary strings, and they count the number of zigzag paths from the top of the triangle to any entry. They see that the number in any location of Pascal's triangle represents the number of different zigzag paths from the top of the triangle to that position in the triangle.

In the context of this activity, a "zigzag path" always moves downward, veering either to the left or to the right at each step. Students should understand that it is possible for a zigzag path in this activity to move always left or always right.

Before students start working on the activity, you might help them understand the context by doing some warm-up activities. Choose a specific location in the triangle, and ask a student to show several paths from the top (START) to that location. Then ask a student to describe the paths in terms of binary strings with a 0 representing a hop to the left and a 1 representing a hop to the right. Tell your students that in the activity "left" and "right" always relate to an "aerial view" of the triangle—the students' own viewpoint as they work on paper rather than the frog's viewpoint as it hops.

To make this part of the activity very concrete and help the students become engaged, you might tape a large copy of the triangle on the floor or show it on an overhead transparency. Then ask a student to walk or trace the path described by a specific binary string and find its endpoint. Point out that when the walker steps to his or her left, the class sees this as a movement to the right, and vice versa. The binary string describes the movement from the observers' point of view.

Be certain that students understand the labeling conventions for this activity. Row 1 is the first row after START (row 0), row 2 is the second row, and so on. In this activity, students do not need to label the entries in a row explicitly. If the subject comes up, however, explain that students should begin with 0 to label the entries in a row—that is, entry 0 in each row is the left-edge entry, entry 1 is the next entry to the right, and so on. This labeling is necessary to make connections with combinations—$C(n, k)$—in subsequent activities.

In problems 1 through 5, the students consider zigzag paths that the frog might take while hopping through the triangular array of lily pads, and they represent the paths as binary strings. At the location of each lily pad, they record the binary strings representing all the zigzag paths from the top of the triangle to that location.

In problems 6 through 10, the students consider Pascal's triangle (see the margin) and its relationship to the lily-pad triangle. Remind your students that the numbering of the rows in Pascal's triangle and the entries in each row begin with 0. In problem 6, the students complete row 10 of Pascal's triangle to ensure that they understand how to construct the triangle. In problem 7, they find and explain the connection between Pascal's triangle and the lily-pad triangle. (Each number in Pascal's triangle is the number of binary strings in the corresponding location in the lily-pad triangle; that number is the number of zigzag paths from the apex of the triangle to that location.) In particular, students explain the addition rule for Pascal's triangle—that is, compute each entry by adding the entries above it to the left and right—in terms of binary strings and zigzag paths. Thus, this activity provides a concrete interpretation of what would otherwise be an abstract rule.

In problems 8 and 9, students explore counting problems related to the connections between the lily-pad triangle and Pascal's triangle, such as counting all zigzag paths of a specific length or determining the number of binary strings of a fixed length that contain a certain number of 1s. In problem 10, they explore and explain the line symmetry in Pascal's triangle in terms of zigzag paths.

Part 3—"Combinations and Subsets"

Part 3 introduces a new notation, $C(n, k)$, to describe the locations of numbers in Pascal's triangle (see the first few rows in the margin). This notation is, of course, the notation for combinations, and the work in this activity relates to combinations. However, instead of giving a formal definition of combinations or using them in a formal manner, this part of the activity uses the $C(n, k)$ notation to represent the number in row n, entry k, of Pascal's triangle. Then students interpret $C(n, k)$ in terms of zigzag paths, binary strings, subsets, and choosing k digits to be 1s in a binary string of n digits. This part of the investigation informally introduces students to the notion of combinations in terms of choosing. The next investigation treats combinations more formally.

Students use and compare three different representations of Pascal's triangle in part 3—the "binary strings" triangle from part 2, the triangle with numerical values that is presented later in that part of the activity, and the representation using $C(n, k)$ notation that appears at the beginning of part 3. Students should refer to all three representations while they work through this final part of the investigation.

In problem 1, the students use $C(n, k)$ notation to complete row 6 of the triangle. In problem 2, they investigate $C(n, k)$ in terms of zigzag paths. They learn that $C(n, k)$ is the number of zigzag paths to entry k in row n, or equivalently, the number of paths of length n that have k

Part 2, Pascal's Triangle

S
1   1
1   2   1
1   3   3   1
1   4   6   4   1

Part 3, Combinations

$C(0, 0)$

$C(1, 0)$ $C(1, 1)$

$C(2, 0)$ $C(2, 1)$ $C(2, 2)$

$C(3, 0)$ $C(3, 1)$ $C(3, 2)$ $C(3, 3)$

$C(4, 0)$ $C(4, 1)$ $C(4, 2)$ $C(4, 3)$ $C(4, 4)$

zigs to the right or $(n - k)$ zags to the left. In problem 3, they investigate $C(n, k)$ in terms of binary strings. They learn that $C(n, k)$ is the number of strings of length n that include k 1s. Problem 4 introduces the "choose" terminology for the numbers $C(n, k)$.

In problem 5, students explore the numbers $C(n, k)$ and explain two basic patterns that are also fundamental patterns of Pascal's triangle. The first of these patterns is

$$C(n, k) = C(n, n - k),$$

which indicates the vertical line symmetry of Pascal's triangle, and the second is

$$C(n, k) = C(n - 1, k - 1) + C(n - 1, k),$$

which represents the basic construction rule of Pascal's triangle.

In problem 6, the students learn about the fundamental connection between $C(n, k)$ and subsets, discovering that $C(n, k)$ is the number of subsets of k elements taken from a set with n elements. Problem 7 introduces the term *combinations,* and students solve a related applied problem involving pizza toppings. Problem 8 takes the students to another context, inviting them to solve an applied problem about a soccer team with eight members, only six of whom can play at a time. The students must restate the problem in terms of the different representations that they have been using. Finally, problem 9 is a summary task, in which the students describe the connections among zigzag paths, binary strings, subsets, $C(n, k)$, and Pascal's triangle.

The Mathematics in the Investigation

The digits 0 and 1 are *binary digits,* or *bits.* The term *binary strings,* or *bit strings,* refers to sequences of 0s and 1s—such as 01001, 111000000, and 001100110011001. Such strings can serve as codes, and they are useful in developing counting techniques and solving counting problems, as shown in this investigation.

A *combination* can be defined in two equivalent ways. One definition is as a collection in which no repetitions occur and a different ordering of the same elements does not count as a different collection. The second definition is as a subset of a set. Students see both characterizations of combinations in this investigation.

The process of making combinations is commonly described as choosing k elements from n elements. Several different notations are possible for the number of combinations, including $C(n, k)$, $_nC_k$, and

$$\binom{n}{k}.$$

This book uses the $C(n, k)$ notation to make an implicit connection with functions.

This investigation gives students a gentle introduction to the notation for combinations and helps them make sense of the ideas in concrete settings without using formal definitions and technical formulas. However, for your own reference, you may find it useful to consider the formal factorial formula for combinations and the related formula for permutations.

The basic construction rule of Pascal's triangle can be stated as follows: To derive each entry in the triangle, add the numbers above it to the left and to the right. This procedure can be expressed as $C(n, k) = C(n - 1, k - 1) + C(n - 1, k)$.

A formula for the number of combinations of k elements chosen from n elements is

$$C(n, k) = \frac{n!}{k!(n-k)!},$$

where the definition of $n!$ (or "n factorial") is

$$n! = n(n-1)(n-2) \dots (2)(1).$$

Combinations do not allow repetition, and the order of the elements does not matter. An important related idea is *permutation*, which again does not allow repetition, but the order of the elements does matter. A formula for the number of k-element permutations from an n-element set is

$$P(n, k) = \frac{n!}{(n-k)!}.$$

Although students do not use these formulas in this investigation, they use them in the following investigation, Combinations, Pascal's Triangle, and the Binomial Theorem.

Pascal's triangle is a triangular array of numbers. The top row, which is the top vertex of the triangle, consists of the single number 1; however, in this investigation, the top vertex is S, or START. Each succeeding row begins and ends with 1, and each remaining entry in the row refers to entries in the row above it. Each number in a given row represents the following sum:

(*Number just above and to the left*) + (*Number just above and to the right*).

The segments connecting 2, 1, and 3 in the triangle in figure 2.1 illustrate this computation.

Row 0					1					
Row 1				1		1				
Row 2			1		2		1			
Row 3		1		3		3		1		
Row 4	1		4		6		4		1	
Row 5	1	5		10		10		5		1

Fig. **2.1.**

Constructing Pascal's triangle

Pascal's triangle bears the name of the seventeenth-century French philosopher and mathematician Blaise Pascal, who explored many of the triangle's properties, particularly those related to the study of probability. However, other mathematicians—including Chu Shih-Chieh in China in 1303—knew about this triangular array well before the time of Pascal.

It is possible to interpret the entries of Pascal's triangle in many ways. In this investigation, students see that each number in Pascal's triangle is the number of zigzag paths from the top of the triangle to that number. Also, the number in row n and entry k is the number of subsets containing k elements from a set with n elements, and it is the number of combinations of k objects chosen from n objects. Thus, the number in row n and entry k of Pascal's triangle is $C(n, k)$.

The $C(n, k)$ notation can express the basic construction rule for Pascal's triangle, illustrated in figure 2.1, as a fundamental combinatorial identity:

$$C(n, k) = C(n - 1, k - 1) + C(n - 1, k),$$

for integers n and k with $0 < k < n$ (see fig. 2.2). The identity $C(n, k) = C(n, n - k)$ expresses the vertical line symmetry of Pascal's triangle for integers n and k with $0 \leq k \leq n$. Students informally explore both of these important patterns in this investigation. They study them more extensively in the following investigation, Combinations, Pascal's Triangle, and the Binomial Theorem.

Fig. **2.2.**

Pascal's triangle, using $C(n, k)$ notation

Row 0	C(0, 0)
Row 1	C(1, 0) C(1, 1)
Row 2	C(2, 0) C(2, 1) C(2, 2)
Row 3	C(3, 0) C(3, 1) C(3, 2) C(3, 3)
Row 4	C(4, 0) C(4, 1) C(4, 2) C(4, 3) C(4, 4)
Row 5	C(5, 0) C(5, 1) C(5, 2) C(5, 3) C(5, 4) C(5, 5)

Combinations, Pascal's Triangle, and the Binomial Theorem

In this investigation, students study connections among Pascal's triangle, combinations, and the binomial theorem. They begin by expanding binomial expressions and looking for patterns. They examine the patterns of exponents and coefficients in binomial expansions, explore connections with Pascal's triangle and combinations, and investigate the role of combinations in the binomial theorem. After finding and describing relationships among combinations, Pascal's triangle, and the binomial theorem, they prove some of the relationships.

Goals

- Understand and apply combinations
- Use reasoning and formulas to solve counting problems in which repetition is not allowed and in which ordering does not matter
- Understand, apply, and describe relationships among the binomial theorem, Pascal's triangle, and combinations
- Use combinatorial reasoning, including for proofs

Materials and Equipment

For each student—

- A copy of the activity sheet "Combinations, Pascal's Triangle, and the Binomial Theorem"

pp. 130–34

Prior Knowledge

The previous investigation—Paths, Strings, and Combinations in Pascal's Triangle—was exploratory and informal. By contrast, the present investigation requires some prior systematic formal knowledge of counting. Students may complete the earlier investigation before they begin this investigation, or they may not; however, to succeed in the current investigation, they will need prior knowledge that extends beyond the previous investigation.

Students should already understand combinations, be able to compute combinations by using the factorial formula

$$C(n, k) = \frac{n!}{k!(n-k)!},$$

and be able to perform algebraic manipulations with factorial notation. They should be able to expand binomial expressions and know how to construct Pascal's triangle. In this investigation, students synthesize their knowledge of combinations, binomial expressions, and Pascal's triangle.

Discussion

Carefully read through or work the problems on the activity sheet before continuing. In problem 1, the students expand $(a + b)^n$ for several values of n and look for patterns in the exponents and the coefficients. Encourage them to see that the exponents in each term add to n, that they increase for one variable and decrease for the other, and that a "hidden" exponent of 0 occurs at the beginning and end of the expansion. Subsequent problems emphasize the pattern of coefficients. Students should be able to describe the patterns in problem 1 well enough to expand $(a + b)^5$ and add that expansion to the table.

In problem 2, the students investigate connections between Pascal's triangle and the expansion of $(a + b)^n$. Although they should be familiar with Pascal's triangle, you may need to give them some reminders. Be sure that they remember the numbering scheme for Pascal's triangle—that is, the rows and the entries in each row are numbered beginning with 0. In this problem, students discover that the coefficients of the binomial expansions are the same as the numbers in the rows of Pascal's triangle.

Students can see the connections among combinations, Pascal's triangle, and the binomial theorem more clearly if you focus on powers of b in the expansion of $(a + b)^n$, as in the investigation, because the expansion of $(a + b)^n$ is conventionally written with decreasing powers of a. Thus, the powers of b increase from 0 to n, matching the entries in Pascal's triangle, which are numbered from 0 to n.

In problem 3, the students investigate connections between combinations and the expansion of $(a + b)^n$. They see that the coefficients of the binomial expansion are the same as the combination numbers $C(n, k)$. They should also notice that $C(5, 3)$, $C(5, 2)$, and the coefficients of the a^2b^3 term and the a^3b^2 term in $(a + b)^5$ are all equal.

In problems 4 and 5, the students take a closer look at the role of combinations in the expansion of binomial expressions of the form $(a + b)^n$. They discover the reasons that the coefficients are the numbers $C(n, k)$, and they formalize this relationship as the binomial theorem.

In problem 6, the students investigate connections between combinations and Pascal's triangle. They identify the entries in Pascal's triangle as the numbers $C(n, k)$. In problem 7, they learn that the construction rule for Pascal's triangle is in fact a fundamental combinatorial identity:

$$C(n, k) = C(n - 1, k - 1) + C(n - 1, k).$$

The students prove this identity in two ways in problem 8—by using the factorial formula for combinations and by using combinatorial reasoning. Students should know the factorial formula for combinations and have some experience in manipulating factorials before they begin this investigation. Finally, in problem 9, they summarize the main points that they have learned by explaining the topics and connections shown in figure 2.3.

The Mathematics in the Investigation

The three main topics in this investigation are combinations, Pascal's triangle, and the binomial theorem. For a discussion of the mathematics of Pascal's triangle, see the previous investigation (particularly pp. 40–42).

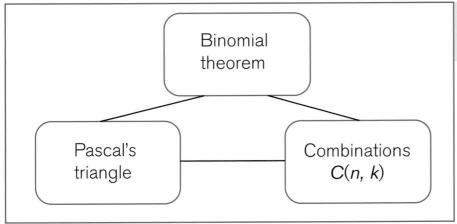

Fig. **2.3.**

The students summarize the topics and connections in the diagram.

The notation $C(n, k)$ denotes the number of combinations, which can be defined as the number of k-element subsets that can be taken from a set with n elements. Equivalently, $C(n, k)$ is the number of ways of choosing k elements from a set of n elements when repetition is not allowed and when different orderings of the same elements do not count as different choices. For example, $C(8, 3)$ is the number of possible three-member committees that can be formed from a group of eight people when the members of the committees are not ranked in any way.

A related idea, although not part of this investigation, is *permutation*. Permutations also involve selecting k elements from a set of n elements with no repetition allowed. Permutations, however, differ significantly from combinations because different orderings of a given k elements count as different selections. The notation $P(n, k)$ or $_nP_k$ denotes permutations. For example, $P(8, 3)$ is the number of different president-vice president-treasurer slates that can be made from a group of eight people. In contrast to an unranked committee of three members, which is a combination, a ranked officer slate consisting of a president, vice president, and treasurer is a permutation.

The binomial theorem gives the expansion of binomial expressions of the form $(a + b)^n$ and shows the relationship between the coefficients of the expansion and the number of combinations, $C(n, k)$. Specifically, the binomial theorem states that for the integers n and k with $0 \le k \le n$ (and $a \ne 0, b \ne 0$),

$$(a + b)^n = C(n, 0)a^nb^0 + C(n, 1)a^{n-1}b + C(n, 2)a^{n-2}b^2 + \ldots + C(n, k)a^{n-k}b^k +$$

$$\ldots + C(n, n - 2)a^2b^{n-2} + C(n, n - 1)ab^{n-1} + C(n, n)\, a^0b^n.$$

The article "Photographs and Committees: Activities That Help Students Discover Permutations and Combinations" (Szydlik 2000) gives further information about permutations and combinations.

Extensions

Possible extensions for this investigation include the following:

1. You can ask your students to prove several classic combinatorial identities by using combinatorial reasoning, the factorial formulas, or mathematical induction. You can also have students relate each identity to Pascal's triangle. For example, you might give your students one of the following challenges:

    a. "Prove that $C(n, k) = C(n, n - k)$, for integers n and k with $0 \le k \le n$. Describe how this identity appears in Pascal's triangle."

  b. "Prove that $C(n, k) = 2^n$, where n is a nonnegative integer and the summation runs from $k = 0$ to $k = n$. Describe how this identity appears in Pascal's triangle."

  c. "Prove that $C(n, k) = C(n - 1, k - 1) + C(n - 1, k)$, for integers n and k with $0 < k < n$."

The classical identity in (*c*) is the one proved in the investigation and is related to the construction rule for Pascal's triangle.

2. Although proving the binomial theorem may be too challenging for most students, you can ask some students to use mathematical induction to prove the following special case of the binomial theorem:

$$(x + 1)^n = C(n, 0)x^n + C(n, 1)x^{n-1} + \ldots + C(n, n - 1)x^1 + C(n, n)x^0,$$

where n is a nonnegative integer.

Conclusion

  This chapter and the previous chapter have presented recommendations and examples for teaching systematic listing and counting in grades 6–12. In addition to systematic listing and counting, NCTM's *Principles and Standards for School Mathematics* (NCTM 2000) recommends that two other discrete mathematics topics be an integral part of the school curriculum. The following chapters discuss ways of teaching these topics—vertex-edge graphs and recursion—in grades 6–12.

NAVIGATING *through* DISCRETE MATHEMATICS

Chapter 3
Vertex-Edge Graphs in Grades 6–8

All students in grades 6–8 should—

- *represent concrete and abstract situations by using vertex-edge graphs and represent vertex-edge graphs with adjacency matrices;*

- *describe and apply properties of graphs, such as vertex degrees, edge weights, directed edges, and isomorphism (whether two graphs are the "same");*

- *use graphs to solve problems related to paths, circuits, and networks in real-world and abstract settings, including explicit use of Euler paths, Hamilton paths, minimum spanning trees, and shortest paths;*

- *understand and apply vertex coloring to solve problems related to avoiding conflicts;*

(continued)

For students in prekindergarten through fifth grade, working with vertex-edge graphs is a very rich hands-on experience that furnishes many opportunities to encounter important ideas gradually and concretely. By the time that students reach grades 6–8, they should have experimented with and constructed vertex-edge graphs in a variety of concrete settings, such as those presented in the graph investigations in *Navigating through Discrete Mathematics in Prekindergarten–Grade 5* (DeBellis et al. forthcoming). Students should have used intuitive reasoning to explore such basic properties as the number of vertices and edges of a graph and neighbors of a vertex. They should have assigned weights to edges; analyzed networks, including distinguishing between a path and a circuit; and examined graphs to determine whether they are the same or different. Students should also have done some informal coloring of maps and vertices and learned to follow and create step-by-step systematic directions to solve problems.

In the middle grades, students should take a closer look at many of these ideas and expand them at the concrete and abstract levels. They can now make a more explicit study of many types of graph problems that they studied informally, including problems involving Euler paths, Hamilton paths, minimum spanning trees, and shortest paths. For example, they should explore problems that enable them to compare and contrast Euler and Hamilton paths and circuits. They should informally consider algorithms for coloring vertices and determining shortest paths, Hamilton and Euler paths, and minimum spanning trees. Students should realize that vertex-edge graphs are powerful tools for

(continued from previous page)

- *use algorithmic thinking to solve problems related to vertex-edge graphs;*

- *use vertex-edge graphs to solve optimization problems.*

representing and solving problems—particularly optimization problems—which detail relationships among a finite number of elements. In the following investigations, students solve optimization problems involving Euler and Hamilton paths, vertex coloring, and minimum spanning trees, all in the context of a summer camp.

Students in the middle grades should also learn about representing a vertex-edge graph with a matrix. They should be able to construct an adjacency matrix for a vertex-edge graph and know how to analyze and interpret the matrix and some of its properties. For example, they should decide whether the adjacency matrix is always a square matrix (it is) and whether it is typically symmetric with respect to its main diagonal (it is not necessarily symmetric for graphs whose edges have an assigned direction). A brief activity with adjacency matrices appears in this chapter.

Students should become aware that people use additional representations of vertex-edge graphs at more advanced levels. In many formal arguments or proofs, for example, points and lines do not represent a graph geometrically; nor does an adjacency matrix represent it numerically. Instead, two sets represent the graph—one is a set of vertices, the other is a set of edges.

Middle school students should also investigate how to recognize when two graphs are "the same." Two graphs are the same, or *isomorphic*, when it is possible to set up a one-to-one correspondence between their vertices and a one-to-one correspondence between their edges so that corresponding edges join corresponding vertices. Students should explore this important concept intuitively in the middle grades, particularly when they are modeling problems, and discover somewhat different-looking graphs in the process.

The two graphs shown in figure 3.1, for example, are essentially the same; they are isomorphic. They both have four vertices that can match so that each letter partners with its corresponding "prime letter." This matching ensures that both corresponding vertices and corresponding edges match. In the middle grades, teachers do not expect students to set up formal one-to-one correspondences, but students should be able to explain intuitively and by redrawing that two graphs are isomorphic.

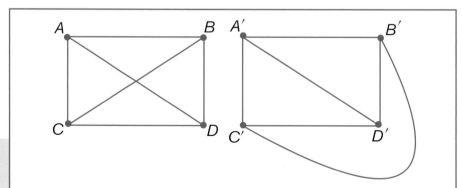

Fig. 3.1.

Isomorphic graphs

Paths at Camp Graffinstuff

This investigation offers a look at Euler and Hamilton paths in vertex-edge graphs. It consists of activities that examine properties and applications of the graphs. The primary focus is on comparing and contrasting Euler paths and circuits with Hamilton paths and circuits. In addition to giving students experience in working with tracings that cover all edges or all vertices of graphs, the investigation challenges them to reason more deeply. They find patterns while they trace more complex graphs and use Hamilton circuits to solve a seating-arrangement problem. The investigation also introduces students to a visual optimization problem related to Euler paths that they can approach through a systematic trial-and-error process.

Goals

- Represent concrete and abstract situations by using vertex-edge graphs
- Describe and apply properties of graphs, such as vertex degrees and directed edges
- Use graphs to solve problems related to paths and circuits, including explicit use of Euler and Hamilton paths
- Use algorithmic thinking to solve problems related to vertex-edge graphs
- Use vertex-edge graphs to solve optimization problems

Materials and Equipment

For each student—

- (Optional) A copy of the activity sheet "Sample Vertex-Edge Graphs"
- A copy of the activity sheet "Paths at Camp Graffinstuff"
- Colored markers
- (Optional; templates available on the CD-ROM) Geodot or grid paper for use in problem 2

pp. 135; 136–40

You can use the templates on the CD-ROM to print geodot or grid paper for your students to work with in problem 2 in the investigation.

Prior Knowledge and Activities

On the basis of their work in previous grades, your students should be able to draw vertex-edge graphs to represent concrete situations, and they should have explored simple properties of graphs. They should also have a command of introductory vocabulary and a basic understanding of terms that enable them to talk about problems involving Euler and Hamilton paths and circuits.

Paths at Camp Graffinstuff allows flexibility in working with students in the middle grades. The investigation is appropriate for students who have done some work on graph tracing but do not yet know how to tell by looking at the degrees of vertices whether a graph has an Euler path or circuit. In addition, since the emphasis is on comparing and contrasting Euler and Hamilton paths, you can use the investigation with students who are ready to apply their knowledge after they have previously done some edge tracing of graphs and are familiar with the conditions required for a graph to have an Euler path or circuit.

To make the most of these investigations, begin by carefully reading the section "The Mathematics in the Investigation" (pp. 53–54)—especially if you are unfamiliar with the extensive vocabulary of graph theory. Learning and exploring the terms gradually is helpful.

You can assign numerous activities to build your students' knowledge of graphs and their uses, providing background and practice before students undertake the investigation. For example, students in the middle grades should learn how and when graph theory began by studying the famous Königsberg bridge (K-bridge) problem and Euler's solution for it. History records that the townspeople of Königsberg tried to devise a route through the city that would cross each of the seven bridges over the river Pregel just once (see fig. 3.2).

Königsberg is a real city. In 1736, it was in East Prussia. Now called Kaliningrad, it is located in Russia.

Fig. **3.2.**

The seven bridges of Königsberg. The river Pregel runs through the city, creating two islands.

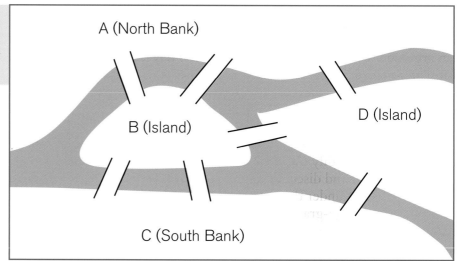

Although many believed that the K-bridge task was not possible, no proof of its impossibility existed until 1736, when the mathematician Leonhard Euler gave a mathematical solution that led to the use of vertex-edge graphs. Students should be able to represent the actual map of Königsberg with a vertex-edge graph, as shown in figure 3.3. Have students attempt to solve the K-bridge problem before they have formal knowledge of Euler paths. That is, ask them to find a route that crosses each bridge exactly once.

As another preliminary activity, have your students work together to generate a set of connected graphs. (For example, see the graphs shown on the blackline master "Sample Vertex-Edge Graphs.") Then let the students work, individually or in groups, to identify the following types of graphs among those that they have created or in those on the optional blackline master:

- Graphs that they can trace completely so that they traverse each edge exactly once, and the starting vertex is the same as the ending vertex
- Graphs that they can trace completely so that they traverse each edge exactly once, and the starting vertex differs from the ending vertex
- Graphs that they cannot trace by traversing each edge exactly once

Fig. **3.3.**

In the vertex-edge graph model of the seven bridges of Königsberg, the vertices represent the four land masses, and the edges represent the bridges.

Ask the students to describe the properties of graphs that fall into each of the three categories. Have them study sample graphs in each category, and ask them to find and verbalize a successful tracing rule. Ask them to make conjectures that summarize their findings and to test their conjectures by examining more graphs.

While your students are working on these activities, you can introduce or reinforce such terms as *degree of a vertex* (the number of edge ends touching the vertex) and *connected graph* (a graph that is all in one piece). Observe that all edges are arcs, line segments, or loops. Edges that are segments or arcs have two distinct vertices as endpoints, whereas loops have just one vertex as an endpoint. A loop adds 2 to the degree of its vertex.

Many students are likely to discover that the tracing secret lies in the degrees of the vertices, and they should be able to articulate the difference between an Euler circuit and an Euler path and understand how to determine whether a graph has either one. If necessary, propose the following conjecture: If a graph has an Euler circuit, then all the vertices of the graph must have even degree. Encourage the students to furnish an argument that supports this conjecture. They should also consider a similar conjecture for a graph that has an Euler path that is not a circuit. You may need to direct the discussion so that they realize that an Euler circuit is a special type of Euler path.

After the students have devised a rule for Euler paths and circuits, revisit the K-bridge problem and verify that a tour of the seven bridges is not possible. Modify the problem in various ways by adding or subtracting bridges, and discuss whether tours that cross all the bridges just once are possible under the changed conditions. For example, figure 3.4 shows a vertex-edge-graph representation of a modified K-bridge problem with eight bridges. A tour crossing all eight bridges exactly once is possible.

After students know what an Euler circuit is and the condition under which it exists, they should try to formulate some sort of strategy for finding such a circuit in a graph and be able to list a sequence of steps that accomplishes that result. They should realize that determining whether a graph has an Euler circuit is one problem, and actually

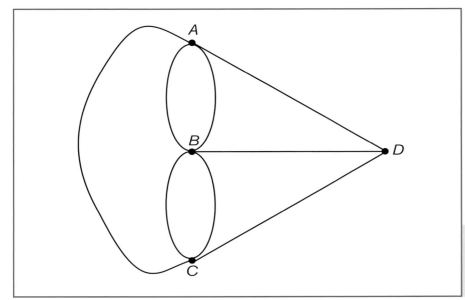

Fig. **3.4.**

A vertex-edge graph adding an eighth bridge to the Königsberg bridge problem

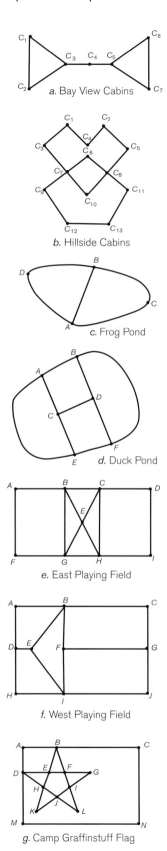

a. Bay View Cabins

b. Hillside Cabins

c. Frog Pond

d. Duck Pond

e. East Playing Field

f. West Playing Field

g. Camp Graffinstuff Flag

finding an Euler circuit may be a separate problem. Using a systematic procedure to find an Euler circuit is an example of algorithmic thinking. Students in the middle grades should devise systematic procedures, but more formal work with algorithms does not ordinarily take place until grades 9–12.

Emphasize the practical value of Euler and Hamilton paths by engaging the class in a discussion about the ways that various businesses and occupations use such paths in their work. Edges matter in some circumstances, such as plowing snow, cleaning streets, collecting money from parking meters, delivering mail, and making security patrols. It is possible to represent these situations with graphs that may have Euler paths and circuits. Contrast these examples with others in which specific delivery and pickup points—that is, vertices—are the crucial feature, such as deliveries to mail storage boxes, salespersons' visits to companies, airline routes to various cities, and collecting money at ATM machines. Hamilton paths and circuits can represent such situations.

Discussion

Read through the activity pages for the investigation carefully before continuing. Note that your students can readily work on the problems individually, in pairs, or in groups. Be certain that they can distinguish between a path and a circuit and that they understand the difference between an Euler path and a Hamilton path.

In problem 1, the students examine graphs of different portions of Camp Graffinstuff as well as the camp's flag design (see the margin) to determine whether the graphs have Euler paths, Euler circuits, Hamilton paths, or Hamilton circuits. Encourage the students to decide on an acceptable path, trace it with a colored marker, and then follow up by producing a sequence of letters or numbers that represents their path. Urge them to use just the subscripts to describe their paths in 1(*a*) and 1(*b*); for example, a Hamilton path in 1(*a*) is 1234567. The students encounter an example on the activity sheet. When they have completed problem 1, they should discuss their solutions with partners, resolve any differences, and determine which graphs have more than one acceptable path or circuit.

The students explore two methods of tracing a rectangular grid in problem 2. The *minimum-lift* method requires that each edge be traced exactly once but allows "lifting" the tracing tool to avoid retracing an edge. The goal is to minimize lifts. By contrast, the *minimum-retracing* method requires that the complete graph be traced with no lifts but allows retracing an edge. The goal is to minimize retraced edges. The numbered edges in problem 2 make it easier for students to describe—as well as represent and draw—the path that shows the tracings with the smallest number of lifts or edge retracings. Emphasize the importance of the word *minimum* and the way to use the word in both methods. An often-used term for a problem that seeks the minimum or maximum as a solution is *optimization problem*. Urge students to be systematic in seeking the best route with the smallest number of edge retracings or pencil lifts as the size of the rectangular grids increases. Caution them to be sure to count the last lift of the pencil.

You may want to challenge students to make a connection between the minimum-lifts part of the activity and the Euler path rule—that is, an Euler path that is not a circuit occurs in graphs that have exactly two odd vertices. The grids all have an even number of odd vertices. The minimum number of pencil lifts needed is one-half the number of odd vertices, since paths can begin at one odd vertex and end at another.

Carefully probe your students' responses to problem 3. This problem calls on the students to make a seating arrangement for eight campers at a circular table, with two campers sitting at adjacent places only if they participate in the same sport. Ask the students to explain how they determined their seating arrangement and, in particular, how a Hamilton circuit helped them find the arrangement. As an extension, you might ask students what criteria, other than participation in the same sport, they can use for determining the campers' seating arrangement. Students can then devise and solve similar problems on the basis of those other criteria.

Note that some edges of the graph intersect at points that are not given as vertices of the graph. You can introduce the term *planar graph* at this time. A planar graph is a graph that can be drawn in the plane so that no two edges intersect, except at the vertices of the graph. Students may think that the graph in this activity is not a planar graph, although it in fact is planar. Ask them to produce an isomorphic graph that clearly shows that the graph is planar (see the margin for one possibility).

Problem 4 tells the students that a new award medallion for the camp must have neither an Euler nor a Hamilton circuit. The students are to examine two graphs (see the margin) to decide if either fits the criteria. In problem 4, as in problems 1 and 2, encourage students to show their answers pictorially and with a sequence of numbers representing the subscripts. They need to do this only if one of the designs has an Euler or Hamilton circuit. The pentagonal graph is the *Petersen graph*. Observe that all the vertices have degree 3. Thus, since all vertices are not even, the graph has no Euler circuit. After students have explored making paths systematically on the graph, they should conclude that traveling to all vertices exactly once is not possible by starting inside with vertices on the tips of the star and then going outside to those that are vertices of the pentagon, or vice versa, or by alternating between the two types of vertices. They should agree that no Hamilton circuit exists. Suggest that students design their own medallions that meet the criteria in the problem.

The Mathematics in the Investigation

This investigation features Euler and Hamilton paths and circuits. Students need to know some terminology to understand the introductory graph theory described in this activity. In particular, they should know the following terms: *vertex, edge, graph, connected graph, path, circuit, degree of a vertex, Euler circuit* and *Euler path*, and *Hamilton circuit* and *Hamilton path*.

A graph consists of points called *vertices*, as well as line segments, arcs, or loops called *edges*, as in figure 3.5. Figure 3.6 is a graph with five vertices and five edges.

Graphs such as the one in figure 3.6 are *connected graphs*. In a connected

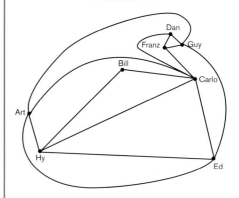

An Isomorphic Graph for Problem 3

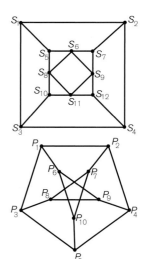

Medallion Designs in Problem 4

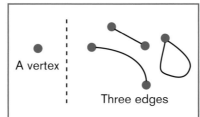

A vertex

Three edges

Fig. **3.5.**

Graph components

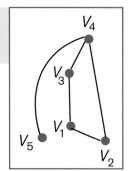

Fig. **3.6.**

A graph with five vertices and five edges

A connected graph has an Euler circuit if and only if all of its vertices have even degree. A connected graph has an Euler path that is not an Euler circuit if and only if among its vertices exactly two have odd degree.

graph, it is possible to travel from any vertex to any other vertex along adjacent edges of the graph.

The *degree of a vertex* is the number of edge ends at the vertex. In figure 3.6, the degree of V_5 is 1; V_1, V_2, and V_3 all have degree 2; and the degree of V_4 is 3. Methods of labeling vertices of a graph include using subscripts, as in figure 3.6, and using different letters, as in figures 3.7a and 3.7b.

An *Euler path* is a tracing or route on a connected graph that traces each edge of the graph exactly once. An *Euler circuit* is an Euler path in which the starting vertex and the ending vertex are the same.

Fig. **3.7.**

Two graphs with five vertices

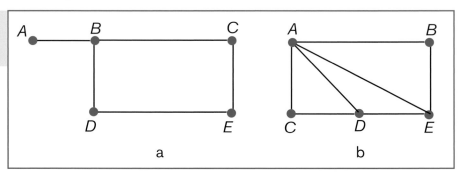

a   b

A *Hamilton path* is a tracing or route on a connected graph that visits each vertex of the graph exactly once. A *Hamilton circuit* is a tracing or route on a connected graph in which the first vertex and the last vertex are the same and all other vertices are visited exactly once.

As students develop their own graphs or work through various problems on given graphs, they should conclude that a straightforward way exists to find out whether a graph has an Euler circuit or path. The note in the margin (upper left) presents useful theorems. They imply that simply by determining the degrees of the vertices, students can look at a graph and decide whether it has an Euler circuit or an Euler path that is not a circuit.

Students can identify paths and circuits by tracing them directly on a graph, or they can describe them by indicating a sequence of vertices. Students can represent a path on the graph of figure 3.6 as V_5, V_4, V_3, V_1, V_2 or more simply as 5 4 3 1 2. The graph in figure 3.7a has exactly two odd vertices—*A* and *B*. It has an Euler path (*ABCEDB*) and it has a Hamilton path (*ABDEC*), but it has no circuit of either type. The graph in figure 3.7b has a Hamilton path (*ABEDC*) and a Hamilton circuit (*ABEDCA*).

Students should also learn that determining whether an arbitrary connected graph has a Hamilton circuit or path is essentially a trial-and-error process. That is, no one knows an if-and-only-if theorem for Hamilton paths. This is a famous unsolved problem in mathematics. However, there are some theorems that are helpful in making a decision about particular graphs. For example, if a connected graph has *n* vertices, with *n* greater than 2, and each vertex has degree of at least *n*/2, then the graph has a Hamilton circuit.

Graph theory has an interesting and relatively recent history. By investigating significant contributors to the field, students can obtain a broader picture of the development of the topic. Their explorations might include the following important graph theorists. Leonhard Euler (1707–1783), for whom Euler paths are named, was one of the greatest of all mathematicians. Sir William Rowan Hamilton (1805–1865), for whom Hamilton paths are named, was a child prodigy who was talented in mathematics as well as in other disciplines. Students can explore the Internet and other sources for biographical information that can make these mathematicians more than just names. You might challenge your class to find out about Euler's polyhedral formula (*Vertices* − *Edges* + *Faces* = 2) and Hamilton's icosian game, which involves finding a Hamilton circuit on a vertex-edge graph of a dodecahedron.

Decisions … Decisions … Decisions at Camp Graffinstuff

This investigation consists of three situations that feature vertex coloring, Hamilton paths, and minimum spanning trees as ways to solve problems. In the first two parts, "The Sports Director's Dilemma" and "The Tour Director's Dilemma," the students use vertex coloring to help solve problems about scheduling to avoid conflicts. In general, vertex coloring can help solve problems in many contexts that call for avoiding conflicts. For instance, vertex coloring can help determine the smallest number of habitats to build in a zoo so that animals in a group are not predators or prey of one another. The students solve the coloring problems in the investigation informally. They do not need to know a particular algorithm in advance; they develop their own strategies by trial and error and describe them.

The third part of the investigation, "The Bus Director's Dilemma," asks students to find bus routes and make plans for painting center stripes on roads that satisfy certain criteria. This investigation uses Hamilton paths and prepares the way for studying a special kind of graph called a *tree* and for learning how minimum spanning trees can be useful mathematical models for certain types of optimization problems.

You can use these activities with students who are unfamiliar with specific vertex-edge graph topics but who can follow the directions and are willing to experiment. After the class has completed the activities, you can lead a directed discussion of shared thinking to develop summaries of the main ideas and methods that students tried.

Goals

- Represent concrete and abstract situations by using vertex-edge graphs
- Describe and apply properties of graphs, such as vertex degrees, edge weights, and directed edges
- Use graphs to solve problems related to paths, circuits, and networks in real-world and abstract settings, including explicit use of Hamilton paths and minimum spanning trees
- Understand and apply vertex coloring to solve problems related to avoiding conflicts
- Use algorithmic thinking to solve problems related to vertex-edge graphs
- Use vertex-edge graphs to solve optimization problems

Materials and Equipment

For each student—

- A copy of each of the following activity sheets:

pp. 141–42; 143; 144–45

○ "The Sports Director's Dilemma"
○ "The Tour Director's Dilemma"
○ "The Bus Director's Dilemma"
• Colored markers or colored pencils

Prior Knowledge and Activities

Students should have a basic familiarity with vertex-edge graphs. They should be able to draw graphs that represent situations in the real world. A crucial part of this representation process is deciding what items to represent by vertices and what items to represent by edges. Examining a wide variety of problems, persisting, and systematically eliminating possibilities will help build students' skill in making the correct choices.

Students should have a command of some introductory vocabulary and a basic understanding of such terms as *connected graph*, *degree of a vertex*, *directed edges*, and *weighted edges* so that they can use these terms when they discuss problems involving paths and circuits. Prior work with situations that emphasize *the least* and *the most* can help prepare students for the type of optimization problems presented in these activities.

Before doing vertex coloring, students should have completed activities similar to those in the investigation Paths at Camp Graffinstuff. Also, if they have not done map coloring in previous grades, you should give them an opportunity to color various maps by using the rule that requires that regions sharing a common border have different colors. Emphasize that the objective for completing such a map coloring is to use the minimum number of colors. Students should experiment with real maps, as well as contrived maps, so that they encounter a variety of color counts in their results.

After your students have done some map coloring to determine the minimum number of colors needed for a map, make the transition to vertex-edge graphs and vertex coloring—that is, have the students make the vertex-edge graph for a map by asking them to represent each region of the map with a vertex and to join two vertices with an edge if the two regions share a common border. They can then establish a routine for coloring the map by coloring the vertices in the graph. This chapter describes one possible algorithm, the Welsh and Powell vertex-coloring algorithm.

Are four colors always enough to color a planar map? Students in the middle grades should become aware of this famous map-coloring problem, which went unsolved for more than one hundred years. The first written reference to the four-color map-coloring problem surfaced in 1852, when Augustus De Morgan wrote to William Rowan Hamilton about a question posed by one of his students. From then until 1976, many mathematicians tried to prove that four colors were enough to color any planar map. In 1976, Kenneth Appel and Wolfgang Haken produced a computer proof of the four-color theorem that took more than 1200 hours of computer time to run. Their proof, which the mathematical community ultimately accepted, has sparked continuing controversy over the validity of computer proofs.

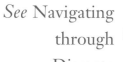

See Navigating through Discrete Mathematics in Prekindergarten–Grade 5 *(DeBellis et al. forthcoming) and the map-coloring activities in* NCTM Student Math Notes *(Dick 1990) on the* CD-ROM.

Discussion

Read through the activity pages before proceeding further. This investigation presents three dilemmas. The first and second dilemmas are scheduling problems that seek the minimum number of time slots needed to create a schedule that avoids conflicts. The investigation encourages students to develop their own schemes for solving the dilemmas. Prior study of algorithms for solving conflict problems is unnecessary.

Part 1—"The Sports Director's Dilemma"
Part 2—"The Tour Director's Dilemma"

The sports director at Camp Graffinstuff wants to allow campers to participate in all the sports that they select, but she needs to come up with an efficient schedule, using as few time slots as possible. Twelve campers have made their selections from seven sports: basketball (BB), tennis (T), soccer (SO), softball (SB), hiking (H), archery (A), and swimming (SW). Meanwhile, the tour director at Camp Graffinstuff is also working out a schedule, this time for six tours, each offering three attractions, some of which may overlap with the attractions of other tours. All the tours must be offered each week, but no two tours can be available on the same day if they have an attraction in common.

After students convert the information in "The Sports Director's Dilemma" and "The Tour Director's Dilemma" into graphs, they can develop their solutions visually. For example, the graph in figure 3.8a, which resolves the dilemma faced by the sports director, implies that three colors are necessary, since the edges form many triangles and each vertex of a triangle must be a different color because the vertices are all adjacent to one another. Similarly, students may notice that the graph in figure 3.8b, which solves the tour director's problem, contains a quadrilateral with its two diagonals included. Such a quadrilateral configuration requires four colors, since all four vertices in this situation are adjacent to one another. Thus, this graph requires four colors.

After the students have devised their own methods to achieve solutions, you can use the problems as a catalyst to develop an informal algorithm. However, if students already know a vertex-coloring method for solving conflict problems, they can resolve "The Sports Director's Dilemma" and "The Tour Director's Dilemma" by using that method.

You might ask students to do a brief report on the famous four-color theorem and its proof by using such Internet sources as http://mathworld.wolfram.com/Four-ColorTheorem.html or such print publications as the book Four Colors Suffice: How the Map Problem Was Solved *(Wilson 2002).*

Fig. **3.8.**

Three colors (*a*) and four colors (*b*) are necessary for the vertices of the graphs in parts 1 and 2 (the numbers in parentheses indicate vertex degrees).

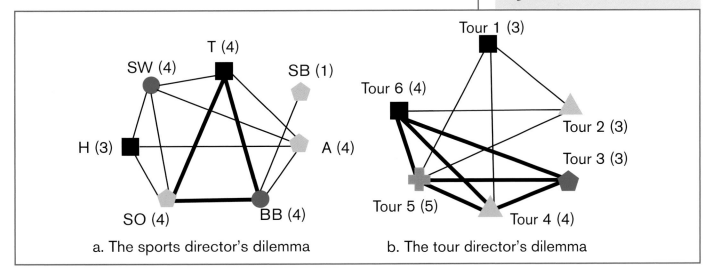

a. The sports director's dilemma

b. The tour director's dilemma

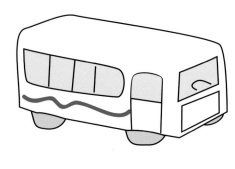

Students can achieve a deeper understanding if they have time to compare and contrast their coloring schemes after they have found their solutions.

Part 3—"The Bus Director's Dilemma"

"The Bus Director's Dilemma" reviews Hamilton paths and provides an informal introduction to the traveling salesman problem (TSP) and the idea of a minimum spanning tree. The camp bus travels on fourteen roads, making eight stops. The bus director, who knows the distance from any location to any other one, wants to design a route that will take the bus to every location without backtracking or visiting any location more than once. The bus does not need to return to its starting point.

This problem applies the word *minimum* to two things—road counts and mileage for a road system that connects all locations. This problem features a *weighted graph*, which is a graph whose edges have numerical values. The numbers are the lengths of the roads, expressed in miles, that edges of the graph represent. Students will probably use a trial-and-error process to approach this problem. When they consider the separate parts, they should realize that many possible bus routes and paths cover all eight locations.

All questions in the third dilemma target spanning trees as a central idea. In problems 1 and 2, the students find a route that visits each vertex exactly once—that is, they find a Hamilton path. Such a path is also a spanning tree, since it is connected, has no circuits, and includes all vertices. Problem 2 also considers the lengths of the roads, so it indirectly provides an informal introduction to the TSP—the problem of finding a least-weight Hamilton circuit in a graph. Students should explore the TSP in more detail in grades 9–12.

Problem 3 focuses on the notion of a minimum spanning tree, exemplified here as a set of roads with the least total mileage that connects all eight locations. The bus driver has a friend who owns the Bright Stripe Company, which has proposed painting a center stripe on any or all roads near Camp Graffinstuff at a cost of $25 per mile. The bus director is assisting the owner in finding a minimum spanning tree in this situation.

The students may offer interesting strategies and arguments while they attempt to find their minimum spanning tree. Be sure to allocate class time for the students to describe their work. Students should notice a basic difference between the solutions to problem 3, which are networks that span all the vertices, and the solutions to problems 1 and 2, which are routes through the graph with no backtracking. Specifically, the minimum spanning trees in problem 3 would not work as typical bus routes unless backtracking were allowed, because of the dead-end branches of the tree, as shown in figure 3.9. Minimum spanning trees have many interesting properties and practical applications that students should explore further in grades 9–12.

The Mathematics in the Investigation

The two major ideas from graph theory that are central to this investigation are the use of vertex coloring as a means of optimally avoiding conflicts and the use of minimum spanning trees as a way to minimize a desired condition in a problem.

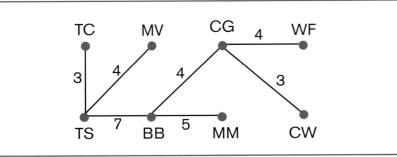

Fig. **3.9.**

A minimum spanning tree for painting stripes (a connected set of roads that joins all eight location and has the minimum total mileage)

After the students have had time to make sense of the situations presented in the dilemmas and have designed their own approaches and solutions, summarize the results in a discussion so that they have a reasonable algorithm to use in each situation. Although there are several efficient algorithms for finding a minimum spanning tree in any connected graph, no one knows an efficient algorithm that is guaranteed to find a minimal coloring for any graph. However, students should consider systematic procedures for coloring graphs.

Welsh and Powell Vertex-Coloring Algorithm

The Welsh and Powell vertex-coloring algorithm may be similar to an algorithm that students suggest. If their ideas do not include this algorithm, present it as a systematic procedure that is easy to follow.

The objective is to use the minimum number of colors to color the vertices of a graph so that adjacent vertices have different colors. The steps of this algorithm are as follows:

1. Order all vertices in the graph according to their degree. Start with the highest, and end with the lowest. Whenever two or more vertices have the same degree, list them in any order.

2. Choose a color for the leading vertex and continue down the list, using that color for any vertices that do not share an edge with that leading vertex or with any other vertex assigned that color.

3. Return to the top of the list, choose a second color for the first uncolored vertex, and proceed down the list as in step 2.

4. Continue the process until you have colored all vertices.

D. J. A. Welsh and M. B. Powell, mathematicians in the United Kingdom, formally developed the Welsh and Powell algorithm in 1967. In general, their popular algorithm gives an upper bound for the minimum number of colors needed for the vertices. In many instances—but not all—this upper bound turns out to be the actual minimum number of colors for the vertices.

Figure 3.10a, for example, is a simple graph that requires two different colors for coloring its vertices, as shown in figure 3.10b. Figure 3.11 shows vertex coloring that is based on the Welsh and Powell algorithm and uses three colors for the same graph. A step-by-step application of the Welsh and Powell algorithm for the graph follows:

1. The result of ordering the vertices by degree is *C*-4, *G*-3, *D*-2, *E*-2, *H*-2, *I*-2, *A*-1, *B*-1, *F*-1.

2. Vertices *C* and *G* use the first color.

Fig. **3.10.**

Two colors suffice for the vertices of the simple graph in (*a*), as shown in (*b*).

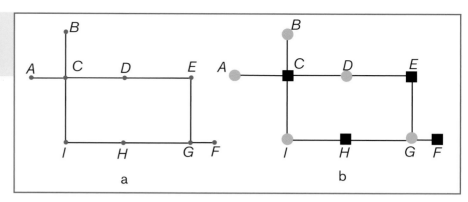

a

b

Fig. **3.11.**

The Welsh and Powell algorithm gives an upper bound of three colors for the vertices of the graph in figure 3.10a.

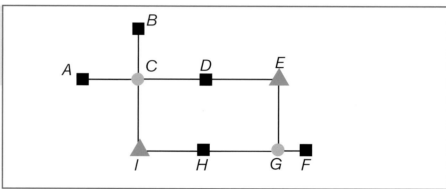

3. Vertices *D*, *H*, *A*, *B*, and *F* use the second color.
4. Vertices *E* and *I* use the third color.

In this example, the Welsh and Powell algorithm gives an upper bound that is not the actual minimum number of colors. Different vertex colorings can result, depending on how vertices with the same degree are listed. However, each application of the algorithm gives the same upper bound of three colors.

When the number of vertices is large, the Welsh and Powell algorithm is easy to implement and fast to run on a computer. However, as in the example, it does not necessarily give the optimal result. In fact, the search continues for an efficient algorithm that can determine the minimum number of colors needed for the vertices of any graph.

The search continues for an efficient algorithm that can determine the minimum number of colors needed for the vertices of any graph.

Minimum Spanning Trees and Kruskal's Algorithm

Students also explore minimum spanning trees in the investigation. Trees are a special kind of connected graph. Some connected graphs contain *circuits*, which are paths that begin and end at the same vertex with no repeated edges; trees are connected graphs that do not contain circuits. A spanning tree of a given connected graph is a tree that reaches all the vertices of the graph; it is therefore a graph that contains all the vertices and at least some of the edges of the given graph. If the connected graph has *n* vertices, a spanning tree contains (*n* – 1) edges. In some circumstances, numbers, or weights, are associated with the edges of a connected graph. A minimum spanning tree in such a weighted connected graph is a spanning tree in which the sum of the weights is as small as possible. Several different efficient algorithms exist for finding a minimum spanning tree. Kruskal's algorithm, a commonly used efficient algorithm, correctly finds a minimum spanning tree. Joseph B. Kruskal, a research mathematician at Bell Laboratories, developed the algorithm in the mid-1950s.

The objective of this algorithm is to determine a minimum spanning tree for a connected graph with n vertices. The steps of the algorithm are as follows:

1. Draw only the vertices of the graph.
2. List all the numbers, or weights, of the edges of the given connected graph according to size, starting with the smallest. Be sure to include repeats.
3. Draw one of the edges with the smallest weight. If more than one edge has that weight, draw all such edges, provided that no circuits exist.
4. Choose the next weight on the list, and draw corresponding edges, omitting those that would make a circuit.
5. Continue the process until you have drawn $(n - 1)$ edges.

The vertices and drawn edges are a minimum spanning tree for the graph. Students can use Kruskal's algorithm to solve problem 3 of "The Bus Director's Dilemma." (See fig. 3.9 and the solution to the problem on pp. 190–91.)

Additional Activity: Adjacency Matrices for Vertex-Edge Graphs

Students in the middle grades routinely work with grids, tables, and arrays. They encounter matrices in their mathematics courses at least on an informal level. In this activity, a matrix is a rectangular array of objects, called *entries*. The entry a_{ij} is in the ith row and jth column. The number of rows and columns determines the size of the matrix, which students record as *row × column*. For example, the 2×5 matrix in figure 3.12 has ten entries, and a_{23} is 8.

Middle school students can experiment with representing graphs by a special kind of matrix called an *adjacency matrix*. Adjacency matrices can represent graphs on a computer. To introduce adjacency matrices, present the following problem to your students:

> Five friends are comparing their course schedules. Molly takes history with Sean and English with Lea. Sean has mathematics with Rico and science with Han. Lea takes fine arts with Han and physical education with Rico. Rico takes history with Molly and health with Han. Which of the five students is taking the most classes with friends?

Guide your students to the solution with the following instructions:

1. "Draw a vertex-edge graph in which each vertex represents a student. Use an edge to join two vertices if the two students are in a class together." (Figure 3.13 shows the solution.)

2. "Represent the data in the question by using an adjacency matrix. That is, construct a matrix in which the rows and columns are labeled with the vertices (i.e., the students). Make the a_{ij} entry 1 if an edge connects the two vertices v_i and v_j. That is, make an entry 1 if the two students have a class in common; otherwise, use 0 as the entry." (Figure 3.14 shows a solution.)

Although no known efficient algorithm gives the minimum number of colors needed for vertex coloring, several different efficient algorithms exist for finding a minimum spanning tree.

Fig. **3.12.**

A 2 × 5 matrix

$$\begin{pmatrix} 1 & 2 & 3 & 4 & 5 \\ 6 & 7 & 8 & 9 & 10 \end{pmatrix}$$

The next chapter, "Vertex-Edge Graphs in Grades 9–12," includes further work with adjacency matrices.

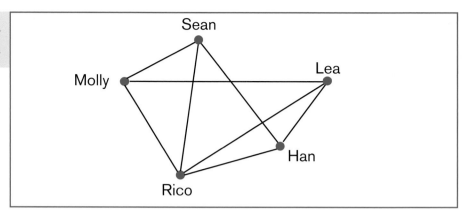

Fig. **3.13.**

A graph based on course data

Fig. **3.14.**

An adjacency matrix

$$\begin{array}{c} \\ H \\ L \\ M \\ R \\ S \end{array} \begin{array}{ccccc} H & L & M & R & S \\ \begin{pmatrix} 0 & 1 & 0 & 1 & 1 \\ 1 & 0 & 1 & 1 & 0 \\ 0 & 1 & 0 & 1 & 1 \\ 1 & 1 & 1 & 0 & 1 \\ 1 & 0 & 1 & 1 & 0 \end{pmatrix} \end{array}$$

3. "How can you tell by looking at the matrix which student is taking the most classes with other friends?" (Rico is taking the most classes with other friends. To obtain this answer, look for the row or column with the most 1s, or equivalently, look for the greatest row or column sum.)

Conclusion

This chapter has provided guidance and examples for teaching vertex-edge graphs in middle school. It presents several investigations that allow students in the middle grades to explore the use of vertex-edge graphs to solve problems. In particular, the chapter compares and contrasts Euler and Hamilton paths and circuits, uses vertex coloring to solve problems related to avoiding conflicts, and introduces a particular kind of graph known as a tree. As students become engaged in this work, they increase their problem-solving ability, build reasoning power, gain deeper understanding, and develop and apply algorithmic thinking. They also become acquainted with optimization problems and ways of solving them. This work lays the foundation for further study of vertex-edge graphs in grades 9–12, as discussed in the next chapter.

NAVIGATIONS SERIES

GRADES 6–12

NAVIGATING *through* DISCRETE MATHEMATICS

Chapter 4
Vertex-Edge Graphs in Grades 9–12

All students in grades 9–12 should—

- *understand and apply vertex-edge graph topics including Euler paths, Hamilton paths, the traveling salesman problem (TSP), minimum spanning trees, critical paths, shortest paths, vertex coloring, and adjacency matrices;*

- *understand, analyze, and apply vertex-edge graphs to model and solve problems related to paths, circuits, networks, and relationships among a finite number of elements in real-world and abstract settings;*

- *devise, analyze, and apply algorithms for solving vertex-edge graph problems;*

(continued)

The study of vertex-edge graphs, which is more formally called the study of *graph theory*, gives students a wonderful opportunity to investigate important mathematics, actively gaining experience in such powerful mathematical processes as problem solving, reasoning, and modeling. The topics in graph theory recommended for study in grades 9–12 are fundamental and widely applicable. Moreover, these topics can engage students in doing mathematics, often without a lot of technical prerequisites, and can provide success and enjoyment for students who have struggled with other topics in mathematics.

Students should have had some experience in previous grades with Euler paths, Hamilton paths, minimum spanning trees, shortest paths, and vertex coloring. Children in prekindergarten through fifth grade study these topics quite informally. More formal terminology and analysis should begin in grades 6–8 and continue in grades 9–12. In grades 9–12, students study two new graph topics: the traveling salesman problem (TSP) and critical paths. They compare and contrast all recommended graph topics, and they do more work with matrix representations of graphs.

The terminology in graph theory is not entirely standardized. For example, Euler and Hamilton paths are sometimes called *Eulerian* or *Hamiltonian* paths. Another name for the traveling salesman problem, which originated when most sales representatives were men, is the *traveling salesperson problem*; and a common abbreviation for it is TSP. Even the term *path* can have slightly different meanings and relates to similar terms like *walk* and *trail*. Terms and their meanings as used in this book are common but not universal. In teaching graph theory in high school

(continued from previous page)

- *compare and contrast topics in terms of algorithms, optimization, properties, and types of problems that can be solved;*

- *extend work with adjacency matrices for graphs through such activities as interpreting row sums and using the nth power of the adjacency matrix to count paths of length n in a graph.*

The traveling salesman problem (TSP) is a famous problem in mathematics: If a salesman starts at one city, visits all the other cities in the sales area exactly once, and returns to the starting city, then what is the minimum number of miles that the salesman travels?

(and in earlier grades), it is important to avoid becoming mired in the terminology but instead to let students focus on the ideas and visual nature of graph theory.

Students study algorithms, or step-by-step procedures, for graph problems more carefully in grades 9–12 than they did in previous grades. Before grade 9, students should have devised their own algorithms, either implicitly or explicitly, or they should have followed directions to carry out algorithms given to them. High school students should continue in this vein, in addition to analyzing graph algorithms in more detail. In particular, they should explore both the correctness and efficiency of graph algorithms. In considering correctness, students learn, for example, that a "nearest-neighbor" algorithm does not solve the TSP for any graph. In considering efficiency, they learn that a brute-force algorithm, although guaranteed to solve the TSP, is not efficient, because the world's fastest computer would require hundreds of years to carry it out even with a relatively small graph.

This chapter includes investigations related to critical paths, the TSP, and matrices. Before we present those investigations, we briefly discuss the other graph topics with respect to recommendations for grades 9–12.

Before students enter ninth grade, they should have learned that the vertex-coloring problem is unsolved. That is, no one knows an efficient way to color all the vertices of any graph so that adjacent vertices have different colors and the minimum number of colors is used. Students should have explored coloring algorithms such as the Welsh and Powell algorithm and should have discovered that, although these algorithms are useful, they do not always produce the minimum number of colors.

Students should also have learned before ninth grade that they can determine whether a given graph has an Euler circuit (that is, a circuit that uses each edge exactly once) by using the following theorem: *A connected graph has an Euler circuit if and only if all vertices have even degree.* Students should have explored the intuitive reason for one direction of this theorem: traveling around an Euler circuit involves going in and out of every vertex, and this "in-and-out" criterion makes every vertex have even degree. The other direction of the theorem is more difficult to prove and is an optional extension topic in grades 9–12.

Changing the criterion of using each *edge* exactly once (as in an Euler circuit) to using each vertex exactly once results in the Hamilton circuit problem. Students should have learned in previous grades that this change in perspective changes the problem from a solved problem to an unsolved one. That is, in contrast to the situation with Euler circuits, no known set of testable criteria completely determines whether a graph has a Hamilton circuit. There is no nice theorem that states, "A graph has a Hamilton circuit if and only if…." Putting weights on the edges of a graph and then trying to find a Hamilton circuit of least total weight results in the TSP.

In grades 9–12, students begin their study of critical paths. A critical path problem, whose solution sometimes uses a *program evaluation and review technique* (PERT), considers a large project that consists of many tasks, some of which are prerequisites for others. A directed graph—that is, a graph in which the edges have a specified direction—can represent the prerequisite relationships among all the tasks in the project.

Then the problem solver employs the graph to find the earliest completion time for the whole project, the scheduling times for each task, and the critical tasks, which are tasks that prevent the project from being completed at the earliest possible completion time if they are behind schedule.

Students in grades 9–12 should be able to compare and contrast the different graph topics that they have been studying: Euler paths, Hamilton paths, shortest paths, critical paths, minimum spanning trees, the TSP, and vertex coloring. For example, they should understand and be able to explain the following concepts and connections:

- The ideas of optimization and algorithmic problem solving are central to all these topics.
- Finding an optimal path or circuit is an important problem that relates to all topics except minimum spanning trees and vertex coloring.
- Minimum spanning trees, Hamilton circuits, and solutions to the TSP represent optimal spanning networks; minimum spanning trees span all the vertices in the graph with a tree, whereas Hamilton circuits and solutions to the TSP span all the vertices with a circuit.
- Euler and Hamilton paths differ significantly by shifting perspective from edges to vertices. An Euler path traverses each edge of a graph exactly once; a Hamilton path visits each vertex exactly once.
- Critical paths contrast with shortest paths in that a critical path is a longest path.
- Finding the "shortest" is a basic problem that is related to several of these topics—finding the shortest path, the shortest tree (minimum spanning tree), or the shortest circuit (TSP).
- Some problems—such as finding Euler paths, shortest paths, critical paths, and minimum spanning trees—are generally solvable and have efficient algorithms, but others—vertex coloring, finding Hamilton paths, and the TSP—are still unsolved.

For more information about graph topics, see the section "Vertex-Edge Graphs: Summary and Additional Information for Grades 6–12" in this chapter (pp. 77–80).

Chapter 3, "Vertex-Edge Graphs in Grades 6–8," includes a discussion of the Welsh and Powell vertex-coloring algorithm (see pp. 59–60).

Using Critical Paths to Schedule Large Projects

In this investigation, students learn one of the most commonly used mathematical management methods—the *critical path method* (CPM), also called the *program evaluation and review technique* (PERT). Students learn this technique by solving two scheduling problems, one in the context of organizing a Peace Day festival and the other in the context of building a house. They learn how to find and use a critical path to determine the earliest finish time for a project, and they also explore more detailed scheduling of each individual task in a project.

Goals

- Understand, analyze, and apply critical paths to model and solve problems related to paths, networks, and relationships among a finite number of elements (in this case, prerequisite relationships among a finite number of tasks in a large project)
- Devise, analyze, and apply algorithms for solving vertex-edge graph problems

Materials and Equipment

For each student—

- A copy of each of the following activity sheets
  ○ "Planning a Festival"
  ○ "Building a House"

pp. 146–48; 149–50

Prior Knowledge

This investigation has no specific prerequisites; students simply need some general experience with graphs. If students do not have any knowledge of graphs, give them a few examples and quickly discuss the basic terminology of vertices and edges.

Discussion

Critical paths are used to find the optimal schedules for large projects that consist of many tasks, some of which are prerequisites for others. Vertices represent the tasks, and a directed edge (an arrow) connects two vertices if one task is an immediate prerequisite of another. In this investigation, students learn how to use such a vertex-edge graph model to schedule a project.

Part 1—"Planning a Festival"

In part 1, the students suppose that they are on the planning committee for a Peace Day Festival at their school. In problem 1, they list tasks that they might need to do to organize the festival. The goal is for students to think about the complexity of a large project and consider how they might break it down into many individual tasks. In problem 2, they consider two fundamental types of tasks—those that are prerequisites for others and those that can be done concurrently with others.

Understanding these types of tasks is crucial for successfully modeling and solving the problem with a vertex-edge graph.

One important detail in this analysis is the difference between a prerequisite and an immediate prerequisite. Students explore this difference in problem 3, which describes a simple Peace Day festival project, represented as a table and a directed graph. The directed edges show the prerequisite relationships. This project digraph, shown in figure 4.1, includes vertices labeled "START" and "END" to show clear beginning and ending points. The remaining vertices represent the following tasks: deciding on the number and types of booths (T), finding volunteers to build the booths (V), obtaining materials to build the booths (M), and building the booths (B).

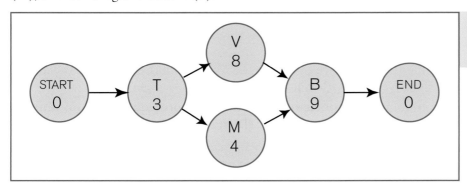

A directed graph, or digraph, *is a graph with direction on its edges.*

Fig. **4.1.**

A simple project digraph

In problem 3, students begin to reason about the situation to find the earliest finish time (EFT), and then they move on to specific techniques and analysis. In part (*c*) of problem 3, they consider the EFTs proposed by three hypothetical students. These three sample responses point out three methods that students commonly use in attempting to determine the EFT. These methods are finding the sum of all task times, finding the length of the shortest path through the project digraph, and finding the length of the longest path through the project digraph. After discussing these three alternatives, students should agree that, perhaps surprisingly, the longest path gives the earliest finish time. Since students often have trouble understanding that the longest path yields the earliest completion time, ask them to explain this result.

In parts (*d*) and (*f*) of problem 3, students investigate critical paths and tasks. A longest path through a project digraph is a *critical path*, and tasks on the critical path are *critical tasks*. For convenience, the digraph includes the START and END vertices as critical tasks. In part (*d*), students find a critical path. In part (*e*), they confirm that the length of a critical path through the project digraph is the EFT for the project. In part (*f*), to help students understand why the term *critical* is used, they explore what happens when a task that is on the critical path falls behind schedule, as well as what happens when a task that is not on the critical path falls behind schedule. Delays on critical tasks increase the EFT though delays on noncritical tasks may not.

In addition to finding the EFT for the whole project, determining scheduling times for all the individual tasks is also important. Thus, in part (*g*) of problem 3, students determine the earliest start time (EST) and the latest start time (LST) for each of the four tasks so that achieving the EFT for the entire project is possible. Students should explain their reasoning and method and thereby move toward devising

For All Practical
Purposes *(COMAP 2006)*
*includes further
information about critical
path analysis.*

a specific procedure, or algorithm, for finding these task starting times.

In the final part of problem 3, students determine the slack time for each task by computing (LST – EST). This difference between the latest start time and the earliest start time is called *slack time* because it is the amount of delay in starting the task that does not lengthen the EFT for the whole project.

Part 2—"Building a House"

Now the students use what they have learned in part 1 to investigate a more complicated project—building a house. In problem 1, they draw a digraph, find a critical path, and determine the EFT for this project. In problem 2, they more carefully analyze what happens when tasks on and off a critical path fall behind schedule.

Because this project is more complex, problem 3, in which students find the earliest and latest starting times for all the individual tasks, is an extension activity. Encourage students who do this problem to describe the procedure that they use for finding the start times very carefully. This activity may lead to a formal algorithm.

The Mathematics in the Investigation

As is the case for graph theory in general, the notation and terminology for critical path analysis are not standardized. Although the vertices often represent the tasks, as in this investigation, the edges may also represent the tasks. The edges-as-tasks representation can result in more complicated graphs and analysis.

Terms for the method itself include *program evaluation and review technique* (PERT) and *critical path method* (CPM). PERT and CPM are slightly different techniques, but they both use critical paths. The United States Navy devised PERT in the late 1950s to aid in developing submarine defense systems. CPM was developed at about the same time in the private sector. Business, industry, and government make extensive use of these techniques.

*Teachers may wish to locate
a local businessperson who
uses PERT and ask him or
her to speak to the class.*

This investigation focuses on the overall EFT for the whole project. However, project managers also need to have more detailed scheduling information for each task. Thus, part of the investigation explores ESTs and LSTs for each task, as well as the slack time for each task. In a small graph, project managers can determine these times by examination and reasoning. In larger graphs, they need algorithms.

The EFT for the whole project is the length of any maximum-length path through the graph. Some graphs have more than one maximum-length path. A task on a maximum-length path, also called a *critical path*, is a *critical task*. The EFT for a specific task is the length of a longest path up to and including the task. The EST for a task is the length of a longest path up to but not including the task. The LST for any task on a critical path is the same as the EST for that task because there are no slack times along a critical path.

Finding the LST for tasks not on a critical path is more complicated. The basic idea is that the LST for a given noncritical task depends on the LST for critical tasks further ahead in the project. Roughly, the LST for a given noncritical task equals the LST for a future critical task minus the time needed to get from the noncritical task to the future critical task. However, there are usually several future critical tasks, so it is necessary to take the minimum of all such computations.

More precisely, finding the LST for a task not on a critical path can be accomplished through the steps below:

1. Follow all paths leading from the given task.

2. Find the first critical task on each such path.

3. For each such critical task, find the LST for the critical task and the length of a longest path from the given task up to but not including the critical task.

4. Subtract this longest length from the critical task LST.

5. Perform this computation for each critical task identified.

6. Take the minimum of all these computations. This minimum value is the LST for the given task.

Your students may not come up with this general method; however, you should require them to give a careful description of the method that they use to find the LST for the tasks in the particular graph on which they are working.

Who Is the Winner?

In this investigation, students use matrices and Hamilton paths to help rank the players in a round-robin tennis tournament. Students first construct vertex-edge graph models and find Hamilton paths, and then they use powers of matrices to determine rankings.

Goals

- Understand, analyze, and apply Hamilton paths to model and solve problems related to paths, circuits, networks, and relationships among a finite number of elements (in this investigation, win-loss relationships among a finite number of players in a tournament)
- Devise, analyze, and apply algorithms for solving vertex-edge graph problems
- Extend work with adjacency matrices for graphs through such activities as interpreting row sums and using the nth power of the adjacency matrix to count paths of length n in a graph

Materials and Equipment

For each student—
- A copy of the activity sheet "Who Is the Winner?"

For each student or small group of students—
- Access to the Internet

pp. 151–52

Prior Knowledge

Students have probably had experience with vertex-edge graphs before they began high school. Previous work with Hamilton paths is helpful but not essential. The students need to know how to multiply matrices, with and without a calculator or computer.

Discussion

When students analyze the results of the two round-robin tennis tournaments in this investigation, they discover that the ranking for the boys' tournament is unambiguous, since only one Hamilton path exists, but the ranking for the girls' tournament is more complicated.

In problem 1, the students determine the number of matches played in a round-robin tournament with four players. This problem provides a nice connection with counting, as described in chapters 1 and 2. The students might compute the number of matches as $C(4, 2) = 6$, they might list all the possible matches, or they might use other reasoning.

The students draw digraphs in completing problem 2. These digraphs, which they derive from the given matrices, represent the tournament results. In problem 3, the students find all Hamilton paths in each graph. These paths are really directed Hamilton paths, since the edges have a direction, so be sure that the students follow the arrows when finding their Hamilton paths.

In problem 4, the students use the Hamilton paths to rank the players. Only one Hamilton path exists for the boys' tournament graph, so the ranking for the boys (Flavio, Simon, Cos, and Bill) is unambiguous.

However, the girls' graph has many Hamilton paths. Furthermore, there are some circuits of three players—for example, Coral beats Amy, Amy beats Nicole, and Nicole beats Coral. Therefore, on the basis of the Hamilton paths, the ranking for the girls is not clear. Deciding what to do to determine a ranking in this situation is an important part of the activity. Students need to develop the ability to analyze and reason about a problem mathematically to produce a solution even if there is no given solution procedure.

In this situation, no general perfect mathematical solution exists, so students might attempt a variety of strategies. They might look at all the Hamilton paths and try somehow to synthesize all that information, but that method is unlikely to yield a clear ranking. They might begin another strategy by noticing which girls won the most matches. After determining that Coral and Amy share this claim and that Coral beat Amy, the students can then rank the players by using the Hamilton path with Coral and Amy as the first two vertices: Coral-Amy-Melodia-Nicole. The students should describe whatever method they used and explain why it yields a reasonable ranking.

In problem 5, the students use a matrix method to rank the players in the tournament. They first compute the sums of the rows of each matrix. These row sums show the number of matches that each player won. In the boys' matrix, the row sums are 3, 2, 1, and 0 for Flavio, Simon, Cos, and Bill, respectively. So Flavio won a total of three matches, Simon won two matches, Cos won one match, and Bill did not win any matches. These row sums yield a clear ranking, which is the same as the ranking generated by using Hamilton paths.

For the girls, the row sums are 2, 2, 1, and 1, for Coral, Amy, Nicole, and Melodia, respectively. These sums indicate ties between Coral and Amy and between Nicole and Melodia. To resolve these ties, the students compute the square of the girls' matrix. The entries in the squared matrix are the number of paths of length 2 between vertices in the digraph, which is the number of "two-stage wins." For example, the Coral-Nicole entry of the squared matrix is a 2. The digraph has two paths of length 2 from Coral to Nicole: Coral-Amy-Nicole and Coral-Melodia-Nicole. These two paths of length 2 correspond to two two-stage wins for Coral over Nicole—Coral beat Amy, who beat Nicole, and Coral beat Melodia, who beat Nicole.

The row sums of the squared matrix give the number of two-stage wins for each player. These row sums are 3, 2, 2, and 1. Comparing these row sums with the row sums of the original girls' matrix (2, 2, 1, and 1) indicates that the previous ties between Coral and Amy and between Nicole and Melodia have been resolved. The final result is the ranking Coral-Amy-Nicole-Melodia.

We have now presented two different rankings for the girls. The ranking that uses the previous reasoning with a Hamilton path is Coral-Amy-Melodia-Nicole. The ranking with the matrix method is Coral-Amy-Nicole-Melodia. Which ranking is correct? The discrepancy between the rankings reveals the limitations of ranking methods. To decide on a ranking, students must consider the purposes, the context, and other factors. For example, in this situation, they might reason that after they have reduced the possible rankings to the two mentioned, they can resolve the Nicole-Melodia ambiguity by finding

Girls' Tournament Matrix (G)

	Coral	Amy	Nicole	Melodia
C	–	1	0	1
A	0	–	1	1
N	1	0	–	0
M	0	0	1	–

The Square of the Girls' Matrix

$$G^2 = \begin{bmatrix} 0 & 0 & 2 & 1 \\ 1 & 0 & 1 & 0 \\ 0 & 1 & 0 & 1 \\ 1 & 0 & 0 & 0 \end{bmatrix}$$

Girls' Digraph

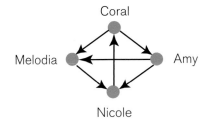

To see how actual tournaments rank players in round-robin matches, go to Internet sites such as http://www.atptennis.com/en/common/TrackIt.asp?file=/posting/2005/605/MDS.pdf and http://www.masters-cup.com.

out who won in Nicole and Melodia's head-to-head match. This strategy yields the ranking Coral-Amy-Melodia-Nicole. This example demonstrates an important type of problem—a problem for which there is no known general solution procedure but which nonetheless requires a solution that will specify some final result. Students must use mathematical analysis and reasoning to solve the problem.

Problem 6 is an extension of the investigation, offering students an opportunity to learn how an actual tennis tournament, the ATP Masters Cup, uses and ranks round-robin tournaments. The students work with information available on the Web at http://www.masters-cup.com.

The Mathematics in the Investigation

The mathematics of voting and ranking underlies this investigation. A seminal result in this area is Arrow's theorem. In 1949, the Nobel Prize–winning economist Kenneth Arrow proposed a set of fairness conditions that he believed any fair voting method should satisfy. Then he proved that no voting method can satisfy all the fairness conditions when the number of candidates is more than two. This striking result applies to the ranking problem in this investigation because the tournament results are similar to voting results, and the outcome must produce a winner. Just as in the situation of Arrow's theorem, no method is guaranteed to determine a winner in a "fair" way in all situations.

The students will have discovered that problems occurred with all the methods used for ranking the players in the girls' tournament. The Hamilton path method did not yield a clear ranking, nor did the method of using the row sums of the original tournament matrix. The row sums of the squared matrix, combined with the original row sums, did yield a clear ranking, but that ranking placed Nicole above Melodia even though Melodia beat Nicole—a result that seems contradictory.

If no perfect ranking method exists that can guarantee a fair result, what should those who must make a ranking do? They can make a decision on the basis of the context, their purposes, and other factors, choosing a reasonable method for a given situation, and all participants must agree to accept the outcome. In the case of the girls' tennis tournament, the tournament's governing board may have to make the decision by creating and enforcing specific ranking rules.

As part of this investigation, students use a matrix method. They look at the square of the original win-loss matrix so that they can examine two-stage wins. More generally, the square of a matrix like this one shows the number of paths of length 2 between each pair of vertices.

To see why, consider the example in the investigation (see fig. 4.2). Multiplying matrices involves taking a row in the left matrix and a column in the right matrix. In this problem, both matrices are the same, since the matrix is squared; in other words, the girls' matrix is multiplied by itself. Think about a ranking that depends on two-stage wins (paths of length 2) between Coral and Nicole. The matrix-multiplication procedure uses Coral's row and Nicole's column. The second entry in Coral's row is a 1, which corresponds to a win against Amy, so a path exists from Coral to Amy (Coral beats Amy). But the second entry in Nicole's column also involves Amy: a 1 there indicates a path from Amy to Nicole. Thus, Coral $\rightarrow$ Amy $\rightarrow$ Nicole is a path of length 2—that is, a path with two edges.

	Coral	Amy	Nicole	Melodia
Coral	0	1	0	1
Amy	0	0	1	1
Nicole	1	0	0	0
Melodia	0	0	1	0

×

	Coral	Amy	Nicole	Melodia
Coral	0	1	0	1
Amy	0	0	1	1
Nicole	1	0	0	0
Melodia	0	0	1	0

Fig. **4.2.**

The 4 × 4 matrix that the students multiply by itself to find the number of paths of length 2

Whenever a matching pair of 1s occurs in the row-column matrix multiplication, there is a connecting vertex. The path goes from the row vertex to the connecting vertex and then from the connecting vertex to the column vertex. Because the matrix multiplication involves multiplying 1s and adding the products as it proceeds, it gives the total number of paths of length 2 as a final result.

The Traveling Salesman Problem (TSP)

In this investigation, students explore the famous traveling salesman problem (TSP), which is the problem of finding an optimal circuit that visits all the vertices in a vertex-edge graph. Students solve the TSP for a problem with four cities. Then they discover that the so-called brute-force solution method quickly becomes impractical as the number of cities grows.

Goals

- Understand, analyze, and apply the TSP to model and solve problems related to paths, circuits, networks, and relationships among a finite number of elements
- Devise, analyze, and apply algorithms for solving vertex-edge graph problems

Materials and Equipment

For each student—

- A copy of the activity sheet "The Traveling Salesman Problem (TSP)"

pp. 153–54

Prior Knowledge

This investigation has no definite prerequisites. However, previous experience with vertex-edge graphs— specifically, with Hamilton circuits—is helpful, although not essential. Students should be able to recall previous work with systematic listing and counting, in which they listed all possibilities in a counting situation or constructed a tree diagram to show the possibilities. Finally, students should know how to use factorial notation, with or without a calculator or computer.

Discussion

In this investigation, students explore the TSP, in which a salesperson wants to visit several cities efficiently by starting at a given city, visiting each of the other cities exactly once, returning to the original city, and traveling the minimum total number of miles. To solve this problem, students first create a graph that represents the information in a matrix showing distances between pairs of cities in a group of four cities. Then they find the shortest circuit through the graph. This circuit starts at a vertex that represents city A, visits each other vertex exactly once, and returns to A. In the language of graph theory, students are finding a *minimum-weight Hamilton circuit*. They solve the problem by using a brute-force method—that is, they find all possible Hamilton circuits, find the total length of each, and choose the shortest.

To learn the limitations of the brute-force method for larger graphs, students next consider the same problem with twenty-five cities. In this situation, they find that even a fast computer—one that can find and compute the length of 70 trillion Hamilton circuits every second—will require approximately 281 years to solve the problem! This fact may be very surprising to them. After all, twenty-five is not a large number of cities; and in many real-world settings, there are many more than twenty-five vertices.

Also, students in this technological age may have developed the misconception that any problem can be solved—quickly—with a computer that is fast enough and software that is good enough. However, this analysis of the TSP dramatically shows the limitations of using the brute-force method and raw computer power to try to solve problems. It also illustrates the phenomenon of "combinatorial explosion," which is the often surprisingly huge number of possibilities that can occur in counting problems, particularly when they involve factorials.

The Mathematics in the Investigation

The investigation Who Is the Winner? relates to a famous problem that addresses Arrow's theorem about fair voting and ranking methods. This investigation presents another famous problem: the TSP. Although Arrow's theorem states that no fair voting method exists (on the basis of Arrow's fairness conditions), no one has come up with a similar theorem— at least, not yet—stating that no efficient method exists for solving the TSP. However, no one knows an efficient method for solving the TSP, and many mathematicians believe that no such method exists. The brute-force method used in this investigation solves the TSP, but, as indicated above, this method is not efficient. Some efficient algorithms are used in practice to solve specific examples of the TSP or to find approximate solutions. But no one knows a method that is efficient and works for all graphs.

Since solving the TSP has so many applications, both inside and outside mathematics, research on the problem continues. Over the years, mathematicians have solved the problem for an increasing number of cities (vertices). A breakthrough occurred in 1954, when a 49-city problem was solved. Fifty years later, in 2004, the record was 24,978 cities.

Extending and Connecting with Algebra: Chromatic Polynomials

How to color the vertices of a graph is an important type of graph problem that students should encounter before high school. The topic of chromatic polynomials can extend the students' work with vertex coloring and provide an interesting connection with algebra.

A k-coloring of a vertex-edge graph is an assignment of one of k possible colors to each vertex of a graph so that no two vertices connected by an edge have the same color. Sometimes someone might simply want to know whether a k-coloring exists. Sometimes the number of k-colorings is useful information (where k is a nonnegative integer and the number of possible 0-colorings of a graph is assumed to be zero). The *chromatic polynomial* for a graph G is a polynomial C_G, such that $C_G(k)$ is the number of different k-colorings of G. Two colorings are different if at least one vertex has a different color.

For example, consider the most "extreme" graphs—graphs with no edges and complete graphs (graphs in which there is exactly one edge

For All Practical Purposes (COMAP 2006) includes an introductory discussion of algorithms used in attempting to solve the TSP. *Applied Combinatorics* (Roberts and Tesman 2004) contains a more rigorous treatment of this topic.

You might ask your students to do some research on the Internet to find the current record for the TSP. For example, they can visit the TSP site at Georgia Tech University: http://www.tsp.gatech.edu.

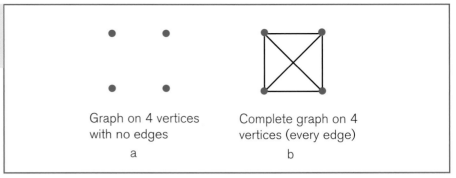

Graph on 4 vertices
with no edges

a

Complete graph on 4
vertices (every edge)

b

For vertex-edge graph activities for students before they reach high school, see chapter 3 "Vertex-Edge Graphs in Grades 6–8," as well as the chapters on vertex-edge graphs in Navigating through Discrete Mathematics in Prekindergarten–Grade 5 *(DeBellis et al. forthcoming).*

between every pair of vertices). Figure 4.3 shows (*a*) a graph with four vertices and no edges and (*b*) a complete graph with four vertices. Note that there is no vertex where the diagonals intersect. Several problems about chromatic polynomials for these graphs follow. You can offer these to your students to extend their experience with vertex coloring.

1. "Let G be a graph with four vertices and no edges. Explain why the chromatic polynomial for G is $C_G(k) = k^4$." (Because edges connect none of the vertices, there is no restriction on the colors used for the vertices. Thus, if k colors are available, k choices are possible for the color of each of the four vertices, and the number of different k-colorings is therefore k^4.)

2. "Let G be a complete graph on four vertices. Explain why the chromatic polynomial for G is $C_G(k) = k(k-1)(k-2)(k-3)$. Explain the connection with counting permutations." (In this case, every vertex is connected by an edge to all other vertices. Therefore, no color can be used twice to color the vertices. Also, different orderings of colors count as different colorings. For example, if the vertices are listed clockwise from the top left in figure 4.3b, blue-green-red-yellow is a different coloring from green-red-yellow-blue. Thus, this counting situation is one in which there are no repetitions and order counts. In other words, the situation calls for counting permutations. The number of k-colorings is therefore

$$P(k, 4) = k(k-1)(k-2)(k-3).)$$

3. "What are the zeros for the polynomial in problem 2? Explain, in terms of coloring, why the chromatic polynomial must be 0 for these values of k." (The zeros are 0, 1, 2, and 3. Because every vertex in a complete graph is connected by an edge to all other vertices, each vertex must be a different color. To color a complete graph on four vertices, at least four colors are necessary. Therefore, $C_G(k)$, which is the number of ways of coloring the graph with at most k colors, must be 0 for $k = 0, 1, 2,$ and 3.)

4. "What is the chromatic polynomial for a graph G on p vertices with no edges? What is the chromatic polynomial for a complete graph G on p vertices?" (The chromatic polynomial for a graph G on p vertices with no edges is $C_G(k) = k^p$, and the chromatic polynomial for a complete graph G on p vertices is

$$C_G(k) = k(k-1)(k-2)(k-3) \ldots (k-(p-1)).)$$

Vertex-Edge Graphs: Summary and Additional Information for Grades 6–12

You may have a limited acquaintance with the mathematics of vertex-edge graphs, since it is a relatively new topic, which some teacher education programs may not yet include. This section provides a brief summary and additional information about graph topics for grades 6–12.

Euler Paths

1. An Euler path is a route through a graph that uses each edge exactly once. An Euler circuit is an Euler path that starts and ends at the same vertex.

2. The game of tracing a figure without retracing and without lifting the pencil is exactly the problem of finding an Euler path:

   - "Tracing the figure" means "using all edges."
   - "Without retracing" means "using an edge only once."
   - "Without lifting the pencil" means "finding a route that proceeds from one vertex to an adjacent vertex."

   For example, figure 4.4 shows a drawing of a house. Try to trace this house without retracing or lifting your pencil.

3. A connected graph has an Euler circuit if and only if all vertices have even degree. The reason for the "only if" statement is, roughly, that traveling around the Euler circuit involves going in and out of every vertex; each "in and out" contributes 2 to the degree of a vertex; so every vertex must have even degree.

4. A connected graph has an Euler path that is not a circuit if and only if there are exactly two vertices of odd degree. In this case, one of the odd vertices is the start and the other one is the end of the path.

5. There are at least two different algorithms for constructing an Euler circuit in a connected graph in which all vertex degrees are even:

   - *Hierholzer's algorithm* (sometimes called the *onion-skin algorithm*): Start anywhere, and "follow your nose" without retracing any edges until you are back where you started. If you have used all the edges, you are finished. If you have not used all the edges, choose any vertex on your initial circuit that is incident to an untraced edge. Start at that vertex, and "follow your nose" until you return to your starting point. Splice that circuit into the original circuit. Continue building incomplete circuits like this until you have traced all edges. When no untraced edges remain, you have an Euler circuit.

   - *Fleury's algorithm:* Start anywhere, and trace an edge that you could remove from the graph, leaving a graph that is still connected. (In other words, the removal of the traced edge would not break the graph into disjoint components.) Darken or color that edge as a reminder that you cannot use it again. Start again at an endpoint of this edge, and repeat the process. When you

Good general resources for vertex-edge graphs include Graphs: An Introductory Approach *(Wilson and Watkins 1990) and* Applied Combinatorics *(Roberts and Tesman 2004), both listed in "A Bibliography of Print Resources for Discrete Mathematics" on the CD-ROM.*

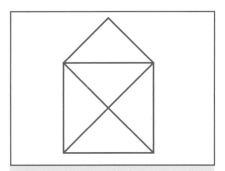

Fig. **4.4.**

Can you trace this house without retracing or lifting your pencil?

The famous *highway inspector problem* converts the TSP from a question about a Hamilton circuit to a question about an Euler circuit. The traveling salesman wants a route that visits each town (vertex) in a given network exactly once. By contrast, the highway inspector, who must be sure that all the roads connecting the towns are in good repair, wants a route that traverses each road (edge) exactly once.

For more information about the Chinese postman problem, see http://people.bath.ac.uk/tjs20/introduction.htm.

have traced all the edges in this manner, you have completed an Euler circuit.

6. When a graph does not have an Euler circuit, adding edges until it does is sometimes desirable. Depending on the situation and your goals, you might allow the addition of new edges or only the duplication of existing edges. In either case, you add an edge by finding the vertices of odd degree and adding edges incident to those vertices in such a way that all vertices have even degree. Such a process is called *Eulerizing the graph*. Often the problem is to Eulerize by using the minimum number of additional edges.

7. The two conditions of an Euler path are that it (1) uses every edge and (2) does not retrace any edge. Two natural extensions result from considering what happens when a path meets one condition but fails the other. Using every edge but allowing some retracing leads to the so-called *Chinese postman problem*, in which the goal is to trace a graph by using as few retraced edges as possible—an activity that relates to Eulerizing a graph. Alternatively, if you do not retrace any edges but perhaps do not use every edge, the result is a problem called the *longest stroll*, in which you try to find a path that uses as many edges as possible with no retracing.

Vertex Coloring

1. Vertex coloring can be used to model situations involving conflict among objects. That is, the vertices represent the objects, the edges join vertices that conflict in some way, and adjacent vertices (i.e., conflicting objects) are colored with different colors. The goal in a vertex-coloring conflict problem is to avoid conflict in an optimal way. For example, suppose that you want to schedule six committee meetings in as few time slots as possible, but you have to avoid conflicts in meeting times because some committees share members and therefore cannot meet at the same time. In this situation, you can let the vertices represent the committees and draw an edge between two vertices if the committees that they represent share a member. Then let colors represent different time slots for meetings, and color the vertices—that is, assign times for committee meetings—with as few colors as possible so that adjacent vertices have different colors. Figure 4.5 represents this situation.

2. No *efficient* algorithm is known for coloring the vertices of any graph with the minimum number of colors, with the condition that any two vertices connected by an edge must have different colors.

3. A *greedy* algorithm for coloring a graph is simply to color each vertex of the graph one by one, as it is encountered, while being careful to avoid coloring any vertex the same color as an adjacent vertex. This algorithm is efficient, in the sense that a computer can implement it in a reasonable amount of time; but it is not correct, because it will not in general provide a minimal coloring.

4. Most efficient coloring algorithms use one or more of the following strategies:

- Color vertices of high degree before vertices of lower degree.
- Color as many vertices as possible with the same color.
- Use the same color for vertices that are adjacent to the same set of vertices but not to one another.

5. Every map in a plane can be colored with at most four colors. This theorem is the famous four-color problem, which Kenneth Appel and Wolfgang Haken solved in 1976 by using a computer-aided proof. Since every planar map can represent a planar graph, and vice versa, this theorem is valid for planar maps or planar graphs. (A planar graph is a graph that can be drawn in the plane in such a way that the edges intersect only at vertices.)

6. A complete graph on *n* vertices requires *n* colors.

7. It is possible to color a *cyclic graph*—that is, a graph that consists entirely of a single circuit with all vertices of degree 2—with a minimum of two colors if the number of vertices is even, and with a minimum of three colors if the number of vertices is odd.

8. The minimum number of colors needed to color the vertices of a graph is two if and only if the graph contains no circuits with an odd number of vertices.

9. The *chromatic number* of a graph is the minimum number of colors needed to color its vertices.

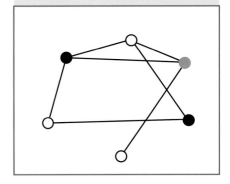

Fig. **4.5.**

The vertices in the graph represent committees. An edge connects two committees that cannot meet at the same time. The colors of the vertices represent meeting times. The minimum number of meeting times needed for all six committees is three.

Minimum Spanning Trees

1. A *tree* is a connected graph with no circuits. It is sometimes useful to try to find a tree in a graph. If the edges of a graph have "weights"—that is, numbers that can represent distance, cost, or some other quantity—then a common problem is to look for a minimum spanning tree in the graph, which is called a *weighted graph*. A minimum spanning tree in a weighted graph is a tree that has minimum total weight and spans—that is, includes—all the vertices of the graph. Figure 4.6 shows (*a*) a tree, (*b*) a graph that is not a tree, and (*c*) a minimum spanning tree (bold lines).

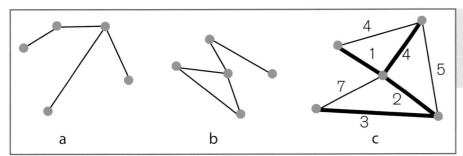

a   b   c

Fig. **4.6.**

Three graphs, including (*a*) a tree; (*b*) a graph that is not a tree; and (*c*) a minimum spanning tree

2. There are several efficient algorithms for finding a minimum spanning tree. When exploring a rich minimum-spanning-tree situation, students often find several reasonable algorithms.

Indeed, this is a good opportunity for students in grades 9–12 to engage in the process of algorithmic problem solving as they devise, implement, and analyze step-by-step procedures for finding minimum spanning trees. Consider the following general strategy. Because a minimum spanning tree is a tree of least total weight,

Principles and Standards for School Mathematics (NCTM, 2000) presents a rich minimum-spanning-tree situation on pp. 317–18.

choosing the edges of smallest weight makes sense. Therefore, the first step is to choose an edge of least weight in the graph. For subsequent edges, three options produce different reasonable algorithms:

- Choose the edge of least weight not already chosen, whether or not it connects to any previously chosen edges.
- Choose the edge of least weight that connects to any edge already chosen.
- Choose the edge of least weight that connects to the "ending vertex" of the last chosen edge, thus traveling to the "nearest neighbor" of the previous vertex.

In all three options, the choice of an edge that completes a circuit is never a possibility, since the goal is to construct a tree, and trees have no circuits. All these options are "natural" strategies that students are likely to try when confronted with a minimum spanning tree problem. The first strategy leads to Kruskal's algorithm (discussed in chapter 3), and the second leads to Prim's algorithm. Both of these are efficient algorithms for finding a minimum spanning tree. By contrast, the third strategy, which leads to the so-called *nearest-neighbor algorithm*, is appealing and sometimes useful, but it does not, in general, produce a minimum spanning tree.

Conclusion

Euler paths, Hamilton paths, the TSP, minimum spanning trees, critical paths, shortest paths, vertex coloring, and adjacency matrices are all topics from graph theory that should appear in school mathematics. Students are likely to encounter critical paths and the TSP for the first time in grades 9–12. During these years, they also develop and extend their knowledge of the remaining graph theory topics, which they now compare, contrast, and analyze more formally and completely than they did in prekindergarten–grade 8.

The next two chapters focus on iteration and recursion, the third main topic of discrete mathematics that *Principles and Standards for School Mathematics* (NCTM 2000) recommends for the school curriculum.

NAVIGATIONS
SERIES

GRADES 6–12

NAVIGATING *through* DISCRETE MATHEMATICS

Chapter 5
Iteration and Recursion in Grades 6–8

All students in grades 6–8 should—

- *describe, analyze, and create simple additive and multiplicative sequential patterns (in which a constant is added or multiplied at each step), as well as more complicated patterns, such as Pascal's triangle (in which each row of numbers, except the first two rows, is constructed from the previous row) and the Fibonacci sequence 1, 1, 2, 3, 5, 8, … (in which each term, except the first two terms is the sum of the previous two terms;*

- *use iterative procedures to generate geometric patterns, including fractals like the Koch snowflake and Sierpinski's triangle;*

- *use informal notation such as NOW and NEXT, as well as subscript notation, to represent sequential patterns;*

(continued)

Some sources describe mathematics as the study of patterns. Others claim that this description is misleading and fails to capture all that mathematics really includes. However, mathematics educators do agree that explorations of patterns should begin in early education and continue throughout the curriculum. The study of sequential patterns involves developing and applying skills that are essential for doing mathematics at every level.

A pattern that underlies a sequential, or step-by-step, process or sequence is called a *sequential pattern*. For example, a sequential pattern in the sequence of even numbers 0, 2, 4, 6, 8, 10, … can be expressed as, "Start with 0 and add 2 to determine the next number in the list." A sequential pattern in the sequence of convex polygons △, □, ⬠, ⬡,… can be stated as, "Each polygon has one more side than the previous polygon."

All students should be able to observe, continue, describe, and create sequential patterns successfully. In prekindergarten through second grade, the emphasis should be on using objects, pictures, sounds, and actions to work with concrete sequential patterns. In grades 3–5, children should explore numeric and geometric sequential patterns by using manipulatives combined with paper-and-pencil activities. Students should learn that they can create some sequential patterns iteratively by repeating the same action or set of steps. They need to identify examples of patterns that grow or shrink. In addition, they should begin to use technology to investigate iterative procedures.

In the middle grades, students should continue the journey of describing, analyzing, and creating sequential patterns, with emphasis on the

(continued from previous page)

- *find and interpret explicit (closed-form) and recursive formulas for simple additive and multiplicative sequential patterns, and translate between formulas of these types;*
- *use iterative procedures and simple recursive formulas to model and solve problems, including those in simple real-world settings;*
- *describe, create, and investigate iterative procedures by using technology, such as Logo-like environments, spreadsheets, calculators, and interactive geometry software.*

iterative process and recursive descriptions. *To iterate* means *to repeat*, so an iterative process is a process that repeats the same procedure or computation over and over again, like adding 3 each time in the sequence 2, 5, 8, 11, …. A recursive description involves describing a given step in a sequential process in terms of the previous steps. For example, NEXT = NOW + 3 describes the pattern in the sequence 2, 5, 8, 11, ….

Students in the middle grades should become engaged at the concrete level, just as they were in previous grades. They should also be able to use different representations to describe patterns and be aware of the advantages and shortcomings of the various representations. They should use NEXT-NOW language and also begin to learn subscript notation and understand that it is a simple yet powerful way to describe sequential patterns. They should understand how to use algebraic symbolism and reasoning to represent the general terms of simple sequences recursively as well as in explicit, or closed, form. For example, an explicit formula describing the sequence 2, 5, 8, 11, … is $s_n = 2 + 3n$, for $n \geq 0$.

Students in grades 6–8 can learn to use spreadsheets to make lists of terms generated by sequential patterns described by recursive and explicit formulas. Students who have used Logo or Logo-like environments on computers should explore recursive processes in those contexts. Graphing calculators are useful tools for working with iteration and recursion. Students should be able to use these technologies to solve problems. Students in the middle grades should also encounter instances in which recursion and iteration occur in everyday situations. For example, eighth-grade students can investigate compound-interest problems and other growth problems from this point of view.

The investigations in this chapter provide situations in which students use recursive and explicit representations to analyze sequential patterns in the mathematical strands of number, algebra, and geometry, as well as in the context of compound interest.

Targeting Squares

This investigation has two parts. Part 1, "Looking at Square Tiles from All Angles," consists of explorations that use the same geometric model, but each exploration focuses on a different characteristic of the model. Part 2, "Squares around the Triangle," also uses one geometric model for its activities; however, its main emphasis is on producing a recursive representation and an explicit representation of the generalization. Students describe and justify their solutions. They also create their own geometric design sequences and apply the same process that they have worked through while investigating their models.

Goals

- Describe, analyze, and create simple additive and multiplicative sequential patterns (in which a constant is added or multiplied at each step), as well as more complicated patterns
- Use iterative procedures to generate geometric patterns
- Use informal notation such as NOW and NEXT, as well as subscript notation, to represent sequential patterns
- Find and interpret explicit (closed-form) and recursive formulas for simple sequential patterns, and translate between these formulas
- Use iterative procedures and simple recursive formulas to model and solve problems, including those in simple real-world settings

Materials and Equipment

For each student—

- A copy of each of the following activity sheets:
  ○ "Looking at Square Tiles from All Angles"
  ○ "Squares around the Triangle"
- Geodot paper (template available on the CD-ROM)
- A supply of square tiles (at least 25)

pp. 155–56; 157–58

The CD-ROM includes a template that you can use to print geodot paper for your students' use in the investigation.

Prior Knowledge and Activities

From previous work, students should be comfortable with patterns in general and with sequential patterns in particular. In addition, students should have acquired at least some intuitive knowledge of iteration and recursion. They should be able to represent patterns in input and output data arranged in tables, whether the tables are oriented horizontally or vertically. The students should also know how to represent patterns by using a NEXT-NOW representation and by using subscripts.

Although a primary goal of these investigations is to enable students to furnish recursive and explicit representations of sequential patterns, they should have had some experience in distinguishing between sequential patterns represented recursively and explicitly. For example, in the sequence of odd numbers 1, 3, 5, 7, …, students should be able to describe the pattern as "NEXT = NOW + 2; start at 1." If s_n represents the nth term of this sequence, then students should know that $s_n = s_{n-1} + 2$, with $s_1 = 1$ and $n \geq 2$, is a recursive representation of the sequence, whereas $s_n = 2n - 1$ is an explicit, or closed-form, representation.

To be successful in these explorations, students should have a good understanding of such basic measurement and geometric concepts as length, angle measure, perimeter, area, symmetry, and similarity. They should be able to perceive details of drawings, be organized when they look for and record data, and have good counting skills. Familiarity with dot and grid paper, as well as with a mix of geometric manipulatives, including square tiles, linking cubes, and pattern blocks, is also helpful so that the students can easily create and construct their own sequential geometric designs.

To review or verify the students' familiarity with subscripts and the NEXT-NOW representation, you might direct students to do the following activity. Depending on the features of your students' calculators, ask them to enter **25**, then press **ENTER** followed by **+** and **2**, and then press **ENTER** repeatedly. This action yields an iterative process that produces 25, 27, 29, 31, 33, …. Students can represent this iterative procedure with a recursive formula by writing "START = 25 and NEXT = NOW + 2." They can also use the more formal subscript notation and write "$s_1 = 25$ and $s_n = s_{n-1} + 2$, for $n = 2, 3, 4, …$" You may need to emphasize that START = 25, or $s_1 = 25$, is an essential part of the recursive formula, since it indicates the starting point from which the iteration begins.

Part 1—"Looking at Square Tiles from All Angles"

Work through the activity sheet "Looking at Square Tiles from All Angles" before reading on. Note that the investigation is appropriate for students to complete alone or in pairs. Square tiles help students generate and generalize the design, and geodot paper is useful for recording results. The design for this activity is a straightforward step pattern that allows visual and analytic approaches to merge easily.

In problem 1, the students examine the first three tile designs in a sequence (see fig. 5.1), and then they draw the next two designs on geodot paper. In problem 2, the students determine the area of each design by counting the square tiles. The table for problem 2 indicates the areas for the given designs and asks the students to supply the areas of subsequent designs. As a built-in self-check, the table also displays the area for the largest design specified. By studying the changes that take place from one design to the next, the students can recognize that the addition of a new row of squares corresponds to the next odd number at each step, and they can articulate the change.

Fig. 5.1.

The first three designs in a sequence of tiles

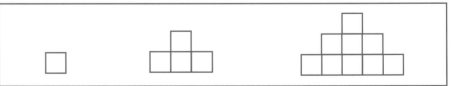

Be sure that the students give the complete recursive formula in problem 2(*b*). Students often include the recursive portion of the generalization but omit the starting point. The complete solution for problem 2(*b*) is $a_1 = 1$ and $a_n = a_{n-1} + (2n - 1)$, for $n \geq 2$.

Moving the tiles around often helps students derive the explicit formula. To solve problem 2(*c*), they should be able to rearrange the tiles at each stage to build squares and thus justify the explicit formula for the area at each stage.

The format of problem 3 is similar to that of problem 2 but this time focuses on perimeter instead of area. In this problem, students can determine the generalization for the recursive formula by inspecting the change in perimeter that occurs from design to design.

Problem 4 focuses on right angles in the interiors of the designs. Some students may give incorrect totals because they have an incorrect understanding of the term *reflex angle*, which is an angle whose measure is greater than 180° and less than 360°. They may count the reflex angles (270°) as right angles. Once the students properly identify right angles, they will discover that the count of the right angles is a familiar number pattern that they can easily generalize in recursive and explicit form.

Problem 5, which investigates the number of 1 × 2 rectangles in the designs, is a challenging one. Caution your students to build their counts for a design column by column. They should look for a familiar pattern that they can simplify by slightly modifying it.

Students create their own designs and analyze them in problem 6. Allow the students enough time to create their own set of designs, and verify that they can make explicit and recursive generalizations. In addition, make time for your students to share their findings with one another.

In this activity, students can readily solve the generalizations because of visual relationships or familiar number patterns. Other designs may have more subtle relationships that call for using such other strategies as the method of finite differences to achieve the explicit generalization; such designs may be more appropriate for students in high school.

Part 2—"Squares around the Triangle"

Work through the activity before reading on. Again you will see that students can work on the activity alone or in pairs. Using geodot paper can help them distinguish between the two sizes of squares in the activity and see how they compare with each other in size. The design for this activity is a straightforward pattern that indirectly features the Pythagorean right-triangle relationship. However, students who are not familiar with the relationship can nonetheless complete the activity successfully. If your students have previously used the Pythagorean theorem, make the connection after they have completed the activities in the investigation.

The format for the activity "Squares around the Triangle" parallels that of the activity "Looking at Square Tiles from All Angles." In problem 1, the students continue the design pattern shown in figure 5.2 by drawing the next two designs in the sequence on dot paper. Students

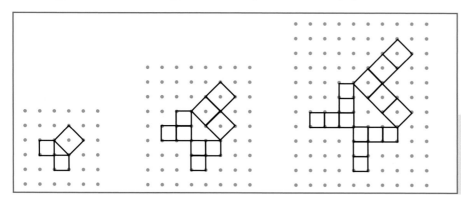

Fig. 5.2.

The first three designs in a sequence that indirectly features the Pythagorean relationship

who have difficulty in continuing to the next design pattern should focus on one aspect of the design at a time and track how it changes from design to design. For example, students might focus on the right triangle. They should observe that in the first design, the legs of the right triangle are one unit in length, in the next design they are two units in length, and so on.

In problem 2, the students investigate the numbers of small squares in each design. The table for the problem shows the small-square counts for the given designs. As a built-in self-check, the table also gives the count for the largest design. By studying the elements that change from design to design, the students can articulate the change and recognize the pairs of L shapes that increase in size in the sequence of designs. Be sure that students give the complete recursive formula, including the starting value. The complete solution for problem 2(b) is NEXT = NOW + 4, starting at 2, or $s_1 = 2$ and $s_n = s_{n-1} + 4$, for $n \geq 2$.

If students have difficulty discovering an explicit formula, suggest that they rewrite and study the data. Students can use any of several methods to arrive at an explicit formula for problem 2(c). For example, they can count the small squares in each L, as shown in the following:

$$s_1 = 2 = 1 + 1 = (2 \cdot 1 - 1) + (2 \cdot 1 - 1)$$

$$s_2 = 6 = 3 + 3 = (2 \cdot 2 - 1) + (2 \cdot 2 - 1)$$

$$s_3 = 10 = 5 + 5 = (2 \cdot 3 - 1) + (2 \cdot 3 - 1)$$

$$s_4 = 14 = 7 + 7 = (2 \cdot 4 - 1) + (2 \cdot 4 - 1)$$

Inductively,

$$s_n = (2n - 1) + (2n - 1) = 4n - 2, n \geq 1.$$

Alternatively, students can iterate by using the recursive formula $s_n = s_{n-1} + 4$, with $s_1 = 2$, look for a pattern, and express the pattern as an explicit formula. Thus,

$$s_1 = 2,$$

$$s_2 = s_1 + 4 = 2 + 4,$$

$$s_3 = s_2 + 4 = (2 + 4) + 4 = 2 + 2 \cdot 4,$$

$$s_4 = s_3 + 4 = (2 + 2 \cdot 4) + 4 = 2 + 3 \cdot 4.$$

Inductively,

$$s_n = 2 + 4(n - 1) = 4n - 2,$$

for $n \geq 1$.

Students should also be able to see that the large-square count, which they investigate in problem 3, is one-half the small-square count. A recursive formula is NEXT = NOW + 2, starting at 1, or $S_n = S_{n-1} + 2$, for $n \geq 1$. An explicit formula is $S_n = 1 + 2(n - 1) = 2n - 1$, for $n \geq 1$. Solutions in problem 3 follow readily from those in problem 2.

In problem 4, the students investigate t_n, the area of the right triangle in the center of the nth design in the sequence. Encourage your students to draw only the triangle from the first design and then draw the triangle for the second design around the first triangle so that the right angle is the location of the overlapping portion. Students should then draw the third triangle around the second triangle in the same way, as

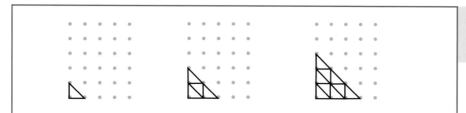

shown in figure 5.3. Using the drawing helps students see the added-on area in the second and third triangles. Continuing in this fashion can facilitate obtaining the recursive and explicit generalizations.

In problem 5, the students must explain why the area of a large square is 2 square units if the area of a small square is 1 square unit. Noticing that two small squares can be cut on a diagonal and their pieces recomposed to make one large square, as shown in figure 5.4, is necessary in solving this problem. Students should use the geodot paper to observe that when a small square region with an area of 1 square unit is divided into two triangular regions, four of these triangular regions produce the larger square region with an area of 2 square units.

If your students know about irrational numbers, work backward from the area of 2 square units to point out that the length of a side of the large square must be $\sqrt{2}$ units. This result may surprise students who are not familiar with geodot paper. Many of them may think that the distance between any two adjacent dots—whether on a horizontal, vertical, or slanted line—is 1 unit.

Problem 5(*e*) gives students an opportunity to think in a new way about the Pythagorean theorem. Students probably will not recognize that this problem is related to the Pythagorean theorem, since they are accustomed to picturing a right triangle with squares, as opposed to L-shaped figures, drawn on the legs and hypotenuse (see the margin). However, the results are the same in this situation: the sum of the areas of the shapes on the legs of the right triangle equals the area of the shape on the hypotenuse of the right triangle. The students can explore other shapes on the legs of the right triangle and see how the areas compare with a similar shape drawn on the hypotenuse.

The Mathematics in the Investigation

"Looking at Square Tiles from All Angles" and "Squares around the Triangle" focus on iteration and recursion in the areas of number, algebra, and geometry. These two parts of the investigation Targeting Squares use both explicit and recursive formulas. Explicit formulas have long been part of algebra and analysis. However, thinking recursively and using recursive formulas are more recent emphases in mathematics. Computers have made this way of expressing relationships indispensable.

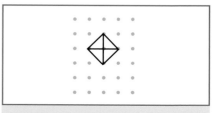

Fig. **5.4.**

The area of a large square is 2 square units.

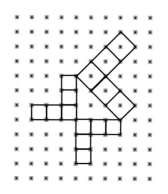

Rózsa Péter (1905–1977) was a Hungarian mathematician who made significant contributions to the theory of recursive functions and advocated their study.

Investing with Lotta Cash

This investigation involves iteration and recursion and emphasizes exponential growth as applied to investments. The students move through explorations that examine the evolution from simple interest to compound interest. Because students who have not formally studied compound interest can proceed through the problems experientially with minimal direction, the investigation can be an effective introduction to compound interest. However, students who have already completed a unit on compound interest can also benefit from the work. While students explore each type of interest, they explain and generalize the behavior of the growth either recursively or explicitly.

Goals

- Find and interpret explicit (closed-form) and recursive formulas for simple additive and multiplicative sequential patterns, and translate between these formulas
- Use iterative procedures and simple recursive formulas to model and solve problems, including those in simple real-world settings
- Describe, create, and investigate iterative procedures by using technology, such as Logo-like environments, spreadsheets, calculators, and interactive geometry software

Materials and Equipment

For each student—

- A copy of the activity sheet "Investing with Lotta Cash"
- A graphing calculator

pp. 159–61

Prior Knowledge and Activities

Students should be familiar with iteration and recursion as presented in the investigation Targeting Squares. They should be aware that the recursive formulas that they developed in that investigation are additive. Specifically, the formulas are of the type $S_n = S_{n-1} + c$, where c is a constant, or $S_n = S_{n-1} + f(n)$, where $f(n)$ is a linear function of n—that is, a constant or other linear function is added to S_{n-1}.

The recursive formulas in this investigation are multiplicative. In other words, multiplying the $(n-1)$th term by a constant yields the nth term. You can introduce these multiplicative recursive patterns with such sequential patterns as 2, 4, 8, 16, 32, 64, …, 2^n, or 2, 6, 18, 54, 162, 486, …, $2 \cdot 3^{n-1}$, for $n \geq 1$, asking for generalizations in recursive and explicit form. You can also ask your students to use calculators to iterate, as described on p. 84, this time using multiplication instead of addition. Introduce other sequential patterns in which the relation is multiplicative rather than additive. Students can consider simple applications that feature some type of exponential growth, such as the doubling of a certain type of bacteria on a surface.

Students should also review or study several topics before undertaking this exploration. They should know how to compute simple interest—that is, interest (I) is the product of principal (P), rate of interest

(R), and time (T)—and know that the formula for computing interest is $I = PRT$. Students should be familiar with and able to use the properties of rational numbers to compute efficiently. They should have had experience with some of the tools of algebra—including symbolic representation and algebraic reasoning. Knowing how to use some special features of a graphing calculator—such as sequence and function modes, tables, and graphs—is helpful but not essential. The class should decide on a process to use for rounding decimal computations, probably rounding up if the digit in the thousandths position is 5 through 9 and retaining the digit in the hundredths position if the digit in the thousandths position is 0 through 4. Thus, $21.546 rounds to $21.55, and $56.234 rounds to $56.23.

Discussion

An examination of the investigation will show you that students can work on it effectively either by themselves or in pairs. Each student should use a graphing calculator. Depending on the background and level of the students, you can revise this exploration to make it more formal or less formal.

This investigation focuses on compound interest, which has been part of the mathematics curriculum for some time. What makes this exploration different is its emphasis on developing both recursive and explicit approaches to the topic. The investigation assumes that the students are not familiar with the topic of compound interest. It presents a series of questions that can provide opportunities for "teachable moments" about compound interest after students have tried the work informally but with some instructional assistance.

The investigation presents Lotta Cash, who received a gift of $2,000 from her grandparents on her twelfth birthday on July 1. Lotta hopes to be able to use the money, plus interest, to purchase a car on her seventeenth birthday. Assuming that a bank's interest rate remains constant at 4 percent over time, the students investigate the growth in Lotta's savings that different compounding schedules will yield.

One issue that surfaces in problems that examine change occurring over a number of years is how best to keep track of the passage of time. Time is an important component of each problem of this investigation. Problem 1, in which the students suppose that Lotta's money earns 4 percent in interest that the bank compounds annually, presents a table that records time both in numbers of years and in terms of Lotta's age. In subsequent problems, the students calculate some of the time details on their own. For example, they need to think about quarters as opposed to years in some problems, and they need to consider years as opposed to Lotta's age in others.

Rounding is another issue. Before students begin the investigation, lead a discussion about the errors that rounding causes and remind your students that different rounding practices can lead to discrepancies in answers. For example, students should realize that rounding at each step of a computation may produce a greater error than rounding only at the end of the computation. Guide your students to a decision to use the computational practice of rounding to the nearest cent only on the final answer. In addition, be aware that students' answers may differ slightly as a consequence of the technology that they use.

This investigation provides many "teachable moments" on compound interest.

The simple interest situation that the students encounter in problem 1 quickly evolves into an iterative process as they consider the passage of time and record data in a table. The students must be able to interpret the recorded data to answer the questions that follow. They need to equate Lotta's age with a particular year of savings in the table—that is, "13 years old" corresponds with year 1, "14 years old" corresponds with year 2, and so on—to answer the questions.

Problem 2 asks the students to describe two different methods of using a calculator to solve problem 1. Depending on the students' experience with calculators, some students may use longer multistep calculations while others use a streamlined one-step approach. For example, some may compute ($2000)(0.04) = $80, add it to $2000 to get $2080, and then continue in the same fashion with the $2080 in place of the $2000. Other students, however, may recognize that they can reduce the two steps to one step and form the product ($2000)(1.04) = $2080. They may continue to multiply by 1.04 to complete the table. Still other students may proceed by using the **ENTER** and **ANS** keys (or similar keys) on their calculators to multiply each previous answer by 1.04. (Calculators vary in the way that they handle iteration.) Another possible calculator strategy is to use the table feature of a graphing calculator. Students can also use spreadsheet software. Ask students to explain to the class how they answered problem 2.

In problem 3, the students suppose that the bank pays interest at a rate of 4 percent, compounding the interest quarterly. Before the students attempt this problem, you may need to explain how to determine the quarterly interest. Be certain that the students understand that Lotta receives the 4 percent in four equal amounts of $\frac{4\%}{4}$, or 1 percent each, at regular intervals during the year.

When students begin problem 4, in which they record the data from problem 3 in a table, be sure that they understand that they should report only the amount in Lotta's account after the fourth quarter—that is, the final amount for each year. Verify that they notice that the recorded amounts are the payments numbered $4 = 4 \cdot 1$, $8 = 4 \cdot 2$, $12 = 4 \cdot 3$, ..., $32 = 4 \cdot 8$. Students need to understand the significance of this pattern, since it will ease their transition from quarterly interest to other distributions, including monthly or daily interest. Ask the students why recording only the results after the final quarter in each year is helpful. They should realize that this process helps them compare the different types of interest distributions.

If students have difficulty writing the recursive generalization in problem 4, suggest that they start with their solution to problem 1(*d*) and modify it. Then they can use their reasoning in problem 4 to help with the generalization in problem 5.

In problem 5, the students suppose that the bank compounds the interest daily. When students work on this problem, verify that they are recording only the end-of-year results—namely, for the periods $365 \cdot 1$, $365 \cdot 2$, $365 \cdot 3$, ..., $365 \cdot 8$.

Students should use a trial-and-error approach to solve problem 6, which asks how long it will take for the money to double if Lotta invests it at 4 percent, with the interest compounded annually. As an extension to this investigation, suggest that they try other starting amounts and interest rates and examine the time needed for an amount of money to double. Then encourage students to look for patterns in their work.

Problem 7 introduces another idea—adding a constant amount and observing how it affects the accumulation of interest. The students probe how close the balances in the various situations are to $4000. You can use this problem to stimulate a discussion that focuses on comparing the interest totals for the three different types of interest distributions presented in the investigation.

The Mathematics in the Investigation

The investigation Investing with Lotta Cash centers on compound interest, so you need to introduce only one specific type of exponential function at this time. Students do additional work with exponential functions and multiplicative sequential patterns in grades 9–12. You can suggest that the students explore other interest problems that are similar to those in the investigation.

Table 5.1 displays a derivation of the recursive and explicit formulas for compound interest. If you decide to share this table with students who have some knowledge of algebra, you should furnish the reasons for each step in the process. The verification of these derived formulas depends on mathematical induction, which this volume describes in chapter 6.

Table 5.1.
Derivation of the Recursive and Explicit Formulas

Compound Interest: Recursive Form		Compound Interest: Explicit Form	
Amount to be invested: A_0 Rate of interest per period: r Number of interest periods: n		Amount to be invested: A_0 Rate of interest per period: r Number of interest periods: n	
Number of Periods	Amount at End of Period n	Number of Periods	Amount at End of Period n
1	$A_1 = A_0 + A_0 r$ $= A_0(1 + r)$	1	$A_1 = A_0 + A_0 r$ $= A_0(1 + r)$
2	$A_2 = A_1 + A_1 r$ $= A_1(1 + r)$	2	$A_2 = A_1(1 + r)$ $= A_0(1 + r)^2$
3	$A_3 = A_2 + A_2 r$ $= A_2(1 + r)$	3	$A_3 = A_2(1 + r)$ $= A_0(1 + r)^3$
$\vdots$	$\vdots$	$\vdots$	$\vdots$
n	$A_n = A_{n-1} + A_{n-1} r$ $= A_{n-1}(1 + r)$	n	$A_n = A_{n-1}(1 + r)$ $= A_0(1 + r)^n$

When students are in high school and study logarithms and methods of solving exponential equations, they learn a formal treatment for determining the number of years needed for an investment to double. A quick summary follows. Let A_0 be the amount to be doubled. The problem is to find n, the number of years, in $2A_0 = A_0(1 + r)^n$, where r is the rate of interest, compounded annually. It follows that

$$2 = (1 + r)^n$$

and

$$\log 2 = n\log (1 + r).$$

Therefore,

$$n = \frac{\log 2}{\log (1+r)}.$$

For example, if

$$r = 4\%$$
$$= 0.04,$$

then

$$n = \frac{\log 2}{\log 1.04}$$
$$= \frac{0.3010}{0.0170}$$
$$\approx 18.$$

The basis of the rule of 72 is the formula for compounding interest continuously, $A = Pe^{rt}$, where P is the amount invested, e is the irrational number 2.71828 … (the base used in calculating natural logarithms), r is the rate of interest per year, t is the time in years, and A is the total returned. Solving by using natural logs yields $t = (\ln 2)/r$, and $\ln 2 = 0.6931$. So the rule is actually the "rule of 69," but 72 is divisible by several positive integers and thus is more useful for easy approximation.

The result, approximately 18 years, depends on the interest rate and is independent of the amount invested. Some students may have heard of the rule of 72, which states that the time in years required to double an investment at x percent interest is approximately $\frac{72}{x}$; that is, $n \approx \frac{72}{x}$. In the previous problem, the rule of 72 gives the doubling time in years as $\frac{72}{4}$, or 18.

Other Recursive Explorations

Depending on your students' interest and skill, you can pursue the topics of recursion and iteration by introducing the following ideas.

Recursive Definitions

Middle school students need to gain broader exposure to and a better grasp of the meaning of recursion. To assist in the process, you can recast familiar definitions in recursive language. For example, the typical way of expressing the meaning of x^n is

$$x^n = x \cdot x \cdot x \cdot \ldots \cdot x,$$

where the number of x's in the product is n. In contrast, the following is a recursive definition of x^n:

$$x^1 = x \tag{1}$$

and

$$x^n = x^{n-1} \cdot x, \text{ for } n = 2, 3, 4, 5\ldots. \tag{2}$$

To have a complete definition of x^n for all natural numbers n, for $n \geq 1$, equation (1) must be part of the definition, since it provides the start. For example, using equations (1) and (2) indicates that

$$x^3 = x^{3-1} \cdot x$$
$$= x^2 \cdot x$$
$$= x^{2-1} \cdot x \cdot x$$
$$= x^1 \cdot x \cdot x$$
$$= x \cdot x \cdot x.$$

Equation (2) does not include the case when $n = 1$. If $n = 1$, then x^0 appears in the expression. Yet, this definition does give meaning to x^0. Substituting 1 for n in equation (2) helps show that x^0 equals 1: $x^1 = x^{1-1} \cdot x = x^0 \cdot x = 1 \cdot x$. Have your students practice the idea of recursive definitions by asking them to give a recursive definition of $n!$ Ask them to find other examples, as well.

Pascal's Triangle

Many students are familiar with Pascal's triangle but may not have recognized that it is indeed a recursively developed triangular array. Except for the first two rows of the triangle, each row is derived from the preceding row. For example, the row 1 5 10 10 5 1 comes from the preceding row 1 4 6 4 1 by starting with a 1, then writing the sums of $(1 + 4)$, $(4 + 6)$, $(6 + 4)$, and $(4 + 1)$, respectively, and concluding with a 1 at the end. Students should construct more rows of the triangle in this manner. They should describe the procedure in which each number in a row, except the two numbers at the ends of the row, is the sum of the two numbers in the row above it immediately to the left and to the right of the number.

Students can also experiment with changing the 2 in row 2 (whose entries are 1 2 1), to another number—say, 3. The students can keep row 0 and row 1 as they are in Pascal's triangle but let the new row 2 be 1 3 1. They can then construct a new triangle by using the same construction procedure as for Pascal's triangle. For example, the new row 3 will become

$$1 \quad (1 + 3) \quad (3 + 1) \quad 1.$$

After students have constructed this new modified Pascal's triangle, shown in figure 5.5, they can compare and contrast the patterns that appear in the two triangles.

```
            1                          1
          1   1                      1   1
        1   2   1                  1   3   1
      1   3   3   1              1   4   4   1
    1   4   6   4   1          1   5   8   5   1
  1   5  10  10   5   1      1   6  13  13   6   1
```

In chapter 2, "Systematic Listing and Counting in Grades 9–12," students investigate this pattern in terms of combinations and discover that the combinatorial identity $C(n, k) = C(n - 1, k - 1) + C(n - 1, k)$, for nonnegative integers $0 < k < n$, describes the procedure for constructing Pascal's triangle.

Fig. **5.5.**

Pascal's triangle and a "Pascal-like" triangle

 The applet Coloring Pascal's Triangle on the CD-ROM allows students to color entries in that triangle on various grids and explore the patterns that emerge.

Fibonacci Sequence

Leonardo of Pisa, popularly known as Fibonacci, described the sequence 1, 1, 2, 3, 5, 8, 13, 21, 34, 55, ... in his book *Liber Abaci* (1202). This sequence is a familiar example of a sequence in which, except for the first two terms, each new term is the sum of the preceding two terms. A recursive representation for the sequence is

$$F_1 = 1, F_2 = 1, F_n = F_{n-1} + F_{n-2}, n \geq 3.$$

You can ask your students to create their own Fibonacci-like sequences by choosing different starting values for F_1 and F_2 and then using the recursive relation for the Fibonacci sequence to enumerate subsequent terms in the new sequence. Students can then compare the new sequence and its properties with those of the Fibonacci sequence. You can ask your students the questions like the following:

- "How does the sum of the first ten Fibonacci numbers compare with F_7?"

- "How does the sum of the first ten Fibonacci-like numbers compare with the seventh term in the Fibonacci-like sequence?"

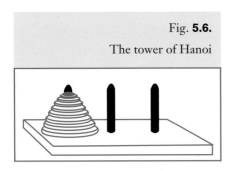

The CD-ROM includes the applet Tower of Hanoi, which students can manipulate to explore this famous problem.

Fig. **5.6.**

The tower of Hanoi

Theodorus of Cyrene (465–398 B.C.) was a Greek mathematician who had a special interest in irrational numbers and was Plato's tutor.

In both instances, the sum of the first ten terms equals 11 times the seventh term. Algebra students can prove this result by letting the first two terms of the sequence be *a* and *b*.

Tower of Hanoi

The *tower of Hanoi problem*, which the French mathematician Edouard Lucas created in 1883, is a great mathematical puzzle that you can present to your students, challenging them to determine a general solution. The problem begins with a conical stack of *n* disks on one of three spikes, as shown in figure 5.6, and seeks the minimum number of moves needed to transfer the stack to one the other "empty" spikes. Two conditions govern the moving of the disks:

- Only one disk may be transferred per move.
- A larger disk may not be stacked on top of a smaller disk.

Students should play the game with one, two, three, and four disks, carefully analyzing their moves. Proceeding systematically and keeping a record of moves will help them determine a pattern, as well as a strategy. A recursive process is important in making a generalization.

The Wheel of Theodorus

Students can approach many problems in geometry recursively and can use iterative processes to reach a solution. One problem that features basic construction skills is producing the wheel of Theodorus, shown in figure 5.7.

Students should begin constructing the wheel by placing the *x*- and *y*-axes on grid paper. Then they should create an isosceles right triangle with legs that are one unit long. One leg should be on the *x*-axis between (0, 0) and (1, 0), and the other should be perpendicular to the *x*-axis at (1, 0). The iterative process involves building a new right triangle adjoining the preceding right triangle by using the preceding hypotenuse as one leg and keeping the perpendicular leg one unit in length.

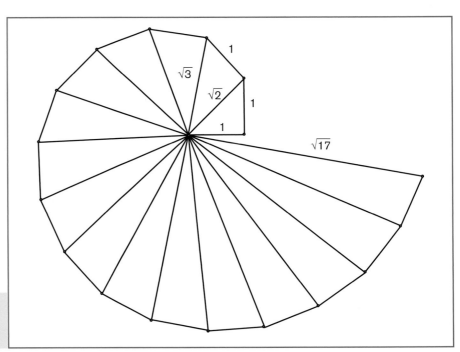

Fig. **5.7.**

The wheel of Theodorus

Navigating through Discrete Mathematics in Grades 6–12

Before your students begin the construction, ask them to guess the length of the hypotenuse of the right triangle whose hypotenuse will be nearest to but below the positive *x*-axis. (It is $\sqrt{17}$.) Then ask students to calculate the length of that hypotenuse by completing the construction. Students should produce their diagram with care, since the final results can vary markedly, depending on the students' ability to create accurate right angles and keep the perpendicular leg one unit long. However, to achieve the correct solution, students do not necessarily need to use a compass and straightedge; a five-by-seven-inch index card with a one-unit mark on an edge will also work well.

The students should be able to describe in words the iterative process of adding a leg and drawing a hypotenuse. Some students may be able to represent the process with the following recursive formula, where H_n is the length of the *n*th hypotenuse:

$$H_1 = \sqrt{2}$$

and

$$H_n = \sqrt{H_{n-1}^2 + 1},$$

for $n \geq 2$.

You can use the template "Centimeter Grid Paper" on the CD-ROM to print grid paper for your students to use in constructing the wheel of Theodorus.

Inductive Reasoning

In addition to having rich connections with the Content Standards of *Principles and Standards for School Mathematics*, iteration and recursion are also relevant to the Process Standards. They play a role in reasoning, representation, communication, connections, and problem solving. For example, middle school students should begin to understand inductive reasoning and see how iteration and recursion can be helpful in articulating this type of reasoning. They should learn the roles that iteration and recursion play in making conjectures and describing patterns on the basis of inductive reasoning. Students should realize that they must be careful in using inductive reasoning to solve a problem, since using such reasoning inappropriately can easily lead to incorrect results.

The following counting situations, for example, blend numeric, algebraic, and geometric strands. These two problems can be misleading. Study the problems and their solutions before sharing the problems with your students:

1. In square dot arrays of varying sizes, how many dots appear on or below the main diagonal that goes from the upper left corner of the array to the lower right corner? (Figure 5.8 shows a dot array.) Students who use a step-by-step, or iterative, approach to answer the question may notice that on or below the square's main diagonal, a 1×1 array contains 1 dot, a 2×2 array contains $1 + 2$ dots, a 3×3 array contains $1 + 2 + 3$ dots, a 4×4 array contains $1 + 2 + 3 + 4$ dots, and a 5×5 array contains $1 + 2 + 3 + 4 + 5$ dots. Students can express this sequential pattern recursively; that is, each new square array's dot count on or below the diagonal is the dot count of the previous square array plus the number of dots on a side of the new square array. In symbols, if S_n is the dot count on or below the main diagonal of a square array with n dots on each side, then $S_n = S_{n-1} + n$, with $S_1 = 1$ and $n \geq 2$. By inductive reasoning, an $n \times n$ array should contain $S_n = 1 + 2 + 3 + \ldots + n$ dots. When students reach high school, they may prove that this conclusion is

Fig. **5.8.**

How many dots are on or below the diagonal?

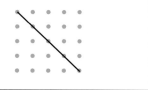

indeed correct by using mathematical induction. The dot counts S_n are the *triangular numbers*.

2. Have the students look again at the square dot arrays. In square dot arrays of varying sizes, how many line segments of different lengths can they draw between two dots that are on or below the main diagonal? Figure 5.9 gives a pictorial representation of this question.

Fig. **5.9.**

How many line segments of different lengths appear in the designs?

Students who use a step-by-step, or iterative, approach to answer this question might notice that the number of line segments of different length on a 1 × 1 array is 0, on a 2 × 2 array is 2, on a 3 × 3 array is 2 + 3, on a 4 × 4 array is 2 + 3 + 4, and on a 5 × 5 array is 2 + 3 + 4 + 5. Students can also express this sequential pattern recursively. That is, for n = 1 through 5, the different-length-line-segment count on each new square array is the line-segment count of the previous array plus the number of dots on a side of the new square array. The data imply that if D_n is the different-length-line-segment count for the square array with n dots on each side, then $D_n = D_{n-1} + n$, with $D_1 = 0$ and $n \geq 2$. By inductive reasoning, an $n \times n$ array should contain 2 + 3 + 4 + ... + n line segments of different length. However, this conclusion is not correct for all $n \geq 2$. Although a sequential pattern is evolving, the leap to a conclusion that is based on inductive reasoning does not consider the actual lengths of the line segments. Two different line segments on or below the main diagonal can have the same length. Such duplications start to appear when n = 6, as indicated in figure 5.10. Both segments drawn below the main diagonal in the figure have a length of 5 units.

For a similar problem, see pp. 266–67 in Principles and Standards for School Mathematics *(NCTM 2000).*

Fig. **5.10.**

Two segments with a length of 5 units

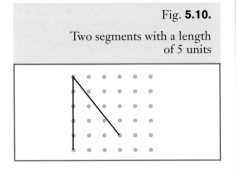

If your students are having trouble determining lengths for comparison, give them a hint. Suggest that they apply the Pythagorean relationship to the segment on the right.

Students should become comfortable in using iterative processes, finding recursive patterns, and using inductive reasoning; however, they must also understand that a pattern deduced from a few—or even many—cases may not be valid and must be verified. The next chapter further develops this important point in the investigation on proof by mathematical induction.

Conclusion

Iteration and recursion are powerful tools that students should develop and apply. Their work with these tools becomes more explicit and formal as they move from elementary school to middle school. In addition, middle school students should compare and contrast recursive and explicit expressions that describe a given situation and decide which representation is more useful under the circumstances. In particular, they should be able to use explicit and recursive expressions to describe situations that change over time. The following chapter gives recommendations and examples that indicate how this development should continue in high school.

NAVIGATIONS SERIES

GRADES 6–12

All students in grades 9–12 should—

- *describe, analyze, and create arithmetic and geometric sequences and series;*
- *create and analyze iterative geometric patterns, including fractals, with an investigation of self-similarity and the areas and perimeters of successive stages;*
- *represent and analyze functions by using iteration and recursion;*
- *use subscript and function notation to represent sequential patterns;*
- *investigate more complicated recursive formulas, such as simple nonlinear formulas; formulas in which the added quantity is a function of* n, *such as* S(n) = S(n − 1) + (2n + 1); *and formulas of the form* A(n + 1) = rA(n) + b, *recognizing that*

(continued)

NAVIGATING *through* DISCRETE MATHEMATICS

Chapter 6
Iteration and Recursion in Grades 9–12

Iteration and recursion are powerful tools for solving problems that deal with *sequential change*. Sequential change is step-by-step change, like the year-to-year change in the amount of money in an interest-bearing savings account or the change from one term to the next in a sequence of numbers. *Iteration* is the process of doing the same procedure or computation over and over again, typically starting from a base step and then generating all the steps or states in a sequence. *Recursion* is the method of describing a given step in a sequential process in terms of previous steps. A recursive formula, also called a *recurrence*, a *recurrence relation*, or a *difference equation*, captures such a description. A recursive formula, such as $a_n = a_{n-1} + 2$, contrasts with an explicit formula, such as $a_n = 2n$.

The development of iteration and recursion begins in a concrete manner in the early grades. In middle school, students build on and extend these concrete and informal approaches. They investigate more complicated patterns and begin to use subscript notation. Students in high school continue to use concrete and informal analysis. They also solve problems related to sequential change in more complicated and abstract settings and by using a more symbolic and formal approach. The representations that they use include informal NEXT-NOW language, subscripts, and function notation. In addition to using function notation to describe recursive patterns, students also deepen their understanding of functions by examining them from a recursive point of view.

Additional topics related to iteration and recursion in high school include finite differences tables, highlighted in the investigation A Recursive View of Skydiving; proof by mathematical induction, featured

97

(continued from previous page)

the resulting sequence is arithmetic when r = 1 *and geometric when* b = 0;

- *use finite differences tables to find explicit (closed-form) formulas for sequences that can be represented by polynomial functions;*

- *understand and carry out proofs by mathematical induction, recognizing a typical situation for induction proofs in which a recursive relationship is known and used to prove an explicit formula;*

- *use iteration and recursion to model and solve problems, including those in a variety of real-world contexts, particularly applied growth situations, such as population growth and compound interest;*

- *describe, analyze, and create iterative procedures and recursive formulas by using technology, such as computer software, graphing calculators, and programming languages.*

in the investigation A Recursive View of Mathematical Induction; and formal analysis of arithmetic and geometric sequences and series. Students extend their understanding of simple exponential explicit formulas and continue the informal treatment of quadratic explicit formulas that they began in middle school. For example, students learn about recursive formulas of the form

$$A(n) = rA(n - 1) + b,$$

along with the corresponding explicit formula, which is a shifted exponential function. This is a function of the form $y = ab^x + c$. Calling it simply an exponential function troubles some people, who reserve that phrase for a function of the form $y = ab^x$.

Students in grades 9–12 also investigate simple recursive formulas that include an added function, like

$$A(n) = A(n - 1) + (n + 1),$$

which yields a quadratic explicit formula, in a more analytic manner than the informal pattern-recognition approach that they used in middle school. Finally, high school students investigate increasingly complex real-world situations involving sequential change, examine fractals in more detail, and make more sophisticated use of technology than they did in the middle grades.

A Recursive View of Some Common Functions

The CD-ROM includes a related applet-based investigation, Trout Pond, which uses recursion to study population changes.

In this investigation, students revisit linear and exponential functions from a recursive point of view. They learn (or review) how to represent linear functions in the form NEXT = NOW + c, where c is the slope or constant rate of change; and they learn how to represent exponential functions in the form NEXT = NOW × c. The simple yet stark difference in the NEXT-NOW equations clearly emphasizes the fundamental difference between linear and exponential functions. Students compare these equations with "$y = \dots$" equations and then use both types of equations, along with tables and graphs, to summarize similarities and differences between linear and exponential functions.

Goals

- Represent and analyze functions by using iteration and recursion
- Investigate more complicated recursive formulas, such as $A(n + 1) = rA(n) + b$
- Use iteration and recursion to model and solve problems

Materials and Equipment

For each student—

- A copy of each of the following activity sheets:
  - "A Constant Rate of Change"
  - "A Constant Multiplier"
- (Optional) Access to a computer and the applet-based investigation Trout Pond on the CD-ROM

pp. 162–63; 164–66

Prior Knowledge

Students should have studied linear and exponential functions, although they need only an elementary understanding of these functions for this activity. In this investigation, students deepen their knowledge, and they compare and contrast these two basic function families while revisiting them from a recursive point of view.

Discussion

The investigation consists of two parts. Students explore linear functions in part 1, "A Constant Rate of Change"; and they explore exponential functions in part 2, "A Constant Multiplier." The class can do the two parts as separate activities at different places in the curriculum. For example, students can do part 1 during a unit on linear functions and part 2 during a unit on exponential functions. However, the investigation is probably best suited for use in its entirety as a synthesizing activity—perhaps during a unit on exponential functions that follows a previous unit on linear functions. The investigation then allows students to compare and contrast linear and exponential functions while

x	y		x	y
0	4		0	4
1	7		1	12
2	10		2	36
3	13		3	108
4	16		4	324
⋮	⋮		⋮	⋮

a · · · · · · · · · b

deepening their understanding of each type of function, particularly by examining the functions from a recursive point of view.

Take a few moments to work through the investigation before reading the rest of this discussion. Throughout the investigation, your students will be looking for patterns in the given tables. Tell them that the patterns shown in the tables are meant to continue in the same way beyond the last row of the given partial tables.

Part 1—"A Constant Rate of Change"

In part 1, "A Constant Rate of Change," students analyze a linear function. They begin by describing all the patterns that they can find in a function table (shown as [a] in the margin). The activity then guides them through a systematic analysis. It is important that students look for patterns vertically, down the y-column of the given table, and then horizontally, from the x-column to the y-column. The x-y horizontal pattern is the more conventional subject of analysis and generates a y = ... equation, but it is often more difficult for students and not as obvious as the y-column pattern, which generates a recursive equation.

Students are likely to notice that the y-values increase by 3 each time. They can intuitively describe this vertical pattern as NEXT = NOW + 3. A nice feature of this recursive formula is that it clearly highlights the constant rate of change and the slope, 3. Students will probably find that the NEXT-NOW recursive formula shows slope and rate of change more clearly and meaningfully than the explicit formula, $y = 4 + 3x$.

After your students complete the graphic organizer that the activity sheet provides for summarizing their work, you can conduct a whole-class discussion in which you ask them to explain each item on the graphic organizer and describe how they determined the item, what it means, and how it connects with other information on the page. Alternatively, you can ask the students to use this information as the basis for reports.

Part 2—"A Constant Multiplier"

After completing the analysis of linear functions in part 1, "A Constant Rate of Change," the students carry out a parallel analysis for exponential functions in part 2, "A Constant Multiplier." In this situation, the pattern in the successive y-values (shown as [b] in the margin) consists of multiplying by 3 each time instead of adding 3. This pattern, NEXT = NOW × 3, is also likely to be an easy one for students to see and describe. The sharp contrast between adding 3 and multiplying by 3 clearly shows the fundamental difference between linear and exponential growth. As in the previous analysis of linear functions, students relate the recursive NEXT-NOW representation for this exponential function to the table, the graph, and the y = ... equation.

Problem 8 in both parts—"A Constant Rate of Change" and "A Constant Multiplier"—asks the students to look back, summarize, and explain their work. Problem 9 of "A Constant Multiplier" asks them to compare and contrast their work in the two parts of the investigation systematically, thereby highlighting several important similarities and differences in the representation and analysis of linear and exponential functions.

Finally, problem 10 of "A Constant Multiplier" offers an extension that uses Trout Pond, an applet-based investigation on the CD-ROM.

In this electronic investigation, students examine the recursive formula

$$\text{NEXT} = r\ \text{NOW} + b$$

Students can work with Trout Pond, an applet-based investigation on the CD-ROM, to extend their understanding of the recursive equation NEXT = r NOW + b.

in the context of a changing trout population, in which r represents the growth rate and b represents an annual restocking amount. Formulas like this one are sometimes called *combined recursive formulas.* Such a formula combines addition and multiplication by a constant. When $r = 1$, the result is an arithmetic sequence with a corresponding linear explicit formula; when $b = 0$, the result is a geometric sequence with a corresponding exponential explicit formula.

The general formula NEXT = r NOW + b can model many similar growth or decay situations—for example, the amount of chlorine in a swimming pool, given that some amount regularly dissipates and some is regularly added; the growth of money in a savings account when the account holder makes regular deposits; or the amount of medicine in the bloodstream when a patient eliminates some and takes a constant dosage.

An important point throughout A Recursive View of Some Common Functions is that recursive NEXT-NOW representations highlight and deepen students' understanding of fundamental features of linear and exponential change. In addition, the NEXT-NOW language can serve as an effective transition to more formal notation for sequences, such as subscript or function notation. For example, NEXT = NOW + 3 translates easily into $A_{n+1} = A_n + 3$ or into $A(n + 1) = A(n) + 3$.

Students often become confused when using different subscript notation such as $A_{n+1} = A_n + 3$, as opposed to $A_n = A_{n-1} + 3$. These expressions look different, but they of course express exactly the same relationship, with 3 added each time. This confusion is probably much less when students use NEXT-NOW language. Most students who understand recursion in NEXT-NOW language have little trouble recognizing that they can express this relationship just as well with the subscripts n and $n - 1$ as with the subscripts $n + 1$ and n. If your students have trouble with this notational subtlety, you might also consider looking at sequential change by using NOW-PREVIOUS language.

NEXT-NOW notation, or similar language, provides a nonthreatening and sense-making basis for formal subscript or function notation. This investigation does not use more formal notation, although you may choose to introduce it if your students are ready. Subsequent activities in this chapter do include more formal notation.

The Mathematics in the Investigation

This investigation presents a recursive view of linear and exponential functions and relates this view to the graphical, tabular, and $y = \ldots$ representations of these functions. As discussed, the recursive view can help emphasize the fundamental properties of slope and rate of change, and it also points toward the connection with arithmetic and geometric sequences. For example, NEXT = NOW + 3 can describe a linear function, and it also clearly describes a sequence that generates the next term by adding 3 to the current term—that is, an arithmetic sequence. Similarly, NEXT = NOW × 3, which can describe an exponential function, as in this investigation, can also describe a geometric sequence, where the current term is multiplied by 3 to obtain the next term.

Other examples of activities of this type include Experimenting with a Dosage in Navigating through Mathematical Connections in Grades 9–12 *(Burke et al. 2006).*

Principles and Standards for School Mathematics *(NCTM 2000, pp. 303–5)*

also presents a recursive activity on the elimination of a prescription drug from the body. Adapted from the National Research Council (1998, p. 80), the activity connects with an associated e-example (http://standards.nctm.org/ document/eexamples/chap7/ 7.2/index.htm).

Three important details related to the NEXT-NOW representations may arise in questions from students.

- NEXT-NOW equations describe only how to progress from one y-value to the next one. A complete description of the sequence of y-values also requires specification of the first value, which can be accomplished in a statement such as START = 4.

- The starting value is the same as the y-intercept only if the table starts at $x = 0$. For example, in part 1, "A Constant Rate of Change," the table starts with $x = 0$, the corresponding starting y-value is 4, and the y-intercept of the graph of $y = 4 + 3x$ is also 4. This correspondence is nice, but since it does not always hold, students should not overgeneralize. If students investigate patterns in a similar table that starts, say, at $x = 1$ instead of $x = 0$, then START = 7, since it is then the first y-value in the sequence of y-values, but the y-intercept is still 4.

- To carry out this type of NEXT-NOW analysis meaningfully, the increment for successive x-values must be constant. In part 1, the constant increment must be 1 so that students can interpret the added constant in the NEXT-NOW equation as slope. The added constant is the change in y, and for this constant to be the same as slope, which is change in y divided by change in x, the change in x must be 1.

Explore these details if they seem appropriate for your students. Do not become sidetracked but keep the major thrust of the investigation simple and straightforward. When the class completes this investigation, you might pose some additional problems that explicitly address these points. For example, with respect to the increment in x-values, consider table 6.1, in which the x-increment is 2.

In this example, you can represent the pattern of y-values in the table by using the equation NEXT = NOW + 8, since each y-value is 8 more than the previous y-value. However, since the constant x-increment is 2, the slope of the corresponding line is not 8 but is instead $\frac{8}{2}$, or 4.

Table 6.1
The x-Increment Is 2

x	y
0	3
2	11
4	19
6	27

A Recursive View of Skydiving

In contrast to the preceding investigation, which provides a recursive analysis of linear and exponential functions, this investigation presents a recursive view of quadratic functions. Students deepen their understanding of quadratic functions, rate of change, and mathematical modeling while analyzing the distance that a skydiver falls because of the effect of gravity. Students also learn how to use finite differences tables to find an explicit formula for certain sequences.

Goals

- Represent and analyze functions by using iteration and recursion
- Use subscript and function notation to represent sequential patterns
- Investigate more complicated recursive formulas, such as formulas in which the added quantity is a function of n and formulas of the form $A(n + 1) = rA(n) + b$
- Use finite differences tables to find explicit (closed-form) formulas for sequences that can be represented by polynomial functions
- Use iteration and recursion to model and solve problems, including problems in a variety of real-world contexts

Materials and Equipment

For each student—

- A copy of the activity sheet "A Recursive View of Skydiving"

For each student or pair of students—

- A calculator with matrix functionality
- (Optional) Access to a computer and the applet-based investigation Trout Pond on the CD-ROM

pp. 167–71

Prior Knowledge

Students should have previously studied quadratic functions, although they need only an elementary understanding for this investigation. Students should also have previously studied matrices. Knowing how to use matrices to solve systems of linear equations is helpful in this investigation, and students at least need to know how to multiply matrices. Students should also have some understanding of arithmetic sequences for the optional problem.

Discussion

Read and work through the investigation before continuing. The overall goal of this investigation is to have students find recursive and explicit formulas for the total distance that a skydiver has fallen after n seconds.

This investigation has three main parts. In problems 1–3, students complete a table showing the time that a skydiver has fallen, the speed at which she falls, and the distance that she falls. In problem 4, they find recursive and explicit formulas for $D(n)$, the distance that the skydiver falls during the nth second. In problems 5–7, they find formulas for $T(n)$, the total distance that the skydiver has fallen after n seconds.

Students must understand and be able to complete the table correctly in problems 1–3, as shown in table 6.2. The data in the table provide the basis for most of the subsequent problems.

Table 6.2.
Table for Problems 1–3

Time n in Seconds	Instantaneous Speed at Time n	Average Speed during Each Second	Distance Fallen during Each Second $D(n)$	Total Distance Fallen after n Seconds $T(n)$
0	0	0	0	0
1 sec	32 ft/sec	16 ft/sec	16 ft	16 ft
2 sec	64 ft/sec	48 ft/sec	48 ft	64 ft
3 sec	96 ft/sec	80 ft/sec	80 ft	144 ft
4 sec	128 ft/sec	112 ft/sec	112 ft	256 ft

In the second and third columns of the table, the students determine the speed at which the skydiver falls. For calculating the instantaneous speed at time n, students need to understand that since acceleration caused by the force of gravity near the surface of the earth is 32 feet per second per second (32 ft/sec²), the instantaneous speed at the end of each second is 32 ft/sec more than the speed at the end of the previous second. Some students may struggle with the third column of the table, which shows the average speed during each second, but after discussing it with their classmates and the teacher, they should figure out how to compute the entries. For example, to compute the average speed during, say, the third second, students might compute the average of the instantaneous speeds at the end of the second and third seconds. Or they might see that the average speed during a given second is 32 ft/sec more than the average speed during the previous second.

The two rightmost columns of the table show distance. Students must make the crucial distinction between distance that the skydiver falls *during* each second and the total distance that the skydiver has fallen *after n* seconds. The basic formula *distance = speed × time* indicates that the distance that the skydiver falls during the nth second, $D(n)$, is the average speed during the nth second multiplied by 1 second. Students can find $T(n)$, the total distance that the skydiver has fallen after n seconds, in several ways. One way is to compute

$$T(n) = D(1) + D(2) + \ldots + D(n).$$

In problem 4, the students use the information in the table to find recursive and explicit formulas for $D(n)$. The recursive formula for $D(n)$ is

$$D(n) = D(n - 1) + 32,$$

since the values for $D(n)$ increase by 32 feet for each second of time. Students may have more difficulty finding the explicit formula. One way to find it is to notice that, for example, to determine $D(4)$, you start with 16 and then add 32 three times. Generalizing this method gives the following explicit formula for $D(n)$ in feet:

$$D(n) = 16 + 32(n - 1)$$
$$= 32n - 16.$$

Problem 4 instructs students to ignore the row in the table for $n = 0$ sec. These formulas apply only when this row is excluded.

Problems 5–7 focus on finding formulas for $T(n)$, the total distance that the skydiver has fallen after n seconds. The students employ three strategies: they use a general analysis, sum an arithmetic sequence, and use a finite differences table.

Problem 5 guides the students through a general analysis. In part (*a*), they describe how they computed $T(3)$. Encourage them to give very careful descriptions and then to use equal care in describing all the different ways in which they can compute $T(n)$. Students should be able to verbalize a statement like this: "For $T(3)$, the total distance that the skydiver has fallen after three seconds is the total distance fallen after two seconds plus the distance fallen during the third second." This statement leads to the recursive formula for $T(n)$, in feet, as requested in part (*c*):

$$T(n) = T(n - 1) + D(n)$$

In problem 6, the students find $T(n)$ by summing an arithmetic sequence. Regard this problem as optional. Your decision to use it will depend on whether your students have previously learned how to sum arithmetic sequences. As in problem 4, the students again must exclude the row for time = 0 sec, since the arithmetic sequence begins with $n = 1$ sec. Summing the arithmetic sequence yields the following result (in feet):

$$T(n) = D(1) + D(2) + \ldots + D(n)$$

$$= 16n^2.$$

Problem 7 uses a finite differences table. By using this method, students should find, once again, that the explicit formula for $T(n)$ is $T(n) = 16n^2$.

Note that using finite differences is effective for finding an explicit formula for many sequences. For example, consider the sequence 1, 3, 6, 10, 15, …, which appears subsequently in this chapter, as well as in chapter 1. In this chapter, students encounter this sequence in the next investigation on mathematical induction, where they determine that the number of edges in a complete graph on 2, 3, 4, 5, 6, … vertices is 1, 3, 6, 10, 15 …, respectively. Using finite differences yields $E(n)$, the number of edges in a complete graph on n vertices, which is equal to

$$\frac{n(n - 1)}{2}.$$

In chapter 1, students considered the triangular numbers 1, 3, 6, 10, 15, …. They can use finite differences to determine that the nth triangular number is

$$\frac{n(n + 1)}{2}.$$

You can therefore reinforce the use of finite differences by applying this method in other discrete mathematics problems. The two explicit formulas in the examples above differ slightly because the sequence starts with $n = 2$ for complete graphs, whereas the sequence of triangular numbers starts with $n = 1$.

For an example of the method that uses algebraic manipulation of the equations without matrices, see Mission Mathematics II: Linking Aerospace and the NCTM Standards, 9–12 *(House and Day 2005, p. 34).*

As part of problem 7, the students solve a system of three linear equations. The main method presented uses matrices. Students can, of course, use other methods, including algebraic manipulation of the equations without matrices.

Problem 8 provides a brief summary, a connection with the investigation A Recursive View of Some Common Functions, and an extension. In part (*a*), students see that they have now taken a recursive view of three important types of functions—linear, exponential, and quadratic functions.

Part (*b*) of problem 8 invites students to explore Trout Pond, the applet-based investigation also suggested as an extension for the preceding activity and available on the CD-ROM. Working with embedded applets, the students can analyze the recursive formula

$$P(n) = rP(n-1) + b.$$

As described in the earlier activity, the context of the investigation is a changing trout population, in which r represents the growth rate and b represents an annual restocking amount. The explicit formula corresponding to this recursive formula is a shifted exponential function.

The Mathematics in the Investigation

This investigation examines recursive and explicit formulas for a quadratic function that models the distance that a skydiver falls. To simplify the analysis, this activity ignores all factors except gravity. The students first find formulas by examining patterns in a table. In problem 6, students find an explicit formula by summing an arithmetic sequence.

In an arithmetic sequence, any given term (after the first term) is computed by adding a constant to the previous term. One way to think about the sum of an arithmetic sequence is as follows:

$$a_1 + a_2 + \ldots + a_n = \frac{\left(\textit{first term} + \textit{last term}\right)\left(\textit{number of terms}\right)}{2}$$

The result in this situation is

$$T(n) = D(1) + D(2) + \ldots + D(n)$$
$$= \frac{\left(16 + \left(32n - 16\right)\right)\left(n\right)}{2}$$
$$= 16n^2.$$

In problem 7, students use finite differences to find an explicit formula for $T(n)$. Since the second differences are constant, this problem uses a given fact about finite differences to conclude that the explicit formula must be of degree 2—that is, quadratic. But why is this statement true? It is actually an "if and only if" theorem: *The second differences in a finite-differences table for a sequence $\{A_n\}$ are constant if and only if the explicit formula for the sequence is a quadratic function.* Consider why this theorem is true.

The first step is to prove that if the explicit formula is quadratic, then the second differences are constant. Suppose that the explicit formula for a sequence $\{A_n\}$ is a quadratic function. That is, suppose that

$$A_n = an^2 + bn + c.$$

The next step is to construct a finite-differences table, as shown in table 6.3, and prove that the second differences are a constant—and also note the connection between the constant second differences and the leading coefficient of the quadratic explicit formula.

Table 6.3.
Finite-Differences Table for the Sequence Given by $A^n = an^2 + bn + c$

n	A_n	First Difference	Second Difference
0	c		
		$a + b$	
1	$a + b + c$		$2a$
		$3a + b$	
2	$4a + 2b + c$		$2a$
		$5a + b$	
3	$9a + 3b + c$		$2a$
		$7a + b$	
4	$16a + 4b + c$		
⋮	⋮	⋮	⋮
n	$an^2 + bn + c$		
		$a(2n + 1) + b$	
$n + 1$	$a(n + 1)^2 + b(n + 1) + c$		$2a$
		$a(2n + 3) + b$	
$n + 2$	$a(n + 2)^2 + b(n + 2) + c$		

Since the computations in the finite-differences table are for an arbitrary n, this process proves that the second differences are constant. In addition, observe that the constant second difference is twice the leading coefficient, a.

Next, consider the other direction of the theorem: If the second differences are constant, then the explicit formula is quadratic. A formal proof involves solving a type of equation called a *second-order nonhomogeneous difference equation*, which is too far afield. However, figure 6.1 shows an informal justification.

Discrete Dynamical Systems *(Sandefur 1990) includes a discussion of second-order nonhomogeneous difference equations.*

For more information about the method of finite differences, see the article "The Method of Finite Differences: Some Applications" (Guillotte 1986) on the CD-ROM.

Another good source for information about this useful method is Finite Differences *(Seymour and Shedd 1973).*

Suppose that the second differences of the sequence $\{A_n\}$ are constant. Let k represent that constant. Then

$$\text{second difference} = (A_{n+2} - A_{n+1}) - (A_{n+1} - A_n) = k.$$

Therefore,

$$A_{n+2} = 2A_{n+1} - A_n + k.*$$

Next, use the equation marked with an asterisk (*) to find an explicit formula for A_n and determine whether it is quadratic. To do so, list the terms of the sequence and look for a pattern:

A_0

A_1

$A_2 = 2A_1 - A_0 + k$ By using the equation marked with an asterisk

$A_3 = 2(2A_1 - A_0 + k) - A_1 + k$

$\quad = 3A_1 - 2A_0 + 3k$ By using the equation with an asterisk again

$A_4 = 2A_3 - A_2 + k$

$\quad = 2(3A_1 - 2A_0 + 3k) - (2A_1 - A_0 + k) + k$

$\quad = 4A_1 - 3A_0 + 6k$

$$\vdots$$

$$A_n = nA_1 - (n-1)A_0 + \frac{n(n-1)}{2}k$$

The sequence of coefficients of k, starting at A_2, appears to be 1, 3, 6, 10, 15, …; this sequence yields $\dfrac{n(n-1)}{2}$ at A_n.

$$= \frac{k}{2}n^2 + \left(A_1 - A_0 - \frac{k}{2}\right)n + A_0$$

By recombining algebraically

This final equation provides an explicit formula for A_n, and it is quadratic. This informal justification, although not a rigorous proof, indicates that if the second differences are constant, then the explicit formula is

Fig. **6.1.**

If the second differences are constant, then the explicit formula is quadratic.

A Recursive View of Mathematical Induction

This investigation provides an initial development of proof by mathematical induction. Students learn about the types of problems in which proof by induction may apply, they make sense of the principle of mathematical induction, and they learn how to carry out proofs by induction.

Goals

- Understand and carry out proofs by mathematical induction, recognizing a typical situation for such a proof, in which a recursive relationship is known and used to prove an explicit formula
- Create and analyze iterative geometric patterns, including fractals, with an investigation of perimeters of successive stages
- Use subscript and function notation to represent sequential patterns
- Investigate more complicated recursive formulas, such as formulas in which the added quantity is a function of n
- Use iteration and recursion to model and solve problems

Materials and Equipment

For each student—
- A copy of the activity sheet "A Recursive View of Mathematical Induction"

For the teacher—
- Books, blocks, or dominoes to illustrate the "falling dominoes" model of induction

pp. 172–77

Prior Knowledge

This investigation provides a first look at proof by mathematical induction, so students do not need to have experience working on such proofs. However, students should have seen and worked with recursive formulas, have had experience in finding such formulas, and be familiar with the recursive point of view in general. If your students do not have this familiarity, you might have them complete the investigation A Recursive View of Some Common Functions before they begin work on this investigation. Students should also be able to use function and subscript notation before beginning the investigation.

Discussion

Acquaint yourself with the problems in the investigation before continuing. Problem 1 confronts students with a situation in which proof by mathematical induction might be useful. The problem asks the

---

This activity is adapted from Coxford and others (2003).

Principle of Mathematical Induction

Suppose that S(n) *is a statement about integers.*

If (i) S(n) *is true whenever* S(n – 1) *is true, for each integer* n > n₀,

and

(ii) S(n₀) *is true,*

then S(n) *is true for all integers* n ≥ n₀.

Fig. 6.2.

Falling dominoes can illustrate the principle of mathematical induction.

A complete graph is a vertex-edge graph that has exactly one edge between every pair of vertices. Chapters 3 and 4 in this volume present more information about these graphs.

students to consider whether the following statement about infinitely many integers is true: $n^2 - n + 41$ is prime for all integers $n \geq 0$. This statement is true for many values of n but clearly fails when $n = 41$. Students need to realize that they cannot prove a statement like this one just by checking several cases. In problem 2, the students find several other values of n for which $n^2 - n + 41$ is not a prime number. They should also understand that one counterexample can disprove such a statement.

After settling these important issues, students next consider how to use the principle of mathematical induction to prove a statement that is asserted to be true for infinitely many integers. Problem 3 presents the common analogy of proof by induction to falling dominoes, as suggested in figure 6.2. You might want to demonstrate this analogy with books, blocks, or dominoes. Discussing the analogy in detail can be a compelling way to help students understand the basic idea of the principle of mathematical induction. In fact, the domino analogy is one reason for stating the principle with the "base step" (prove that the statement is true for n_0) listed second instead of first (see the margin). To use the falling-domino analogy, first set up the dominoes so that each domino will be knocked over by the previous domino, and then knock over the first domino. Thus, although it is possible to list the two parts of the principle of mathematical induction in either order, listing the base step second makes sense for students when they think about falling dominoes. In parts (*a*), (*b*), and (*c*) of problem 3, the students should explain how specific aspects of the domino situation are analogous to condition (i), condition (ii), and the conclusion of the principle.

The investigation next presents the two steps of proof by mathematical induction. These steps correspond to the two conditions of the principle of mathematical induction. The investigation then gives students a sample problem about finding and proving a formula for the number of edges in a complete graph. Figure 6.3 shows two examples of complete graphs.

Before starting the proof, students first consider the two possible types of formulas for the number of edges: a recursive formula and an explicit formula. Emphasize that this example represents a common situation in which proof by induction may apply. That is, the goal is to prove an explicit formula, and a recursive formula is an essential tool in the proof.

Thus, students first need to find a recursive formula for the number of edges in a complete graph. They find that formula in problem 4. In

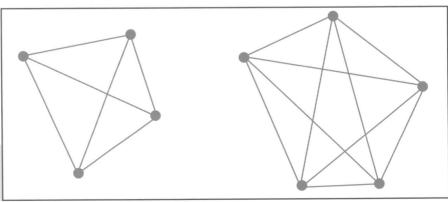

Fig. 6.3.

Complete graphs on four and five vertices

this problem, students sketch graphs, collect data about the number of edges, organize the data, and find a pattern. Being able to use this process is an important skill for students to acquire, so refrain from giving them a blank table to fill in unless they really need that extra help.

After the students have found a recursive formula for the number of edges in a complete graph with n vertices, they encounter a conjecture for an explicit formula:

$$E(n) = \frac{n(n-1)}{2},$$

for every $n \geq 1$. This is the statement that students must prove. In problems 5 and 6, they make sense of and carry out a proof by mathematical induction.

After the investigation has guided students through this first induction proof, they practice their new skill in problems 7 and 8 by doing two more proofs, which represent two interesting and important types of problems. In problem 7, students prove a formula for the sum of the first n odd numbers. Such proofs related to finite sums are common induction proofs in textbooks. In problem 8, the students investigate and prove a formula for the perimeter of the Sierpinski triangle, which is a famous fractal. Figure 6.4 shows the Sierpinski triangle (which starts with a solid triangular region that is 1 unit on a side) at several stages.

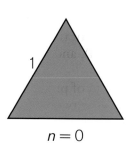 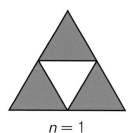 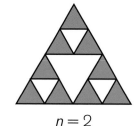 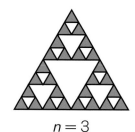

$n = 0$ $\quad$ $n = 1$ $\quad$ $n = 2$ $\quad$ $n = 3$

Fig. **6.4.**

The Sierpinski triangle at various stages

The Mathematics in the Investigation

This investigation is about proof by mathematical induction. The approach used in this investigation has two distinguishing features. First, the investigation encourages students to recognize a common type of situation in which proof by induction may apply—namely, a situation involving infinitely many integers, in which they can use a known recursive relationship to try to prove a conjectured explicit relationship. A crucial detail related to this point is that the recursive relationship must either be taken as known or the students must prove it. If students prove it, the proof is a separate one, independent of the main induction proof, and it usually is not done by induction.

The second distinguishing feature relates to the approach that the investigation takes to resolve a common area of confusion. Students often become confused in an induction proof when the teacher says, "We assume that the statement is true for k and prove that it is true for $k + 1$." This one statement, which is accurate and sensible to the teacher, can be triply confusing for students, who may be asking themselves these questions:

 The accompanying CD-ROM includes the article "Benoit Mandelbrot: The Euclid of Fractal Geometry" (Camp 2000). Another good resource about fractals is *Fractals for the Classroom: Strategic Activities*, Volumes 1 and 2 (Peitgen, Jürgens, Saupe, Maletsky, Perciante, and Yunker 1991, 1992).

- "Where does the k come from, since the problem is stated for n?"
- "Why are we proving it for $k + 1$, since there is no $k + 1$ or $n + 1$ in the problem statement?"
- "Why are we *assuming* that the statement is true—for n or k or whatever—when we are supposed to *prove* that it is true?"

The approach used in this investigation avoids these potential sources of confusion by stating and using the principle of mathematical induction in a form that moves from the $(n - 1)$ case to the n case, rather than from the k case to the $(k + 1)$ case. Because the goal is to prove a statement about n, this method proceeds straight ahead and tries to do just that, while making only a simple notational change that completely preserves the meaning of the principle. It does not introduce a new variable, k, and it does not try to prove the statement for $k + 1$ or $n + 1$. It simply tries to prove that the statement is true for n, since that is what the problem requests and that is what the first condition of the principle of mathematical induction calls for. Then, while students are trying to prove the statement for n, they may assume at any time that the statement is already true for $n - 1$, since that is also part of the first condition of the principle. With this approach, proof by mathematical induction can seem more straightforward to students, and it avoids the classic confusions about k and $k + 1$.

The induction step is typically the largest part of an induction proof, but the base step, which involves proving the statement for the initial value of n, is also essential. You may want to extend this investigation by asking students to construct some proofs in which the initial value of n is something other than $n = 0$ or $n = 1$, as in the proofs in this investigation.

Conclusion

This chapter, like the previous chapter for grades 6–8, has presented recommendations and sample activities for teaching iteration and recursion, this time in grades 9–12. When we combine this material with that in the previous chapters, we have have completed our "navigation" for grades 6–12 through the three fundamental areas of discrete mathematics recommended in *Principles and Standards for School Mathematics* (NCTM 2000): systematic listing and counting, vertex-edge graphs, and iteration and recursion. We hope that this book will help teachers implement the important recommendation in *Principles and Standards* that "these ideas can be systematically developed from prekindergarten through grade 12" (p. 31).

NAVIGATING *through* DISCRETE MATHEMATICS

Looking Back and Looking Ahead

This book presents a vision, based on NCTM's *Principles and Standards for School Mathematics* (2000), for incorporating discrete mathematics into the mathematics curriculum for students in grades 6–12. The companion book, *Navigating through Discrete Mathematics in Prekindergarten–Grade 5* (DeBellis et al. forthcoming), presents an analogous vision for students in prekindergarten through grade 5.

Discrete mathematics is more relevant than ever in today's technology-intensive and information-dense world. It is increasingly "the math for our time" (Dossey 1991, p. 1). Students today need to understand and be able to apply such discrete mathematics topics as combinatorics, vertex-edge graphs, and iteration and recursion so that they can be knowledgeable and competitive as adults in the twenty-first century.

Discrete mathematics topics are engaging, contemporary, and useful. These topics should routinely be part of today's school mathematics. As *Principles and Standards* asserts, "Discrete mathematics should be an integral part of the school mathematics curriculum" (p. 31). We hope that this book will help achieve this recommendation and bring the power of discrete mathematics to all students in all grades.

NAVIGATIONS SERIES

GRADES 6–12

NAVIGATING *through* DISCRETE MATHEMATICS

Appendix

Blackline Masters and Solutions

Flag Trademarks

Name _____

A luggage company is considering two rectangular flag patterns, pattern A and pattern B, for use as a trademark. The company plans to use the winning pattern on one side of a certain brand of luggage in the orientation shown below.

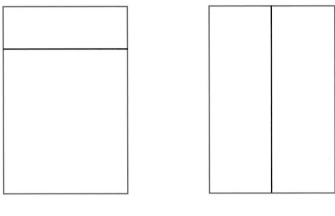

Pattern A   Pattern B

Note that pattern A looks different when it is rotated 180° about its center, though pattern B looks just the same when rotated 180° about its center. Each pattern requires two pieces of cloth.

1. Suppose that the company plans to use red, white, and blue cloth for prototypes of the flag trademarks. You will use red, white, and blue construction paper to cut out the shapes in patterns A and B so that you can create models of the trademarks. You must display all the different possibilities for patterns A and B on a poster. You are trying to save time and space, so you want to be sure that you produce the fewest cutout models that can represent all possible patterns. Use the construction paper to make the flags, and mount them on poster board or paper. But first, count the number of possibilities by following the steps below (write your explanations on a separate sheet of paper).

    a. If the two pieces of cloth can be the same color, how many different pattern A models do you need to make? Explain how you determined your total, and display each pattern on the poster.

    b. If the two pieces of cloth can be the same color, how many different pattern B models do you need to make? Explain how you determined your total, and display each pattern on the poster.

    c. If the two pieces of cloth must be different colors, how many different pattern A models do you need to make? Explain how you determined your total, and display each pattern on the poster board.

    d. If the two pieces of cloth must be different colors, how many different pattern B models do you need to make? Explain how you determined your total, and display each pattern on the poster board.

Navigating through Discrete Mathematics in Grades 6–12

Flag Trademarks (continued)

Name _____

2. Suppose that the company plans to use red, white, blue, and green cloth for prototypes of the flag trademarks. Construct a tree diagram that shows all possible different color pairs. Use the diagram to answer the following questions:

    a. If the two pieces of cloth can be the same color, how many different pattern A models are possible? Explain how you determined your total.

    b. If the two pieces of cloth can be the same color, how many different pattern B models are possible? Explain how you determined your total.

    c. If the two pieces of cloth must be different colors, how many different pattern A models are possible? Explain how you determined your total.

    d. If the two pieces of cloth must be different colors, how many different pattern B models are possible? Explain how you determined your total.

3. Suppose that the company plans to use red, white, blue, green, and yellow cloth for prototypes of the flag trademarks. Use counting principles to answer the following questions:

    a. If the two pieces of cloth can be the same color, how many different pattern A models are possible? Explain how you determined your total.

    b. If the two pieces of cloth can be the same color, how many different pattern B models are possible? Explain how you determined your total.

    c. If the two pieces of cloth must be different colors, how many different pattern A models are possible? Explain how you determined your total.

    d. If the two pieces of cloth must be different colors, how many different pattern B models are possible? Explain how you determined your total.

4. Design your own flag trademark pattern that requires three different colors. If you can choose from a selection of eight colors, how many different models are possible for your pattern? Explain how you determined your total.

Templates for Flag Cutouts

Counting the Kids

Name _____

Solve the problems below. Label all diagrams appropriately. Write all explanations on a separate sheet of paper.

1. The class officers polled all students in the sixth grade at Pythagoras Middle School to determine what they wanted to eat at the class picnic. The students listed the foods that they were willing to eat. The results are shown below:

Student Count	Choices
48*	Hot dogs
36*	Chicken wings
60*	Hamburgers
12*	Hot dogs and chicken wings
20*	Chicken wings and hamburgers
16*	Hot dogs and hamburgers
5	All three items
19	None of the items

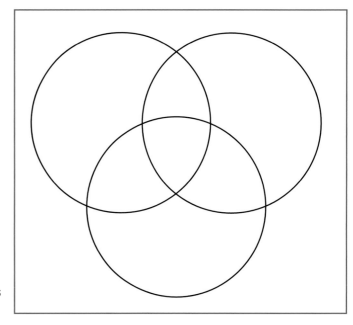

The totals marked with an asterisk (*) are *inclusive* totals. For example, 48 is the total count of students who chose hot dogs only or hot dogs in combination with other selections.

  a. Record these results on the Venn diagram above. How many students were in sixth grade?

  b. How many students preferred hot dogs only? Explain.

  c. How many students preferred exactly two kinds of food? Explain.

2. In the spring, all the seventh-grade students at Pythagoras Middle School participated in a three-act play at the school. Acts I, II, and III included 31, 38, and 35 students, respectively. A total of 9 students appeared in acts I and II, 10 students appeared in acts I and III, and 15 students were in acts II and III. A total of 8 students were in all three acts, and 23 students worked on the production in other ways.

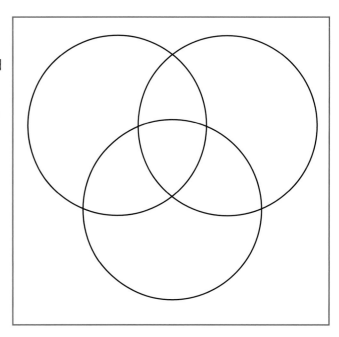

  a. Record these results on the Venn diagram. How many students were in seventh grade?

  b. Does the number of students who performed in exactly two acts exceed the number who performed in all three acts? Explain.

Name _____

3. All 100 eighth-grade students at Pythagoras Middle School participated in at least one of three contests. The history, mathematics, and science contests had 44, 45, and 46 participants, respectively. A total of 12 students participated in the history and mathematics contests, 13 were in the mathematics and science contests, and 14 participated in the history and science contests.

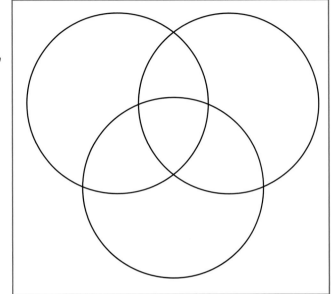

   a. Record these results on the Venn diagram. *Hint:* You need to use a different strategy from the one that you used in problems 1 and 2.

   b. How many students participated in all three contests?

   c. How many students participated in exactly one contest? How many participated in at least one contest?

   d. How many students participated in exactly two contests? How many participated in at most two contests?

4. Use your results for the preceding questions to determine how many students in all attended Pythagoras Middle School in grades 6, 7, and 8.

Binary Strings

Name _____

Paths, Strings, and Combinations in Pascal's Triangle—Part 1

Use a separate sheet of paper to write explanations or make lists.

1. Carl needs to cross three rivers to walk from point *X* to point *Y*. He can cross each river by using a bridge or a tunnel. As Carl walks from point *X* to point *Y*, he flips a coin to determine whether he will go over a bridge or through a tunnel to cross a river. Heads means that he uses a bridge; tails means that he uses a tunnel.

   a. Carl decides to use a 1 to represent a bridge and a 0 to represent a tunnel. The diagram below shows the trail represented by the string 110. This trail is the one that Carl will follow if the results of flipping the coin three times while he walks are heads, heads, tails. The string 011 represents a different trail. Mark that trail on the diagram also, and describe when Carl will use a bridge and when he will use a tunnel.

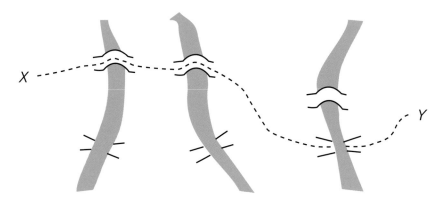

   b. Represent the following trail with 1s and 0s: Take the tunnel under the first river, the bridge over the second river, and the tunnel under the third river.

   c. List the strings of 1s and 0s that describe all possible trails that Carl can take from point *X* to point *Y*.

   d. What is the probability that Carl will use two bridges and one tunnel to travel from point *X* to point *Y* if he bases his decisions on tossing a coin?

2. Consider four points on a line, as shown in the following figure.

   a. How many different line segments do these four points determine? List all of them.

   b. If the string of digits 0011 represents line segment *CD*, what string represents line segment *AC*?

   c. How many 1s are in any string that represents a line segment? Explain.

Zigzag Paths and Binary Strings

Name _____

Paths, Strings, and Combinations in Pascal's Triangle—Part 2

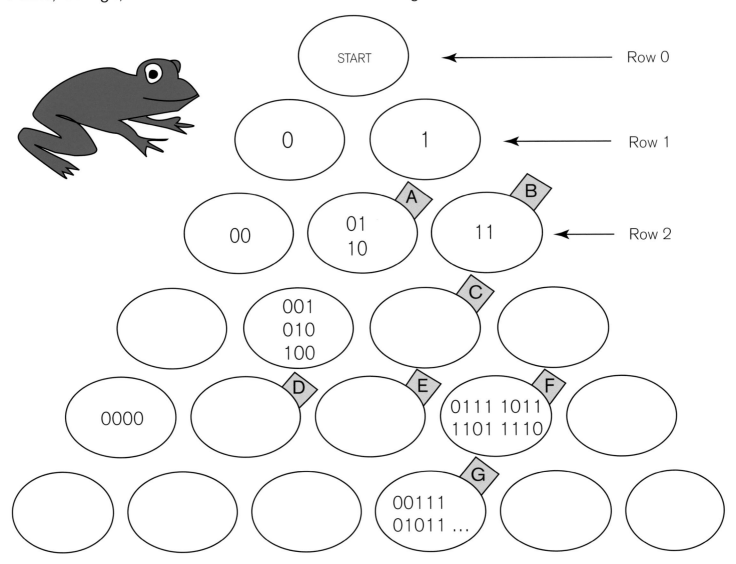

Suppose that a frog hops downward from START through this triangular array of lily pads. The frog can jump only to lily pads that are on the row just below it, so the frog hops downward right or left in a zigzag fashion. You can code its path as a *binary string* of 0s and 1s. Use a 0 to denote a hop downward and to the left *from your perspective* and a 1 to denote a hop downward and to the right. For example, the frog can use any of four zigzag paths to hop from START to location F. These paths are recorded in the figure at location F as four binary strings: 0111, 1011, 1101, and 1110. Respond to the questions below, using a separate sheet of paper, if necessary, for descriptions, explanations, or lists.

1. The figure shows all the binary strings for rows 1 and 2. That is, for each location in rows 1 and 2, the figure shows the binary strings representing all paths from START to that location. (Row 1 is the first row

Zigzag Paths and Binary Strings (continued)

Name _____

after START, row 2 is the second row after START, and so on. START is row 0.) Consider row 3.

    a. Trace the path represented by 010.

    b. Use a different color to trace a path from START to location C. Represent the path as a binary string.

    c. Record all the binary strings for each location in row 3.

    d. Why do all the binary strings in row 3 have exactly three digits?

    e. List all the strings in row 3. List them in a systematic order, and describe the order that you use.

2. Explain why there is just one string in each "outside" location of the triangle.

3. In row 4, consider locations D and F.

    a. Do you think that the number of strings at location D will be the same as the number of strings at location F? Explain your thinking.

    b. List the binary strings for all zigzag paths from START to location D.

    c. Compare the strings for location D with those for location F. What do they have in common? How do they differ? Explain.

4. Consider all the locations in row 4.

    a. How many strings would you need to code all zigzag paths to E? List them.

    b. Find all the binary strings for each location in row 4 (you have already found many of them, so just complete row 4).

    Describe patterns that you see in the strings in row 4.

5. Consider the locations E, F, and G.

    a. Strings for location G represent zigzag paths from START to G. Find several strings for location G.

    b. Study the zigzag paths to G in the triangle. A path that leads from START to G must travel through E or F. Use the strings in locations E and F to determine all the strings for G.

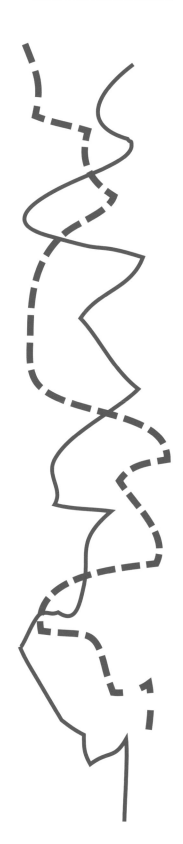

Zigzag Paths and Binary Strings (continued)

Name _____

So far, you have been finding the binary strings for each location in the triangle. Now consider the number of strings at each location. How many zigzag paths can the frog take from START to each one? The following array can help you answer this question. The name of the array is Pascal's triangle.

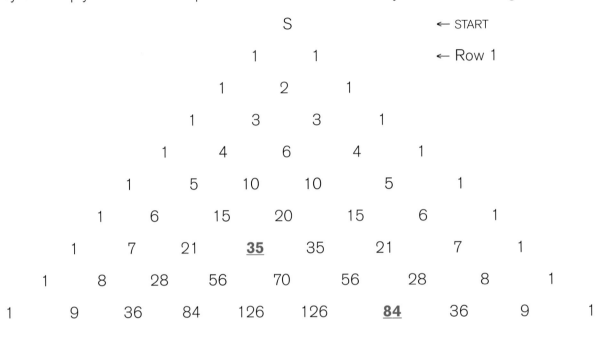

You can calculate the numbers in the array by using the following rules:

- **Row 1 consists of two 1s.**
- **Each row begins and ends with a 1.**
- **To compute any other number in any row, add the two numbers that are just above it to the left and to the right. (This is the "addition rule" for Pascal's triangle.)**

6. Complete row 10 of Pascal's triangle.

7. Compare Pascal's triangle with the triangle of lily-pad locations.

   a. In problem 4, you found all the binary strings for each location in row 4 of the lily-pad triangle.

   - Compare the binary strings with the numbers in row 4 of Pascal's triangle.
   - Describe the relationship between row 4 of the lily-pad triangle and row 4 of Pascal's triangle.

   b. In problem 5, you considered how you can determine the strings for location G from the strings for E and F.

   - Underline the entries in Pascal's triangle that correspond to locations E, F, and G.
   - Describe how the three numbers that you have underlined relate to the numbers of strings in locations E, F, and G.

Navigating through Discrete Mathematics in Grades 6–12

Zigzag Paths and Binary Strings (continued)

Name _____

- The addition rule for Pascal's triangle, the last of the three bulleted rules in bold above, describes how the three numbers in locations E, F, and G are related. Explain why this addition relationship makes sense in terms of paths to E, F, and G in the lily-pad triangle.

c. Explain the addition rule for Pascal's triangle in terms of zigzag paths.

d. State the connection between the number of binary strings in each location of the lily-pad triangle and the corresponding numbers in Pascal's triangle.

8. Consider zigzag paths from the apex (S) of the triangle to the underlined 35.

a. A binary string that describes one such path is 0010011. Sketch this path.

b. Write the binary strings for two other paths from S to the underlined 35.

c. What is the length of each binary string that represents a path from S to the underlined 35? What does the length of the string represent?

d. How many 1s are in each string corresponding to a path from S to the underlined 35?

How many 0s are in each string corresponding to a path from S to the underlined 35?

Explain the number of 1s and 0s in terms of zigzag paths.

e. Consider all zigzag paths of length 7. If you assume that all paths are equally likely, what is the probability that such a path stops at the underlined 35?

9. Consider zigzag paths to locations in row 9.

a. What is common to every path from S to the underlined 84 in the triangle?

b. What is the length of any path from S to any location in row 9?

c. How many nine-step paths from S contain four downward steps to the right? Explain how you determined your answer.

d. How many strings of length 9 contain three digits that are 1s?
Explain your answer in terms of zigzag paths.
List two such strings, and mark the paths that they represent in the triangle.

10. Pascal's triangle has left-right symmetry. Explain the reasons for this left-right symmetry in terms of zigzag paths.

Combinations and Subsets

Name _____

Paths, Strings, and Combinations in Pascal's Triangle—Part 3

In part 2, "Zigzag Paths and Binary Strings," you learned that any number in Pascal's triangle tells you how many zigzag paths there are from the top of the triangle to that number. Continue your analysis by using the following notation to locate numbers in Pascal's triangle. Use a separate sheet of paper to provide descriptions, explanations, and lists.

$C(n, k)$ represents entry k in row n of Pascal's triangle. The top, or START (S), is row 0, and the initial entry in each row is entry 0. With this notation, you can represent Pascal's triangle as follows:

Row 0						$C(0, 0)$					
Row 1					$C(1, 0)$		$C(1, 1)$				
Row 2				$C(2, 0)$		$C(2, 1)$		$C(2, 2)$			
Row 3			$C(3, 0)$		$C(3, 1)$		$C(3, 2)$		$C(3, 3)$		
Row 4		$C(4, 0)$		$C(4, 1)$		$C(4, 2)$		$C(4, 3)$		$C(4, 4)$	
Row 5	$C(5, 0)$		$C(5, 1)$		$C(5, 2)$		$C(5, 3)$		$C(5, 4)$		$C(5, 5)$

1. Complete row 6 of this triangle.

You now have three representations of Pascal's triangle—the "binary strings" triangle at the beginning of "Zigzag Paths and Binary Strings," the triangle with numerical values following problem 5 from that part of the investigation, and the representation above, which uses the $C(n, k)$ notation. As you work through the following problems, you will find that all three of these representations of Pascal's triangle can be useful.

2. Think about $C(n, k)$ in terms of zigzag paths.

   a. $C(3, 2)$ refers to zigzag paths that are how long?

   b. $C(3, 2)$ refers to zigzag paths with how many "zigs" to the right?

   c. $C(5, 1)$ refers to zigzag paths that are how long?
   How many zigs to the right do these paths have?

   d. Describe $C(n, k)$ in terms of zigzag paths and zigs to the right.

3. Think about $C(n, k)$ in terms of binary strings. In "Zigzag Paths and Binary Strings," you learned that you can represent zigzag paths as binary strings and can think of each entry in Pascal's triangle as indicating all the binary strings corresponding to that location.

Combinations and Subsets (continued)

Name _____

a. How long are the strings at the location represented by $C(3, 2)$?

b. How many 1s are in the strings at the location represented by $C(3, 2)$?

c. How many strings are at the location represented by $C(5, 1)$?

How long are the strings?

How many 1s are in each string? How many 0s?

d. How many binary strings of length 4 contain exactly three 1s?

Which location in Pascal's triangle corresponds to these strings?

e. Describe $C(n, k)$ in terms of the number of strings of a certain length that have a certain number of 1s.

4. As you learned in problem 3, $C(n, k)$ is the number of binary strings of length n that contain k 1s. In other words, $C(n, k)$ is the number of ways that you can choose k digits to be 1s in a string of n digits. Thus, you can read the notation $C(n, k)$ as "*n* choose *k*."

a. In how many ways can you choose three digits to be 1s in a string of four binary digits? Represent your answer by using $C(n, k)$ notation.

b. How many binary strings of length 6 contain exactly four 1s?

c. What is the value of "5 choose 2"?

Restate this question in terms of zigzag paths.

Restate the question in terms of binary strings.

5. You can find many interesting patterns related to the numbers $C(n, k)$ and Pascal's triangle.

a. Without finding the numerical values, explain why $C(6, 2) = C(6, 4)$. As part of your explanation, include answers to the following questions:

- How do these numbers appear in Pascal's triangle?

- How do these numbers relate to binary strings?

- How do these numbers relate to zigzag paths?

b. Find two other $C(n, k)$ numbers that fit the pattern in part (*a*), and state a general rule.

c. Given that $C(7, 4) = 35$ and $C(7, 5) = 21$, explain how to use these two numbers to find $C(8, 5)$.

How do all three of these numbers appear in Pascal's triangle?

Combinations and Subsets (continued)

Name _____

d. State three other $C(n, k)$ numbers that fit the pattern in part (*c*), and then state a general rule.

6. Binary strings and the numbers $C(n, k)$ also relate to subsets. Consider the set

$$L = \{v, w, x, y, z\}.$$

Subsets of *L* are sets whose elements come from *L*. A subset can contain some, all, or none of the elements of *L*. For example, the following are three subsets of *L*: the empty set, written as $\emptyset = \{\}$; the entire set *L*; and $\{w, y\}$. Note that the subset $\{w, y\}$ is the same as $\{y, w\}$, since only combinations of the elements of *L* are of interest here—not the order in which the items are listed. The set *L* has many other subsets. Binary strings and $C(n, k)$ can help you find all the subsets of a set.

a. List three subsets of *L* that differ from the subsets given thus far. For convenience, list the elements of your subsets alphabetically.

b. The set *L* has five elements, so consider binary strings of length 5.

- To what subset does 01011 correspond?

- To what subset does 11111 correspond?

c. What binary string represents the subset $\{w, y\}$?

What binary string represents the empty set?

What binary strings represent the subsets that you listed in part (*a*)?

d. Suppose that you want to know how many subsets of *L* contain three elements.

- What kind of binary strings relate to this problem?

- How many such binary strings are there?

- Where does this number appear in Pascal's triangle?

- Which number $C(n, k)$ represents the number of subsets of *L* that contain three elements?

e. Describe how you can use binary strings to represent subsets.

Describe how you can use $C(n, k)$ to count subsets.

Combinations and Subsets (continued)

Name _____

7. A term for the numbers $C(n, k)$ is *combinations*, since these numbers count the number of combinations of n objects taken k at a time. In the "choose" language, you are choosing a combination of k objects from the n objects. With subsets, you are forming combinations of k elements from a set with n elements.

   a. Describe $C(3, 2)$ in terms of subsets of a set.

   b. Think about a very concrete set—the set of toppings that you can put on a pizza. Suppose that the possible toppings for a pizza are black olives, green olives, mushrooms, tomatoes, and green peppers.

   • How many different pizzas containing three of these toppings are possible?

   • Which number $C(n, k)$ answers this question?

8. Kathie coaches a first-grade soccer team. Eight children are on the team, and six can play at one time. The team members are Amy, Bobbi, Caitlin, Diem, Earl, Floricel, Guillermo, and Hilary.

   a. If you place the team members in alphabetical order, what team of six does the string 01101111 represent?

   b. What string represents the team when Amy and Hilary are not playing?

   c. How many different teams of six are possible?
   Restate this question in terms of each of the following ideas or representations:

   • binary strings

   • subsets

   • zigzag paths

   • Pascal's triangle

   • $C(n, k)$

9. To summarize this investigation, describe the connections among Pascal's triangle, binary strings, zigzag paths, and the numbers $C(n, k)$.

Combinations, Pascal's Triangle, and the Binomial Theorem

Name _____

In this investigation, you will explore some of the relationships among combinations, Pascal's triangle, and the expansion of binomial expressions of the form $(a + b)^n$. Provide descriptions, explanations, or lists on a separate sheet of paper.

1. Use the following steps to consider patterns in the expansion of $(a + b)^n$.

   a. Complete the table below.

n	$(a + b)^n$	Expansion of $(a + b)^n$	Coefficients
0			
1			
2	$(a + b)^2$	$a^2 + 2ab + b^2$	1, 2, 1
3			
4			

   b. Examine the exponents in the expansions. Describe all the patterns that you notice.

   c. Examine the coefficients in the expansions. Describe all the patterns that you notice.

   d. By looking at the patterns in the table, make a conjecture for the expansion of $(a + b)^5$. Check your conjecture by expanding (you might use a computer algebra system). Add this expansion to the table.

2. Think about connections between Pascal's triangle and the expansion of $(a + b)^n$.

   a. Construct or obtain a copy of Pascal's triangle through at least row 5.

   b. Compare the pattern of coefficients in the table in problem 1(*a*) to the pattern of numbers in Pascal's triangle. Describe this connection.

   c. Compare the coefficient of the ab^2 term in $(a + b)^3$ with entry 2 in row 3. (Remember to start with row 0 when you number the rows of Pascal's triangle, and begin with entry 0 when you number the entries in a given row.)

Combinations, Pascal's Triangle, and the Binomial Theorem (continued)

Name _____

d. What is the coefficient of the a^2b^3 term in $(a + b)^5$?

Where does this coefficient occur in Pascal's triangle?

e. Describe how to use Pascal's triangle to find the coefficient of the $a^{n-k}b^k$ term in $(a + b)^n$.

f. Use Pascal's triangle to expand $(a + b)^6$. Check your answer by expanding by hand or with a computer algebra system.

3. Think about connections between combinations and the expansion of $(a + b)^n$. Recall that a formula for the number of combinations of k objects chosen from n objects, $C(n, k)$, is

$$C(n,\ k) = \frac{n!}{k!(n-k)!}.$$

a. For $n = 2$, $n = 3$, and $n = 4$, use the following steps to compute $C(n, k)$ for all values of k:

- For $n = 2$, compute $C(2, 0)$, $C(2, 1)$, and $C(2, 2)$.

- For $n = 3$, compute $C(3, 0)$, $C(3, 1)$, $C(3, 2)$, and $C(3, 3)$.

- For $n = 4$, compute $C(4, 0)$, $C(4, 1)$, $C(4, 2)$, $C(4, 3)$, and $C(4, 4)$.

b. Compare the values that you found for $C(n, k)$ in part (*a*) with the list of coefficients in the table in problem 1.

Describe connections between the coefficients of $(a + b)^n$ and the combination numbers $C(n, k)$.

c. For what values of n and k is $C(n, k)$ equal to the coefficient of the ab^2 term in $(a + b)^3$?

d. For what values of n and k is $C(n, k)$ equal to the coefficient of the a^2b^3 term in $(a + b)^5$?

e. Compute $C(5, 3)$ and $C(5, 2)$.

Compare these numbers with the coefficients of the a^2b^3 term and the a^3b^2 term in $(a + b)^5$.

Explain the relationships among these numbers.

f. Make a conjecture about a general rule that uses combinations to determine the coefficient of the $a^{n-k}b^k$ term in $(a + b)^n$.

4. In problem 3, you made a conjecture about a connection between combinations and the expansion of $(a + b)^n$. Consider reasons for that connection. One student gave the following explanation of the method for using combinations to find the coefficient of the $a^{87}b^{13}$ term in $(a + b)^{100}$:

Combinations, Pascal's Triangle, and the Binomial Theorem (continued)

Name _____

"$(a + b)^{100} = (a + b)(a + b)(a + b) \ldots (a + b)$; 100 factors of $(a + b)$. If you carried out this multiplication, you would multiply each entry in the first set of parentheses—that is, a and b—by each entry in the second set of parentheses, then multiply each of those products by each entry in the third set of parentheses, and so on. To get b^{13}, you need to multiply by b in 13 of the 100 sets of parentheses; and in the other sets of parentheses, you multiply by a. So the total number of ways to get b^{13} is the number of ways of choosing 13 sets of parentheses from the 100 sets of parentheses, which is $C(100, 13)$. Hence, the coefficient of the $a^{87}b^{13}$ term in $(a + b)^{100}$ is $C(100, 13)$."

a. In reasoning about the coefficient of the $a^{87}b^{13}$ term in $(a + b)^{100}$, you could focus on a^{87} instead of b^{13}. If you do, which $C(n, k)$ number do you obtain as the coefficient?

b. Reason in the same manner as in problem 4(a) to find the coefficient of the $a^{13}b^{87}$ term in $(a + b)^{100}$.

c. Explain why $C(100, 13) = C(100, 87)$.

d. State a general rule that uses combinations and the preceding reasoning for determining the coefficient of the $a^{n-k}b^k$ term in $(a + b)^n$.

5. The relationship between combinations and the coefficients in the expansion of $(a + b)^n$ gives rise to the *binomial theorem,* which states that for integers n and k with $0 \le k \le n$,

$$(a + b)^n = C(n, 0)a^n + C(n, 1)a^{n-1}b + C(n, 2)a^{n-2}b^2 + \ldots + C(n, k)a^{n-k}b^k + \ldots$$
$$+ C(n, n - 2)a^2b^{n-2} + C(n, n - 1)ab^{n-1} + C(n, n)b^n.$$

Use the binomial theorem to expand the following:

a. $(a + b)^5$

b. $(a - b)^5$

c. $(x + 4)^3$

d. $(4x + 2y)^4$

6. You have seen connections between the coefficients in the expansion of $(a + b)^n$ and combinations, as well as connections between these coefficients and Pascal's triangle. These connections suggest an additional connection between combinations and Pascal's triangle.

Combinations, Pascal's Triangle, and the Binomial Theorem (continued)

Name _____

a. Compute $C(4, 2)$.

Where do you find $C(4, 2)$ in Pascal's triangle?

Compute $C(5, 3)$. Where do you find it in Pascal's triangle?

Compute $C(5, 2)$. Where do you find it in Pascal's triangle?

b. Describe how to find $C(n, k)$ by using Pascal's triangle.

c. Pascal's triangle has a vertical line of symmetry. Explain how the binomial theorem shows this symmetry.

7. In problem 6, you saw that the numbers $C(n, k)$ show up systematically as entries in Pascal's triangle. This correspondence is pretty amazing! The rule for constructing a row of Pascal's triangle is to start with 1, then determine the next entries by adding the numbers in the row above that are just to the left and right, and then end with 1. Why does this peculiar construction rule also systematically generate all the values of $C(n, k)$? To learn why, compare the rule for constructing Pascal's triangle with an important recursive property of combinations.

Rule for Pascal's triangle:

(an entry in any row) = (the entry above and to the left) + (the entry above and to the right)

Combination property:

$$C(n, k) = C(n - 1, k - 1) + C(n - 1, k)$$

Explain the similarities between these two formulas.

8. Examine the combination property in problem 7 more closely:

$C(n, k) = C(n - 1, k - 1) + C(n - 1, k)$, for integers n and k with $0 < k < n$.

a. Choose several specific values of n and k, and verify the property for those values.

b. Use the factorial formula for $C(n, k)$ and algebraic reasoning to prove that the property is true in general.

c. Consider how you can use combinatorial reasoning to prove this property. Explain each step of the following argument:

Combinations, Pascal's Triangle, and the Binomial Theorem (continued)

Name _____

Explanation

$$C(n, k) \quad = \text{number of } k\text{-element subsets}$$
of the set $\{1, 2, 3, \ldots, n\}$

$= [\text{number of } k\text{-element subsets}$
$\text{that include } n] + [\text{number of } k\text{-element}$
$\text{subsets that do not include } n]$

$= [\text{number of } (k - 1)\text{-element subsets}$
$\text{of the set } \{1, 2, 3, \ldots, n - 1\}$
$\text{(and automatically include } n \text{ in each}$
$\text{of these subsets)}] + [\text{number of}$
$k\text{-element subsets of } \{1, 2, 3, \ldots, n - 1\}]$

$= C(n - 1, k - 1) + C(n - 1, k)$

d. Compare the proof methods in parts (*b*) and (*c*). Which method focuses more on the counting process? Which method makes more sense to you? Why?

9. Summarize your investigation of connections among combinations, Pascal's triangle, and the binomial theorem by briefly describing each topic and each connection shown in the diagram below.

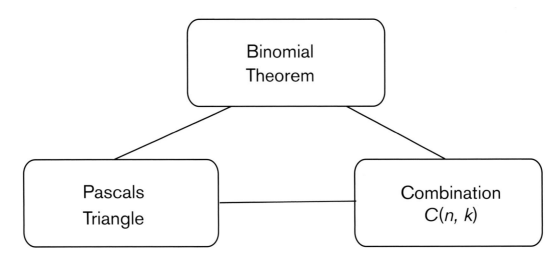

Sample Vertex-Edge Graphs

Name _____

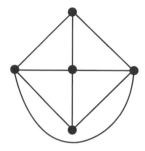

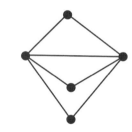

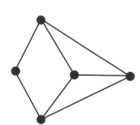
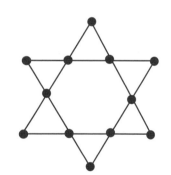

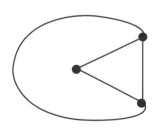

Paths at Camp Graffinstuff

Name _____

A *connected graph* can have different types of paths. An *Euler path* on a connected graph is a tracing or route that traces each edge of the graph exactly once. An *Euler circuit* is an Euler path in which the starting vertex and the ending vertex are the same.

On a connected graph, a *Hamilton path* is a tracing or route that visits each vertex of the graph exactly once. A *Hamilton circuit* is a tracing or route in which the first vertex and the last vertex are the same and all other vertices are visited exactly once.

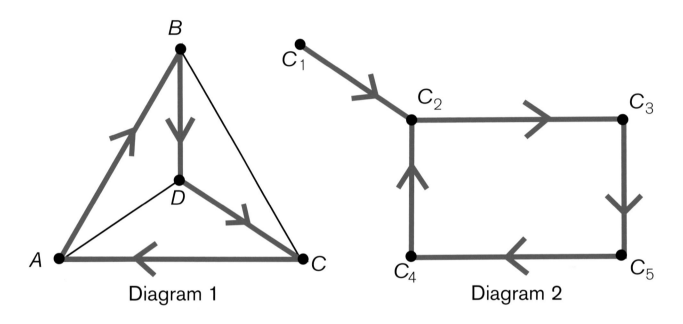

Diagram 1   Diagram 2

In diagram 1, *ABDCA* describes a path on the graph that moves from *A* to *B* to *D* to *C* to *A*. It is a Hamilton circuit. In diagram 2, the path 1 2 3 5 4 2 moves from C_1 to C_2 to C_3 to C_5 to $C4$ to C_2. It is an Euler path that is not a circuit.

1. Graphs of portions of Camp Graffinstuff and the camp flag design appear on the next page. For each of the diagrams, determine whether the graph has any of the following:

   • An Euler circuit, an Euler path (that is not a circuit), or neither

   • A Hamilton circuit, a Hamilton path (that is not a circuit), or neither

   Describe these paths on a separate sheet of paper, using a labeling scheme that is similar to the ones shown for diagram 1 and diagram 2.

Paths at Camp Graffinstuff (continued)

Name _____

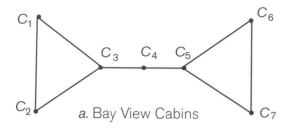

a. Bay View Cabins

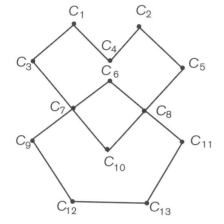

b. Hillside Cabins

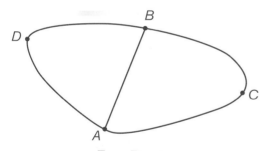

c. Frog Pond

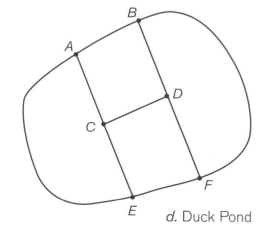

d. Duck Pond

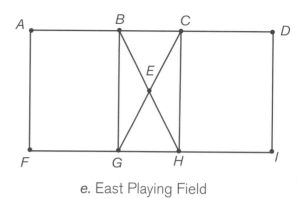

e. East Playing Field

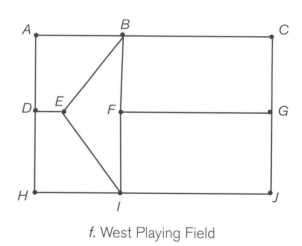

f. West Playing Field

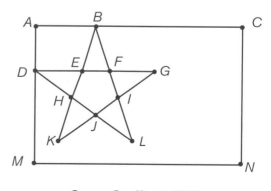

g. Camp Graffinstuff Flag

Paths at Camp Graffinstuff (continued)

Name _____

2. As part of a mathematics challenge from their counselors, the campers in Hillside 6 are tracing grids on the tarmac with chalk. They are comparing two methods: the *minimum-lift method* and the *minimum retracing method.*

Group 1 is using the minimum-lift method, which requires that the campers trace each edge of the grid exactly once. The rules do not allow this group to retrace any edge, but the campers can lift the chalk to avoid retracing an edge. They keep track of the total number of lifts, including the last one. Their goal is to lift the chalk the minimum number of times.

Group 2 is using the minimum-retracing method, which requires that the campers trace the complete grid without lifting the chalk until they are done. These campers sometimes need to retrace an edge to avoid lifting the chalk. Their goal is to retrace the minimum number of edges.

In the following grids, the numbers on the edges have been provided so that you can represent your tracing as a string of numbers. For example, 1 2 9 12 6 5 10 7 is a path on the 2 × 2 square. Use the same edge-numbering scheme for any grids that you create on additional sheets of paper.

a. Use the minimum-lift method and the minimum-retracing method for the 2 × 2 grid shown. Verify that the minimum number of lifts is two and that the minimum number of retraced edges is two.

b. Use both methods for the 3 × 3 grid. What is the minimum number of lifts, and what is the minimum number of retraced edges?

Paths at Camp Graffinstuff (continued)

Name _____

c. Which group do you think will win—that is, get the smaller number—when the groups use a 4 × 4 grid like the one at the right?

```
        1         2         3         4
   ┌─────────┬─────────┬─────────┬─────────┐
21 │      22 │      23 │      24 │      25 │
   │ 5       │ 6       │ 7       │ 8       │
   ├─────────┼─────────┼─────────┼─────────┤
26 │      27 │      28 │      29 │      30 │
   │ 9       │ 10      │ 11      │ 12      │
   ├─────────┼─────────┼─────────┼─────────┤
31 │      32 │      33 │      34 │      35 │
   │ 13      │ 14      │ 15      │ 16      │
   ├─────────┼─────────┼─────────┼─────────┤
36 │      37 │      38 │      39 │      40 │
   │ 17      │ 18      │ 19      │ 20      │
   └─────────┴─────────┴─────────┴─────────┘
```

d. Use both methods, and report your results for a 2 × 3 grid and for a 2 × 4 grid like those below.

```
        1         2         3
   ┌─────────┬─────────┬─────────┐
10 │      11 │      12 │      13 │
   │ 4       │ 5       │ 6       │
   ├─────────┼─────────┼─────────┤
14 │      15 │      16 │      17 │
   │ 7       │ 8       │ 9       │
   └─────────┴─────────┴─────────┘
```

```
        1         2         3         4
   ┌─────────┬─────────┬─────────┬─────────┐
13 │      14 │      15 │      16 │      17 │
   │ 5       │ 6       │ 7       │ 8       │
   ├─────────┼─────────┼─────────┼─────────┤
18 │      19 │      20 │      21 │      22 │
   │ 9       │ 10      │ 11      │ 12      │
   └─────────┴─────────┴─────────┴─────────┘
```

e. Which group wins when the groups use a 2 × 5 grid like the one below?

```
        1         2         3         4         5
   ┌─────────┬─────────┬─────────┬─────────┬─────────┐
16 │      17 │      18 │      19 │      20 │      21 │
   │ 6       │ 7       │ 8       │ 9       │ 10      │
   ├─────────┼─────────┼─────────┼─────────┼─────────┤
22 │      23 │      24 │      25 │      26 │      27 │
   │ 11      │ 12      │ 13      │ 14      │ 15      │
   └─────────┴─────────┴─────────┴─────────┴─────────┘
```

Paths at Camp Graffinstuff (continued)

Name _____

3. Counselors plan to assign the eight campers identified in the following diagram to seats at a circular table in the dining hall. In the graph, an edge joins two campers if they participate in the same sport. Two campers will sit at adjacent places at the table only if they participate in the same sport.

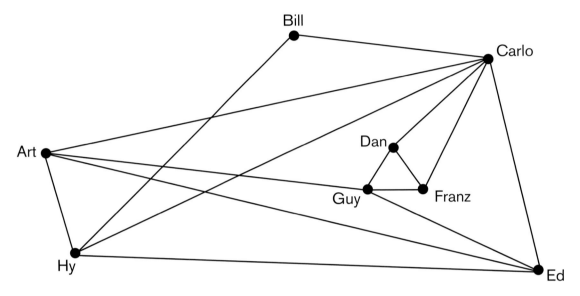

a. Draw a Hamilton circuit to help you assign the eight campers to their places at the table. Explain why a Hamilton circuit is helpful in solving this problem.

b. Sketch the circular table, and label each place with the name of the camper who will sit there.

4. The head counselor at Camp Graffinstuff is designing a new award medallion for the coming summer. However, the counselor has decided that the graph for the medallion cannot have an Euler circuit or a Hamilton circuit. Which, if either, of the two graphs below satisfies these criteria? Give an explanation for your answer, and label any circuits.

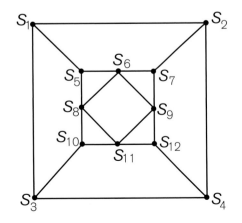 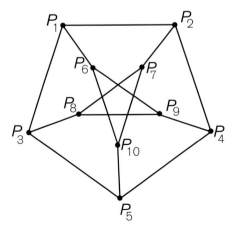

The Sports Director's Dilemma

Name _____

Decisions … Decisions … Decisions at Camp Graffinstuff–Part 1

Several staff members at Camp Graffinstuff are facing dilemmas related to their work. One of these is the sports director, who wants to allow campers to participate in all the sports they select but also must use as few time slots as possible for sports.

Campers at Camp Graffinstuff can participate in the following sports:

Tennis (T)	Softball (SB)	Archery (A)
Basketball (BB)	Soccer (SO)	Hiking (H)	Swimming (SW)

The sports director plans to use a sampling of data from campers to set the sports schedule for the month. She must find the minimum number of time slots that allow the campers in the sample to participate in the sports that they have chosen, and she must identify the sports that Camp Graffinstuff can offer at the same time and sports that the camp should offer at different times.

The following list gives the campers' names and shows the sports that they have selected. Help the sports director solve her dilemma by using a vertex-coloring scheme.

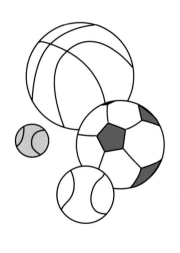

Al	T	SW	SO
Burt	T	A	BB
Corey	A	H	
Dom	T	SW	
Ernie	SW	H	
Felipe	T	A	
Greg	H	SO	
Hank	A	SW	
Ivan	T	SO	
Jose	T	BB	SO
Kevin	SB	BB	
Liam	BB	SO	

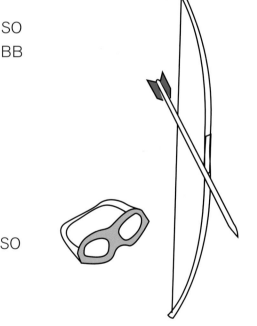

1. Before constructing the vertex-edge graph, decide what the vertices and edges should represent.

2. Construct the graph on a separate sheet of paper.

3. Use as few colors as possible to color the vertices of your graph so that no two neighboring vertices are the same color. Provide a step-by-step description of your coloring plan, and explain why it uses the minimum number of colors.

The Sports Director's Dilemma (continued)

Name _____

4. Solve the problem.

  a. What is the minimum number of time slots that allows campers in the sample to take the sports that they have selected?

  b. Create a schedule that indicates the sports that Camp Graffinstuff can offer at the same time and those that it must offer at different times.

The Tour Director's Dilemma

Name _____

Decisions … Decisions … Decisions at Camp Graffinstuff–Part 2

The tour director at Camp Graffinstuff is another staff member who faces a dilemma. Campers can participate in six all-day tours during their stay at Camp Graffinstuff. The tour director must devise a schedule that meets two conditions:

- The camp must offer all tours each week.
- Two tours cannot operate on the same day if they have an attraction in common.

The following are the six tours:

Tour 1	Splash Sports	Mt. Seemore	Carnival Wharf
Tour 2	Mega Mall	Splash Sports	Sports Museum
Tour 3	Best Beach	Mammoth Zoo	Movie-rama
Tour 4	Movie-rama	Belle Lake	Mt. Seemore
Tour 5	Belle Lake	Movie-rama	Splash Sports
Tour 6	Movie-rama	Best Beach	Mega Mall

1. Before constructing a vertex-edge graph that represents the situation, decide what the vertices and edges should represent.

2. On a separate sheet of paper, construct the graph.

3. Use as few colors as possible to color the vertices of your graph so that no two neighboring vertices are the same color.

4. Provide a step-by-step description of your coloring plan, and explain why it uses the minimum number of colors.

5. Solve the tour director's problem by answering the following questions:

   a. What is the minimum number of days that the tour director can use to schedule all the tours in a week? Explain the reasoning that you used to find this number.

   b. Prepare a schedule that shows the tours to offer on each day.

   c. If more than one schedule enables the tour director to schedule the tours on the minimum number of days, give a second solution.

The Bus Director's Dilemma

Name _____

Decisions … Decisions …Decisions at Camp Graffinstuff–Part 3

The bus director at Camp Graffinstuff also has a dilemma. In studying the road map in the diagram, the bus director sees that the bus travels on fourteen roads, making the eight stops. The graph shows the distance (in miles) between locations.

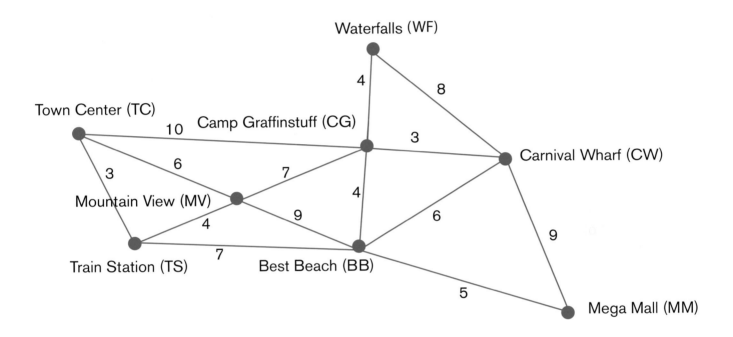

Using a separate sheet of paper if necessary, help the bus director consider several problems:

1. The bus route must include all eight locations. The bus should not backtrack, and it should not visit any of the locations more than once. The bus does not need to return to its starting point.

   a. Regardless of the order in which the bus visits the eight locations, what is the minimum road count that meets the given conditions?

   b. Use the abbreviations for the eight locations shown on the graph to describe three different routes with minimum road count that start with TC and visit all eight locations.

   c. Find three different routes with this same road count that start with CG and visit all eight locations.

   d. Show that a route with minimum road count can start from any point and visit all eight locations.

Navigating through Discrete Mathematics in Grades 6–12

The Bus Director's Dilemma (continued)

Name _____

2. For each of the following starting and ending locations, find a route that visits each of the eight locations only once, and give the total number of miles for that route.

   a. Start at TC; end at CG .

   b. Start at CG; end at WF.

   c. Start at MM; end at BB.

3. The bus director has a friend who owns the Bright Stripe Company, which has proposed painting a center stripe on any or all roads near Camp Graffinstuff at a cost of $25 per mile. The bus director is assisting the owner with this big job. Help them both solve the following problems:

   a. What is the total number of miles of all roads on the map?
   What is the cost of painting a center stripe on all roads?

   b. Find a connected set of roads that joins all eight locations and has the minimum total mileage. (The connected set of roads may not make an appropriate bus route, but remember that this job is painting stripes.)

   • Highlight the connected set of roads on the road map.

   • What is the minimum total mileage?

   • What is the cost of painting a center stripe on these roads?

   c. Provide a step-by-step explanation that describes how you achieved a minimum solution.

   d. If more than one connected set of roads joins all eight locations and has the minimum total mileage, make a copy of the road map, and highlight this connected set of roads.

Planning a Festival

Name _____

Using Critical Paths to Schedule Large Projects–Part 1

Suppose that the students at your school are planning a Peace Day festival. The festival will include booths, speakers, and activities related to creating peace. This project will require careful planning and scheduling. You are on the planning committee.

1. Your first step in scheduling this project is to figure out all the necessary tasks. Working on a separate sheet of paper, list several of these tasks.

2. *a.* Do the students who are working on the festival need to complete some of the tasks that you listed in problem 1 before they can begin working on other tasks? If so, list two tasks, one of which students must finish before they can begin the other one. If no such tasks are on your list in problem 1, think of two additional tasks, one of which is a *prerequisite* for the other one.

    b. Suppose that several teams are working on this project. Can two teams work at the same time on two different tasks that you listed in problem 1? If so, give an example. If not, think of two additional tasks that two teams can work on at the same time.

3. The following table shows the tasks that students at another school need to complete for the booths at their school's Peace Day festival. The table shows the estimated time for completing each task, as well as all the tasks that are *immediate prerequisites*. An immediate prerequisite for a targeted task is a task that must be completed immediately before starting the targeted task, with no other task on the list coming between the immediate prerequisite task and the targeted task. For example, three tasks for painting a house might be setting up, painting, and cleaning up. In this example, setting up is a prerequisite for cleaning up, but it is not an immediate prerequisite.

Peace Day Booths Project

Task	Task Time	Immediate Prerequisites
Decide on the number and types of booths (T)	3 days	none
Find volunteers to build the booths (V)	8 days	T
Obtain materials to build the booths (M)	4 days	T
Build the booths (B)	9 days	V, M

You can represent the information in the table with a vertex-edge graph, as shown on the next page. The graph is called a *directed graph,* or *digraph* for short, because the edges have a direction. The graph includes the tasks at the far left and right, "START" and "END," for convenience, to represent the starting and finishing points.

Navigating through Discrete Mathematics in Grades 6–12

Planning a Festival (continued)

Name _____

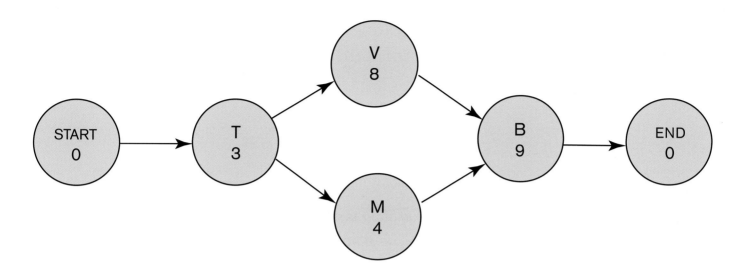

a. What are two tasks that two different teams of students can work on at the same time?

b. If several different teams are working on the project, what is the earliest finish time (EFT)—that is, the minimum amount of time needed to finish the Peace Day booths project?

c. Three students gave the following answers for the EFT for the Peace Day booths project. Explain how you think that each student arrived at his or her answer. Which answer is correct? Why?

Rama's answer: 24 days

Amy's answer: 20 days

Jocey's answer: 16 days

d. A *critical path* is a longest path through the project digraph. What is a critical path in the Peace Day booths project digraph?

e. How does the length of a critical path compare with the EFT?

f. *Critical tasks* are tasks on a critical path.

- What are the critical tasks for the Peace Day booths project?

- What happens to the EFT if a critical task gets behind schedule by two days?

- What happens to the EFT if a noncritical task gets behind schedule by two days?

Planning a Festival (continued)

Name _____

g. In addition to knowing the EFT for the whole project, managers also want to know how to schedule each task. In particular, they want to know the earliest and latest times to start each task so that they can still achieve the EFT for the entire project. For each individual task in the Peace Day booths project, find the earliest start time (EST) and the latest start time (LST). Explain how you determined these times.

h. The formula for computing the *slack time* for each task is LST − EST.

- Compute the slack time for each task.

- Explain why it makes sense to call (LST − EST) *slack time*.

Navigating through Discrete Mathematics in Grades 6–12

Building a House

Name _____

Using Critical Paths to Schedule Large Projects—Part 2

Now that you know how to use critical paths to find the earliest finish time (EFT) for a project, try a larger project. The following table gives the tasks, task times, and immediate prerequisites for a house-building project.

House-Building Project

Task	Task Time	Immediate Prerequisites
Prepare land (L)	3 days	None
Put in foundation (Fo)	4 days	L
Build frame (Fr)	16 days	Fo
Wire for electricity (E)	10 days	Fr
Install plumbing (P)	6 days	Fr
Finish outside (O)	13 days	Fr
Finish inside (I)	11 days	E, P
Landscape (Ls)	7 days	O

1. Analyze the house-building project in the following steps (use a separate sheet of paper for your work):

   a. Draw a digraph for the project.

   b. How many different paths are there from the START vertex to the END vertex of the digraph? List them all, and compute their lengths.

   c. Find a critical path. List the vertices in the critical path.

   d. What is the EFT for this project?

2. With numerous crews working on such a project, many delays are possible. For each delay specified in (a)–(d) below, describe how the delay affects the EFT and the critical path.

   a. Two-day foundation delay

   b. Two-day plumbing delay

   c. One-day landscaping delay

   d. Two-day landscaping delay

   e. Summarize how delays on and off a critical path can affect the EFT and the critical path.

Name _____

3. Project managers usually need detailed scheduling information for each individual task.

    a. Use the original undelayed task times to find the EST and the LST for each task in the house-building project, and enter them in the following table.

Task	Earliest Start Time (EST)	Latest Start Time (LST)	Slack Time
Prepare land (L)			
Put in foundation (Fo)			
Build frame (Fr)			
Wire for electricity (E)			
Install plumbing (P)			
Finish outside (O)			
Finish inside (I)			
Landscape (Ls)			

    b. Carefully describe the procedure that you used to determine these times.

    c. Compute the slack time, (LST − EST), for each task, and enter the slack times in the chart.

Who Is the Winner?

Name _____

A *Hamilton path* is a path through a graph that visits each vertex exactly once. You can use Hamilton paths to analyze tournaments.

In a round-robin tournament, every player has one match against every other player. Consider two round-robin tennis tournaments—one for boys and one for girls—each involving four players. The following matrices show the results of the tournaments (1 indicates a win, and 0 indicates a loss). Read the matrices from side to top; for example, the 1 in the Amy-Melodia cell means that Amy beat Melodia. In solving the problems, use a separate sheet of paper to show your work.

Boys' Tournament

	Cos	Simon	Flavio	Bill
Cos	–	0	0	1
Simon	1	–	0	1
Flavio	1	1	–	1
Bill	0	0	0	–

Girls' Tournament

	Coral	Amy	Nicole	Melodia
Coral	–	1	0	1
Amy	0	–	1	1
Nicole	1	0	–	0
Melodia	0	0	1	–

1. How many matches are played in a round-robin tournament with four players? Explain your answer.

2. For each tournament, draw a vertex-edge graph that represents the information in the matrix. In these graphs, use edges with arrows to indicate who beat whom. For example, the boys' graph should have an arrow from Flavio to Bill.

3. Find all the Hamilton paths in each graph. (Be sure to follow the arrows, since the edges have a direction.)

4. Use the Hamilton paths to help rank the players in the tournaments. Explain what you did. In your explanation, answer the following questions.

   • Does each graph contain a Hamilton path?

   • Can there be more than one Hamilton path?

   • How does a Hamilton path produce a ranking?

   • What do you do if there is more than one Hamilton path?

5. Another way to rank the players is to use the matrices directly, without converting them to vertex-edge graphs.

   a. Compute the row sums for each matrix. Explain how this information helps you rank the players.

Name _____

b. If the row sums do not yield a complete ranking, compute the square of the matrix and then the row sums. Explain how this additional information helps you find a ranking. (For the purpose of squaring the matrix, replace the blank entries with zeros.)

c. Compare the ranking that you found for the girls' tournament by using Hamilton paths with the ranking that you found by using powers and row sums of matrices. Discuss any differences, and decide on a final ranking.

Mathematicians have proved that there is no perfect ranking system that works in all situations. Therefore, you must sometimes decide on a ranking on the basis of the situation, your purposes, and other factors.

6. (Extension) The ATP Masters Cup is one of the most prestigious tournaments in professional tennis. The singles competition of this tournament brings together the top eight players in the world. Play begins with two round-robin tournaments of four players each. Matrices very much like those in this investigation are often used to display the results of the round-robin play. Go to the ATP Masters Cup Web site (http://www.masters-cup.com), and find the results for the most recent Masters Cup. Rank the players in each four-person round-robin tournament by using vertex-edge graphs and matrices, as you have done in this investigation. Then find the ATP rules and rankings and compare them with your ranking. Describe and discuss similarities and differences.

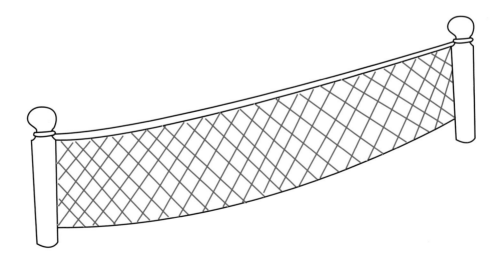

The Traveling Salesman Problem (TSP)

Name _____

The following matrix shows the mileage between pairs of cities in a group of four cities—A, B, C, and D. A salesperson wants to visit each city to check on customers.

$$
\begin{array}{c}
 & \begin{array}{cccc} A & B & C & D \end{array} \\
\begin{array}{c} A \\ B \\ C \\ D \end{array}
\left[\begin{array}{cccc}
- & 20 & 25 & 40 \\
20 & - & 35 & 45 \\
25 & 35 & - & 30 \\
40 & 45 & 30 & -
\end{array} \right]
\end{array}
$$

1. Working on a separate sheet of paper, draw a vertex-edge graph that represents the information in the matrix.

2. The salesperson wants to start at city A, visit the other cities exactly once, and return to A. Such a route through a graph is called a *Hamilton circuit.* Find all the different Hamilton circuits. List the vertices in each circuit, starting at A.

3. Consider these two circuits: ABCDA and ADCBA. Explain how these two circuits are different and how they are similar.

4. Record the total length of each possible different Hamilton circuit.

5. What is the shortest route that the salesperson can take?

   The name of the problem of finding such a shortest route—that is, of finding a Hamilton circuit that has the minimum total length—is the *traveling salesman problem* (TSP).

6. Suppose that you want to solve the TSP for 25 cities. That is, a salesperson wants to start at city A, visit each of 24 other cities exactly once, and finish at A, traveling the minimum total distance. Assume that there is a direct link (an edge) between every pair of cities.

   a. Before doing any computations, make a quick guess of the amount of time that a fast computer would take to solve this problem by checking all possible Hamilton circuits.

   b. Next, start doing some computations:

   - How many Hamilton circuits are there? (*Hint:* You start at A. You can go to 24 cities from A, so a total of 24 two-city routes are possible. For each of these two-city routes, you can then go to any of 23 cities. Thus, the number of three-city routes is 24 × 23.)

The Traveling Salesman Problem (TSP)

Name _____

• Continue to use this strategy to determine how many four-city routes exist.

• How many 25-city circuits exist?

c. In early 2005, the fastest computer in the world was the BlueGene/L Supercomputer. According to the information on the Web (http://www.top500.org), it can carry out 70.2 trillion calculations per second. Suppose that the BlueGene/L computer can find and determine the length of 70 trillion Hamilton circuits every second. How long will this computer take to check all possible 25-city Hamilton circuits?

d. Did your answer to question 6(c) surprise you? Is the amount of time that you computed close to your guess in question 6(a)? This example shows the inefficiency of the so-called brute-force method, in which you check all possibilities to solve the problem. No one knows an efficient way to solve the TSP for any graph, so you are exploring the frontiers of mathematics!

e. Use the Internet to find the speed of the fastest computer in the world today. How long would this computer take to check all possible 25-city Hamilton circuits? All possible 35-city Hamilton circuits?

Looking at Square Tiles from All Angles

Name _____

Targeting Squares—Part 1

Suppose that each side of a square tile is one unit in length, and each square tile has an area of one square unit. The path around each design of square tiles is shown by dark line segments below.

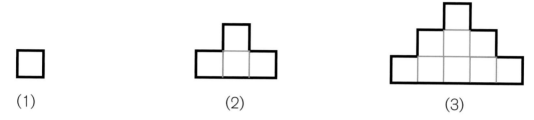

(1) (2) (3)

1. If the square-tile design sequence follows the pattern of the first three designs, draw the next two designs in the sequence on a sheet of geodot paper.

2. Let a_n be the area of the nth design.

   a. Complete the following table.

Design n	1	2	3	4	5	6	7	8	9	10
Area a_n	1	4	9							100

   b. On a separate sheet of paper, explain how to express the area of each new tile design, except the first one, in terms of the one that precedes it. What is the recursive formula for the nth area?

   c. What is the explicit formula for the nth area? Explain how you can use the tiles to justify your answer.

3. Let p_n be the perimeter of the nth design.

   a. Complete the following table.

Design n	1	2	3	4	5	6	7	8	9	10
Perimeter p_n	4	10	16							58

   b. Explain how to express the perimeter of each new tile design, except the first one, in terms of the one that precedes it. What is the recursive formula for the nth perimeter?

   c. What is the explicit formula for the nth perimeter? Explain how you found your answer.

Looking at Square Tiles from All Angles (continued)

Name _____

4. Let r_n be the total number of right angles in the interior of the nth design in the square-tile design sequence. (This total includes only the right angles formed by segments that make the figure's perimeter.)

   a. Complete the following table.

Design n	1	2	3	4	5	6	7	8	9	10
Right-angle count r_n	4	6	8							22

   b. Explain how to express each new right-angle count, except the first one, in terms of the one that precedes it. What is the recursive formula for the nth right-angle count?

   c. What is the explicit formula for the nth right-angle count? Justify your answer.

5. A 1×2 rectangle looks like ⬚. Note that the rectangle is identified as length × height. Working with the same square-tile design sequence as before, let t_n be the total number of 1×2 rectangles in the nth design.

   a. Complete the following table:

Design n	1	2	3	4	5	6	7	8	9	10
1×2 rectangle count t_n	0	1	4							81

   b. Explain how to express each new 1×2 rectangle count, except the first one, in terms of the one that precedes it. What is the recursive formula for the nth 1×2 rectangle count?

   c. What is the explicit formula for the nth 1×2 rectangle count? Explain your reasoning.

6. Now it is your turn. Create your own square-tile design sequence. Investigate area, perimeter, and one other characteristic in your sequence; and express your results recursively and explicitly.

Navigating through Discrete Mathematics in Grades 6–12

Squares around the Triangle

Name _____

Targeting Squares–Part 2

Assume that each small square in the designs below has an area of one square unit and a side length of one unit. Each of the designs also includes one right triangle with an array of these small squares on two legs of the triangle and with an array of larger squares on the hypotenuse of the triangle.

(1)

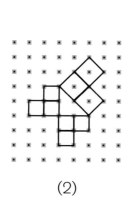

(2)

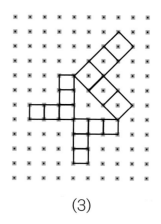

(3)

1. Working on a sheet of geodot paper, use the pattern of the first three designs to draw the next two designs in the triangle-and-squares design sequence.

2. Let s_n be the total number of small squares in the nth design.

   a. Complete the following table.

Design n	1	2	3	4	5	6	7	8	9	10
Small-square count s_n	2	6	10							38

   b. On a separate sheet of paper, explain how to express each new square count, except the first one, in terms of the one that precedes it. What is the recursive formula for the small-square count s_n?

   c. What is the explicit formula for the small-square count s_n? Justify your answer.

3. Let S_n be the total number of large squares in the nth design.

   a. Complete the following table.

Design n	1	2	3	4	5	6	7	8	9	10
Large-square count S_n	1	3	5							19

   b. Explain how to express each new square count, except the first one, in terms of the one that precedes it. What is the recursive formula for the large-square count S_n?

Name _____

c. What is the explicit formula for the large-square count S_n? Justify your answer.

4. If the area of a small square in the designs is 1 square unit and you draw a diagonal of the square (◲), then the area of each of the small right triangles formed is 1/2 square unit. Each of the designs has a right triangle at the center of the design. Let t_n be the area of this right triangle in the nth design.

   a. Complete the following table:

Design n	1	2	3	4	5	6	7	8	9	10
Area t_n	$\frac{1}{2}$	$\frac{4}{2}$	$\frac{9}{2}$							$\frac{100}{2}$

   b. Explain how to express the area of each new right triangle, except the first one, in terms of the one that precedes it. What is the recursive formula for the area of the nth right triangle?

   c. What is the explicit formula for the area of the nth right triangle? Explain how you found your answer.

5. a. If the area of a small square is 1 square unit, explain why the area of a large square is 2 square units.

   b. Let A_n be the sum of the areas of the large squares in the nth design. Complete the following table:

Design n	1	2	3	4	5	6	7	8	9	10
Area A_n	2	6	10							38

   c. Except for the first design, explain how to express the sum of the areas of the large squares in a design in terms of the sum of the areas of the large squares in the design that precedes it. What is the recursive formula for the sum of the areas of the large squares in the nth design?

   d. What is the explicit formula for the sum of the areas of the large squares in the nth design? Explain how you found your answer.

   e. In each design, what connection can you make between the area of the shapes drawn on the legs of the right triangle and the area of the shape drawn on the hypotenuse of the right triangle? Give a reason for the connection that you make.

Investing with Lotta Cash

Name _____

Lotta Cash was twelve years old on July 1. Her very generous grandparents gave her $2000 as a birthday gift so that she could open a new savings account. Lotta hopes to save as much money as possible, since she has permission to buy her first car on her seventeenth birthday. In the following activities, assume that the bank's interest rates do not change over time. Use a graphing calculator to help carry out this investigation. Round all final answers to the nearest cent, and write all explanations and descriptions on a separate sheet of paper. Copy the tables to complete them, if necessary.

1. Suppose that Lotta deposits her $2000 in an account that pays 4% per year in interest, which compounds, or is paid, at the end of each year. Lotta wants to know how much money she will have in the account on her seventeenth birthday and on her twentieth birthday if she does not make any withdrawals.

   a. To help Lotta calculate the amounts that she will have, complete the following table:

End of year n	1	2	3	4	5	6	7	8
Lotta's age	13	14	15	16	17	18	19	20
Amount in account	2080.00							

   b. What is the account balance on Lotta's seventeenth birthday?

   c. What is the account balance on her twentieth birthday?

   d. Describe the computations that you used when you completed the table.

   e. Use your answer to part 1(d) to help you write a recursive formula for the bank balance at the end of year n.

2. You can use any of several methods to solve problem 1 with a graphing calculator. Describe two different methods.

3. Suppose that Lotta Cash deposits her $2000 in a bank that pays 4% per year in interest, which compounds quarterly. In other words, Lotta receives interest at the rate of 1% four times each year. Give the account balance after each of the four quarters in the first year.

First Year Quarters	First Quarter	Second Quarter	Third Quarter	Fourth Quarter
Amount in account at end of each quarter				

Investing with Lotta Cash (continued)

Name _____

4. *a.* Use the data and procedure from problem 3 to complete the following table. Record only the fourth-quarter results for each year.

Year n	1	2	3	4	5	6	7	8
Amount in account at end of fourth quarter of year	2081.21							

  b. What is the account balance on Lotta's seventeenth birthday?

  c. What is the account balance on her twentieth birthday?

  d. Describe the computations that you used in completing the table.

  e. Use your answer to part 4(*d*) to help you write a recursive formula for the account balance at the end of year *n*.

5. Suppose that Lotta Cash decides to deposit her $2000 in a bank that pays interest at the rate of 4% each year, and the yearly interest compounds daily—that is, Lotta receives interest at the rate of $\dfrac{4\%}{365}$ 365 times per year.

  a. Complete the following table. Record only the account balance for the 365th day of each year in the table.

Year n	1	2	3	4	5	6	7	8
Amount in account after 365th payment at end of year	2081.62							

  b. What is the account balance on Lotta's seventeenth birthday?

  c. What is the account balance on her twentieth birthday?

  d. Describe how you completed the table.

  e. Use part 5(*d*) to write an explicit formula for the account balance at the end of year *n*.

Investing with Lotta Cash (continued)

Name _____

6. If Lotta Cash uses the account that credits 4% in interest once a year, how long will it take for her money to double? Give your answer to the nearest year. Describe your method of solving the problem.

7. What happens if Lotta Cash also receives a $1000 gift on her sixteenth birthday and deposits it in her account right away?

a. Complete each of the following three tables. In the first table, the interest compounds once each year; in the second table, the interest compounds quarterly; and in the third, the interest compounds daily.

End of Year n	1	2	3	4	5	6	7	8
Amount in account								

Year n	1	2	3	4	5	6	7	8
Amount in account at end of fourth quarter of year								

Year n	1	2	3	4	5	6	7	8
Amount in account after 365th payment at end of year								

b. In each situation, will Lotta have an account balance of at least $4000 by her twentieth birthday? Explain.

A Constant Rate of Change

Name _____

A Recursive View of Some Common Functions—Part 1

You can represent functions in several ways—by using tables, graphs, and equations, for example. In parts 1 and 2 of this investigation, you will examine representations of two fundamental types of functions. Your goal, by the end of the investigation, is to find answers to these questions:

- How can two different types of equations represent each function—the one that you examine in part 1 and the one that you encounter in part 2?

- How does each equation show fundamental properties of the function and its graph?

- How do the equations help you see similarities and differences between the functions that you encounter in parts 1 and 2?

Consider the function table below. Complete the page by solving the problems on the next page. Use a separate sheet of paper for your descriptions and explanations.

x	y
0	4
1	7
2	10
3	13
4	16

Recursive Formula

Explicit Formula

Slope
Constant Rate of Change

Sketch graph below:

Constant Added (to get from one y-value to the next)

A Constant Rate of Change (continued)

Name _____

1. Examine the function table on the previous page and briefly describe any patterns that you see.

2. Look down the column of *y*-values in the table. If NOW is the *y*-value at a particular place in the table and NEXT is the *y*-value in the next row down, write an equation using NEXT and NOW that describes the pattern in the *y*-values. Write this equation in the box next to the down-arrow.

3. Look across the columns of the function table. Write an equation in the form "*y* = ..." to show the relationship between *x* and the corresponding *y*. Write this equation on the previous page in the box above the right-arrow.

4. What type of function is represented by the table and by the equations that you have found? Describe the basic characteristics of this function.

5. Sketch a small graph of this function in the location shown on the previous page . Slope is a fundamental feature of the graph of a linear function. What is the slope of the graph of this function?

6. The slope of a graph of a linear function also shows the constant rate of change of *y* with respect to *x*. Describe how the table shows this constant rate of change.

7. Examine the equations in the boxes on the previous page.

   • Describe how the slope and constant rate of change are shown in each of the two equations.

   • Circle the number in those equations that corresponds to the slope. To show what the circled number represents, draw an arrow from each circled number to the box at the bottom of the page, and enter the number in the box.

   • Do you think that one equation shows the slope and constant rate of change more clearly than the other? Explain.

8. Review your work. Be prepared to explain all the information on the previous page to your classmates. In particular, for each item, be prepared to answer these questions:

   • What is it?

   • How is it determined?

   • What does it mean?

   • How does it connect with other information on the page?

A Constant Multiplier

Name _____

A Recursive View of Some Common Functions—Part 2

In part 1 of this investigation, you examined representations of a linear function. In part 2, you will examine representations of a function of a different fundamental type. Recall that your goal, by the end of the investigation, is to find answers to these questions:

- How can two different types of equations represent each function—the one that you examined in part 1 and the one that you encounter in part 2?
- How does each equation show fundamental properties of each function and its graph?
- How do the equations help you see similarities and differences between the functions that you encounter in parts 1 and 2?

Consider the function table below. Your task is to complete the page by solving the problems on the next page. Use a separate sheet of paper for your descriptions and explanations. When you are finished, you will compare this work with the work that you did in part 1 of this investigation.

x	y
0	4
1	12
2	36
3	108
4	324

Recursive Formula

Explicit Formula

Sketch graph below:

Constant Multiplier

A Constant Multiplier (continued)

Name _____

1. Examine the function table on the previous page and briefly describe any patterns that you see.

2. Look down the column of *y*-values in the function table. If NOW is the *y*-value at a particular place in the table and NEXT is the *y*-value in the next row down, write an equation using NEXT and NOW that describes the pattern in the *y*-values. Write this equation in the box next to the down-arrow.

3. Look across the columns of the function table. Write an equation in the form "$y = ...$" to show the relationship between *x* and the corresponding *y*. Write this equation on the previous page in the box above the right-arrow.

4. What type of function is represented by the table and by the equations that you have found? Describe the basic characteristics of this function.

5. Sketch a small graph of this function in the location shown on the previous page. Does the graph have a constant slope? Is there a constant rate of change of *y* with respect to *x*? Explain.

6. A fundamental characteristic of exponential functions is that there is a constant multiplier (but not a constant rate of change of *y* with respect to *x*). Describe how the table shows the constant multiplier.

7. Examine the equations in the boxes on the previous page.

    • Describe how the constant multiplier is shown in each of the equations.

    • Circle the number in those equations that corresponds to the constant multiplier. To show what the number represents, draw an arrow from each circled number to the box at the bottom of the page, and enter the number in the box

    • Do you think that one equation shows the constant multiplier more clearly than the other? Explain.

8. Review your work. Be prepared to explain all the information on the previous page to your classmates. In particular, for each item, be prepared to answer these questions:

    • What is it?

    • How is it determined?

    • What does it mean?

    • How does it connect with other information on the page?

A Constant Multiplier (continued)

Name _____

9. Compare the NEXT-NOW equations that you wrote in part 1 ("A Constant Rate of Change") and part 2 ("A Constant Multiplier"). These equations are *recursive formulas,* since they describe one value in terms of the previous value.

   a. Describe how these two NEXT-NOW equations are similar and how they are different.

   b. How do the $y = \ldots$ equations that you wrote in part 1 and part 2 show this difference? (These equations are explicit, or closed-form, formulas.)

   c. How do the graphs of the two functions show this difference?

   d. How do the tables for the two functions show this difference?

10. (Extension) In this investigation you have explored two recursive formulas:

$$\text{NEXT} = \text{NOW} + k$$
$$\text{NEXT} = \text{NOW} \times k.$$

   Consider a "combined recursive formula":

$$\text{NEXT} = r\ \text{NOW} + b.$$

   a. Why do you think that the phrase *combined recursive formula* is used? Specifically, explain why you think that the word *combined* is used.

   b. (Optional; as your teacher directs) Work through the activity Trout Pond, an applet-based investigation in which you will use graphs, tables, and $y = \ldots$ equations to analyze this type of recursive formula in the context of a changing fish population.

A Recursive View of Skydiving

Name _____

Skydiving is an exciting but dangerous sport. Many precautions are necessary to ensure the safety of skydivers. The basic fact underlying these precautions is that acceleration caused by the force of gravity near the surface of the earth is 32 feet per second per second (written as 32 ft/sec^2). Therefore, each second that skydivers are falling, their speed increases by 32 ft/sec. This investigation ignores air resistance and other complicating factors, instead focusing only on acceleration caused by gravity. You must determine recursive and explicit formulas for the distance that a skydiver falls before her parachute opens.

To help find these equations, consider the following table, which you will complete in subsequent problems. Use a separate sheet of paper for all descriptions and explanations.

A Skydiver's Speed and Distance of Fall before Her Parachute Opens

Time n in Seconds	Instantaneous Speed at Time n	Average Speed during Each Second	Distance Fallen during Each Second $D(n)$	Total Distance Fallen after n Seconds $T(n)$
0	0	0	0	0
1 sec	32 ft/sec	16 ft/sec	16 ft	16 ft
2 sec	64 ft/sec	48 ft/sec	48 ft	64 ft
3 sec				
4 sec				
⋮	⋮	⋮	⋮	⋮
n sec				

1. Explain each entry in the row corresponding to time $n = 1$ sec in the table. (Remember that the basis for computing all entries is that acceleration caused by gravity is 32 ft/sec^2).

2. Explain each entry in the row corresponding to time $n = 2$ sec.

3. Complete the table for time $n = 3$ sec and time $n = 4$ sec.

4. Use the information in the table to help find recursive and explicit formulas for $D(n)$, the distance that the skydiver falls during the nth second, as follows. (In completing this problem, ignore the row in the table for time $n = 0$ sec.)

   a. If NOW is the distance that the skydiver falls during any given second and NEXT is the distance that she falls during the next second, write an equation for NEXT in terms of NOW.

   b. Rewrite the NEXT-NOW equation by using $D(n)$ and $D(n-1)$. That is, if $D(n)$ is the distance that the skydiver falls during the nth second and $D(n-1)$ is the distance that she falls during the $(n-1)$st

A Recursive View of Skydiving (continued)

Name _____

second, write an equation for $D(n)$ in terms of $D(n − 1)$. This formula is a *recursive formula,* since it expresses $D(n)$ in terms of a previous value, $D(n − 1)$.

c. If $D(n)$ is the distance that the skydiver falls during the *n*th second, write an equation for $D(n)$ in terms of *n.* A formula like this one, where $D(n)$ is written as a function of *n,* is an *explicit,* or *closed-form, formula.*

The final goal of this investigation is to find formulas for $T(n)$, the total distance that the skydiver has fallen after *n* seconds. In the next three problems, you will use three methods to find these formulas: a general analysis, an analysis using an arithmetic sequence, and an analysis using finite differences.

5. Use a general analysis to find formulas for the total distance that the skydiver has fallen after *n* seconds, as follows.

    Let $T(n) =$ total distance fallen after *n* seconds.

    a. As part of problem 3, you computed $T(3)$. Describe how you computed $T(3)$.

    b. Describe all the methods that you can think of for computing $T(n)$.

    c. Write a formula for $T(n)$ in terms of $T(n − 1)$ and $D(n)$.

    Since the formula expresses $T(n)$ in terms of the previous value, $T(n − 1)$, this formula is a recursive formula.

6. Find $T(n)$ by summing an arithmetic sequence, as follows.

    a. One method of finding $T(n)$ that you may have described in problem 5(*b*) is to sum all the terms to $D(n)$ in the $D(n)$ column. If you did not already describe this method in problem 5(*b*), explain why the method is a valid one for computing $T(n)$.

    b. In problem 4(c), you ignored the row for time $n = 0$ sec and found that, in feet,

    $$D(n) = D(n − 1) + 32.$$

    This formula shows that you add a constant, 32, each time to find the next value of $D(n)$. The terms $D(n)$ therefore form an arithmetic sequence, so $T(n)$ is the sum of the arithmetic sequence $D(1) + D(2) + … + D(n)$. Compute this sum to find a formula for $T(n)$ in terms of *n.*

A Recursive View of Skydiving (continued)

Name _____

7. Find $T(n)$ by using finite differences, as follows:

a. Complete the three remaining entries in the last two rows of the following table.

Finite Differences Table

n	$T(n)$	First Differences (entry in the previous column) − (entry just above it)	Second Differences (entry in the previous column) − (entry just above it)
1	16	—	—
2	64	$64 - 16 = 48$	—
3	144	$144 - 64 = 80$	$80 - 48 = 32$
4	256	$256 - 144 = 112$	
5	400	_____	_____

b. Describe the pattern in the second-differences column.

c. Apply a basic fact: If the nth differences in a finite-differences table are constant, then the formula for $T(n)$ is an nth-degree polynomial. In this example, the second differences are constant, so the formula for $T(n)$ is a second-degree polynomial. In other words, the formula is quadratic. (Proving this fact is not too difficult, but the proof is time-consuming. Your teacher might give you guidance or references for the proof if you are interested.) You now know that $T(n)$ is quadratic:

$$T(n) = an^2 + bn + c.$$

You need to find the coefficients, a, b, and c. One way to find a, b, and c is to generate and solve a system of three linear equations. Because you know the value of $T(n)$ for several values of n, you have the following equations:

$$T(n) = an^2 + bn + c$$
$$n = 1 \rightarrow \quad 16 = a + b + c$$
$$n = 2 \rightarrow \quad 64 = 4a + 2b + c$$
$$n = 3 \rightarrow \quad 144 = 9a + 3b + c.$$

Describe in detail how to generate these three equations.

d. You next need to solve this system of three linear equations. One method is to use matrices. You can represent a system of linear equations like this one by using matrices, as follows:

$$\begin{bmatrix} 1 & 1 & 1 \\ 4 & 2 & 1 \\ 9 & 3 & 1 \end{bmatrix} \begin{bmatrix} a \\ b \\ c \end{bmatrix} = \begin{bmatrix} 16 \\ 64 \\ 144 \end{bmatrix}.$$

A Recursive View of Skydiving (continued)

Name _____

Explain where all the entries in the matrices come from and why this matrix equation is equivalent to the linear system in part (c) of this problem.

e. You can solve this matrix equation by multiplying both sides of the equation at the bottom of the preceding page by the inverse of matrix $\begin{bmatrix} 1 & 1 & 1 \\ 4 & 2 & 1 \\ 9 & 3 & 1 \end{bmatrix}$.

The result of this multiplication is $\begin{bmatrix} a \\ b \\ c \end{bmatrix} = \begin{bmatrix} 1 & 1 & 1 \\ 4 & 2 & 1 \\ 9 & 3 & 1 \end{bmatrix}^{-1} \begin{bmatrix} 16 \\ 64 \\ 144 \end{bmatrix}$.

Find this inverse matrix, and carry out the multiplication to solve the matrix equation. You may want to use your calculator for these computations.

What are the values of a, b, and c?

f. Give the formula for T(n) by using the values for a, b, and c that you just found.

g. Check the formula that you found in part (f) by evaluating it for some values of n and verifying that you obtain the same values for T(n) that you found in the preceding tables.

h. You can also solve systems of linear equations like this one by using algebra without matrices. To do so, you need to combine and manipulate the three equations in part (c) until you can solve them for a, b, and c. This combining and manipulating is similar to what you do for a system of two linear equations, but the process is more complicated because there are more equations. Try this method. Do you obtain the same solution that you found in part (f)?

8. In this investigation and in parts 1 and 2 of the investigation A Recursive View of Some Common Functions, you have explored three types of recursive formulas:

- $A(n) = 3A(n - 1)$

- $B(n) = B(n - 1) + 3$

- $T(n) = T(n - 1) + 32n - 16$

If you did not find this exact formula for T(n) in the preceding problems, reexamine problems 4(c) and 5(c).

a. Which of these three recursive formulas has a corresponding explicit formula that is a linear function? Which one of the three recursive formulas has a corresponding explicit formula that is an exponential function?

Which one of the three recursive formulas has a corresponding explicit formula that is a quadratic function?

A Recursive View of Skydiving (continued)

Name _____

b. (Extension; optional—as your teacher directs) Consider a recursive formula that is a combination of the first two formulas:

$$P(n) = rP(n - 1) + b$$

Work through the activity Trout Pond, an applet-based investigation in which you will use graphs, tables, and explicit formulas to analyze this type of recursive formula in the context of a changing fish population.

A Recursive View of Proof by Mathematical Induction

Name _____

Proof is an important part of mathematics because it establishes, without doubt, the truth or falsity of mathematical statements. Use a separate sheet of paper to show your work on the following problems.

1. Think about statements that are supposed to be true for infinitely many integers. For example, consider this statement: **$n^2 - n + 41$ is a prime number.**

   a. Is this statement true for $n = 0$? Is it true for $n = 1$? Is it true for $n = 2$?

   b. Check out the truth of this statement for some other values of n.

   c. Consider the statement **$n^2 - n + 41$ is a prime number, for all integers $n \geq 0$.** Do you think that it is a true statement? Explain.

   d. Check out the case when $n = 41$. Is $(41)^2 - 41 + 41$ a prime number?

2. In problem 1(c), the statement **$n^2 - n + 41$ is a prime number** is asserted for infinitely many values of n—specifically for all integers $n \geq 0$. In part (d), you found a single value of n for which $n^2 - n + 41$ is not a prime number. This single counterexample shows that the statement asserted for all integers $n \geq 0$ is not true. One counterexample is enough to show that a statement is not true. In this problem, there are in fact many more values of n for which $n^2 - n + 41$ is not a prime number. Find a few more.

You can prove that a statement asserted for infinitely many integers is not true by finding a single counterexample. But what do you do if you believe that such a statement is true? You cannot prove that it is true by checking all the cases, since there are infinitely many. One powerful and ingenious method for proving a statement claimed to be true for all integers greater than or equal to a starting value is *proof by mathematical induction*.

The validity of a proof by mathematical induction rests, in part, on the *principle of mathematical induction*. This principle is a basic property of integers and can be used to prove that a statement about integers, $S(n)$, is true for every integer $n \geq n_0$.

Principle of Mathematical Induction

Suppose that $S(n)$ is a statement about integers.

If (i) $S(n)$ is true whenever $S(n - 1)$ is true, for each
  integer $n > n_0$, and

  (ii) $S(n_0)$ is true,

then $S(n)$ is true for all integers $n \geq n_0$.

This activity is adapted from Coxford, Arthur F., James T. Fey, Christian R. Hirsch, Harold L. Schoen, Gail Burrill, Eric W. Hart, and Ann E. Watkins. *Contemporary Mathematics in Context.* Course 4: Part A, Unit 4. New York: Glencoe McGraw-Hill, 2003.

A Recursive View of Proof by Mathematical Induction (continued)

Name _____

3. An analogy that is commonly used to illustrate this principle involves dominoes. Think about setting up dominoes as shown in the diagram.

   a. Imagine that whenever any given domino falls over, it will knock over the next one. Explain how this condition corresponds to condition (i) in the principle of mathematical induction.

   b. Imagine knocking over the first domino. Explain how this situation corresponds to condition (ii) in the principle of mathematical induction.

   c. Given parts (a) and (b), all the dominoes would fall. Explain how this outcome corresponds to the conclusion in the principle of mathematical induction that $S(n)$ is true for all integers $n \geq n_0$.

The principle of mathematical induction provides the basis for proof by mathematical induction. To use mathematical induction to prove that a statement asserted for all integers $n \geq n_0$ is true, you proceed in two steps:

   (i) Induction Step: Prove that the statement is true for n whenever it is true for $n - 1$.
   (ii) Base Step: Prove that the statement is true for n_0.

(Note that you can complete these steps in either order.)

As an example, consider the following problem:

How many edges does a complete graph on n vertices have?

The discussion below and steps 4–6 will help you find and prove your answer.

A complete graph is a vertex-edge graph that has exactly one edge between every pair of vertices. (Complete graphs on four and five vertices appear on the next page.) Let $E(n)$ be the number of edges in a complete graph on n vertices. There are two fundamental ways to think about $E(n)$. You can find an explicit formula that describes $E(n)$ as a function of n, or you can find a recursive formula that describes $E(n)$ in terms of $E(n - 1)$. You need to do both.

A Recursive View of Proof by Mathematical Induction (continued)

Name _____

A complete graph on 4 vertices

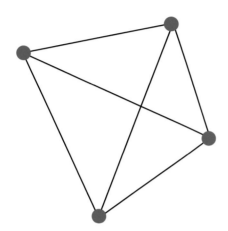

A complete graph on 5 vertices

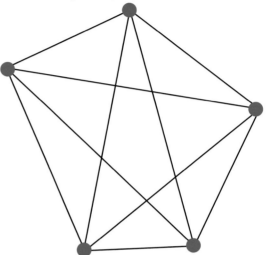

It is the explicit formula that you will prove by using the principle of mathematical induction. The recursive formula is an essential tool in the proof, as you can see from condition (i) in the principle of mathematical induction.

4. Use the following steps to find a recursive formula for $E(n)$. Sketch some complete graphs, and count the numbers of edges. Record your results in a table. Look for a pattern. Find a recursive formula that describes the relationship between $E(n)$ and $E(n-1)$. Explain why you believe that your formula is valid.

You now need a conjecture for an explicit formula. Suppose that some students conjecture that the number of edges in a complete graph on n vertices is

$$E(n) = \frac{n(n-1)}{2}, \text{ for every } n \geq 1.$$

You will now prove this statement by mathematical induction. Problems 5 and 6 guide you through the two steps that you must carry out.

5. **Induction step:** Prove that the statement is true for n whenever it is true for $n-1$.
   You must show that if the statement is true for $n-1$, then it will be true for n. (In terms of the domino analogy, you are showing that the dominoes are set up in such a way that if the previous domino falls, then it will knock over the current domino.)

   Thus, in a proof by mathematical induction, you may assume that the statement is true for $n-1$ while you try to prove it for n.

Navigating through Discrete Mathematics in Grades 6–12

A Recursive View of Proof by Mathematical Induction (continued)

Name _____

a. In this situation, you may assume that the explicit formula for $E(n-1)$ is true. Write the explicit formula for $E(n-1)$ by replacing n with $n-1$ in the formula

$$E(n) = \frac{n(n-1)}{2}.$$

b. Complete the induction step of the proof by filling in the requested details. Give written answers to all the "why" questions.

You must prove that $E(n) = \frac{n(n-1)}{2}$.

You may assume that $E(n-1) = \frac{(n-1)(n-2)}{2}$. Why?

You want to start with $E(n)$, then use the recursive formula to "step back" to $E(n-1)$, then use the formula for $E(n-1)$, and then work to end up with $E(n) = \frac{n(n-1)}{2}$.

Here is one way to lay out the proof:

$E(n) = E(n-1) + (n-1)$ Use the recursive formula from problem 4.

$= \dfrac{(n-1)(n-2)}{2} + (n-1)$ Why?

$= \dfrac{n^2 - 3n + 2}{2} + (n-1)$ Why?

$= \text{???}$ Why?

$= \text{???}$ Why?

$\vdots$ (You may use more or fewer steps.)

$= \dfrac{n(n-1)}{2}$ Why?

Thus, you have completed the induction step. You have shown that the statement $E(n) = \frac{n(n-1)}{2}$ is true for n whenever it is true for $n-1$.

6. **Base step:** Prove that the statement is true for the initial value of n.

In the induction step, you have shown that the explicit formula for the number of edges in a complete

A Recursive View of Proof by Mathematical Induction (continued)

Name _____

graph is true for *n* whenever it is true for *n* − 1. Now you need to show that the explicit formula is true for the initial value of *n*, or in this case *n* = 1.

a. Explain why a complete graph with *n* = 1 vertex has $\dfrac{n(n-1)}{2}$ edges.

b. How is this step related to the domino analogy?

You have completed the two steps of a proof by mathematical induction, and thus you have satisfied the two conditions of the principle of mathematical induction. Therefore, you can conclude that

$$E(n) = \frac{n(n-1)}{2}, \text{ for every } n \geq 1.$$

You are finished!

Practice doing induction proofs problems by solving problems 7 and 8.

7. The principle of mathematical induction is often used to prove statements about finite sums. For example, consider the sum of the first *n* odd positive integers:

$$S_n = 1 + 3 + 5 + 7 + \ldots + (2n - 1)$$

a. Compute S_n for a few values of *n*. Make a conjecture for a concise explicit formula for S_n as a function of *n*.

b. Use mathematical induction to prove your conjecture.

8. Consider the Sierpinski triangle at various stages. This triangle starts with a solid triangular region with one unit on a side. Smaller and smaller equilateral triangular regions are removed from the original triangle, as shown below.

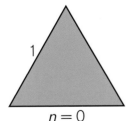
$n = 0$

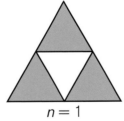
$n = 1$

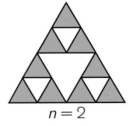
$n = 2$

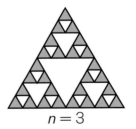
$n = 3$

...

The white triangular regions in each figure are holes. The perimeter of each figure is the sum of the lengths of all edges, including both the outside edges and the inner edges around each hole. Each time that a triangle is cut out, its vertices cut the surrounding line segments in half.

By looking at the pattern in the figure, some students conjectured the following explicit formula for the perimeter at the *n*th stage:

A Recursive View of Proof by Mathematical Induction (continued)

Name _____

$$P_n = \frac{3^{n+1}}{2^n}, \quad n \geq 0.$$

Use mathematical induction to prove that this formula is true.

(Note that to carry out the proof, you need to know a recursive formula for P_n. That is, you will need to figure out how the perimeter at any stage P_n ($n \geq 1$) is related to the perimeter at the previous stage, P_{n-1}.)

Solutions for the Blackline Masters

Solutions for "Flag Trademarks"

1. *a.* Nine pattern A flags are necessary.

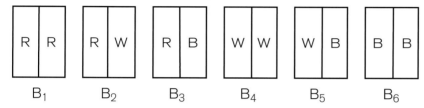

A$_1$ A$_2$ A$_3$ A$_4$ A$_5$ A$_6$ A$_7$ A$_8$ A$_9$

b. Six pattern B flags are necessary.

B$_1$ B$_2$ B$_3$ B$_4$ B$_5$ B$_6$

c. A total of (9 − 3), or 6, pattern A flags are necessary: A$_2$, A$_3$, A$_4$, A$_6$, A$_7$, and A$_8$.

d. A total of (6 − 3), or 3, pattern B flags are necessary: B$_2$, B$_3$, and B$_5$.

2. *a* and *b.* If the colors for the flags are red, white, blue, and green and the two pieces of cloth can be the same color, the number of pattern A models is $4 + 4 + 4 + 4 = 4 \times 4 = 16$, and the number of pattern B models is $4 + 3 + 2 + 1$, or 10. The tree diagrams for (*a*) and (*b*) are combined below; circles show the pattern B models.

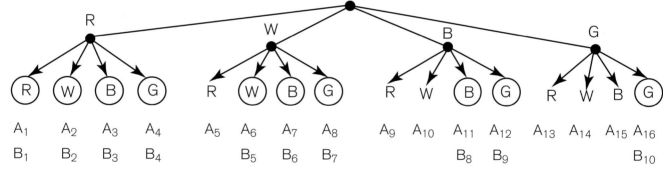

A$_1$ A$_2$ A$_3$ A$_4$ A$_5$ A$_6$ A$_7$ A$_8$ A$_9$ A$_{10}$ A$_{11}$ A$_{12}$ A$_{13}$ A$_{14}$ A$_{15}$ A$_{16}$

B$_1$ B$_2$ B$_3$ B$_4$ B$_5$ B$_6$ B$_7$ B$_8$ B$_9$ B$_{10}$

c and *d.* If the colors for the flags are red, white, blue, and green and the two pieces of cloth cannot be the same color, the pattern A models are A$_2$, A$_3$, A$_4$, A$_5$, A$_7$, A$_8$, A$_9$, A$_{10}$, A$_{12}$, A$_{13}$, A$_{14}$, and A$_{15}$. The number of pattern A models is $(4 \times 4) - 4 = 12$, or $4 \times 3 = 12$, or $3 + 3 + 3 + 3 = 12$. The pattern B models are B$_2$, B$_3$,

B$_4$, B$_6$, B$_7$, and B$_9$; the number of pattern B models is $3 + 2 + 1 + 0 = 6$, or $10 - 4 = 6$, or $\frac{4 \times 3}{2} = 6$.

3. *a* and *b.* If the colors for the flags are red, white, blue, green, and yellow and the two pieces of cloth can be the same color, the total number of pattern A models is $5 \times 5 = 25$, or $5 + 5 + 5 + 5 + 5 = 25$, and the total number of pattern B models is $5 + 4 + 3 + 2 + 1 = 15$, or $\frac{5 \times 4}{2} + 5 = 15$.

c and *d.* If the colors for the flags are red, white, blue, green, and yellow and the two pieces of cloth must be different colors, the total number of pattern A models is $4 + 4 + 4 + 4 + 4 = 20$, or $5 \times 4 = 20$, or $(5 \times 5) - 5 = 20$.

The total number of pattern B models is $4 + 3 + 2 + 1 + 0 = 10$, or $15 - 5 = 10$, or $\frac{5 \times 4}{2} = 10$.

4. Students' answers will vary.

Solutions for "Counting the Kids"

1. *a.* A total of 120 students were in sixth grade: $25 + 7 + 9 + 11 + 5 + 15 + 29 + 19 = 120$.

   b. A total of 25 students preferred hot dogs only: $48 - (11 + 5 + 7) = 25$.

   c. The number of students who preferred exactly two types of food was $11 + 7 + 15 = 33$; 11 preferred hot dogs and hamburgers only, 7 preferred chicken wings and hot dogs only, and 15 preferred chicken wings and hamburgers only.

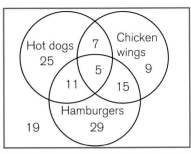

2. *a.* A total of 101 students were in seventh grade: $20 + 1 + 22 + 2 + 8 + 7 + 18 + 23 = 101$.

   b. Yes; the number of students who performed in exactly two acts exceeded the number of students who performed in all three acts: $1 + 2 + 7$, or 10, students performed in exactly two acts, but only 8 students performed in all three acts.

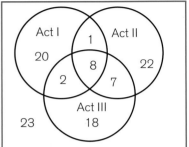

3. *b.* A total of 4 students participated in all three contests.

   c. A total of $22 + 24 + 23$, or 69, students participated in exactly one contest; and 100 students participated in at least one contest.

   d. A total of $8 + 9 + 10$, or 27, students participated in exactly two contests; and $100 - 4$, or 96, students participated in at most two contests.

4. A total of 321 students attended Pythagoras Middle School.

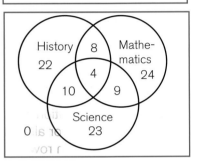

Solutions for "Binary Strings"

Paths, Strings, and Combinations in Pascal's Triangle—Part 1

1. *a.* If Carl follows the trail represented by 011, he will take the tunnel under the first river and the bridges over the other two rivers.

   b. The representation for taking the tunnel under the first river, the bridge over the second river, and the tunnel under the third river is 010.

   c. The eight strings of 1s and 0s that describe all possible trails from point *X* to point Y are 000, 001, 010, 011, 100, 101, 110, and 111.

   d. If Carl bases his decisions on tossing a coin, the probability that he uses two bridges and one tunnel to travel from *X* to *Y* is 3/8, since three of the eight strings in part 1(*c*) contain exactly two 1s.

2. *a.* The six line segments determined by the points are *AB, AC, AD, BC, BD,* and *CD*.

   b. The string that represents line segment *AC* is 1010.

   c. The number of 1s in any string that represents a line segment is always two, since a 1 represents a point and two points determine a line segment.

Solutions for "Zigzag Paths and Binary Strings"

Paths, Strings, and Combinations in Pascal's Triangle—Part 2

1. *a.* The path represented by 010 goes left, then right, then left, ending at row 3, entry 1. (Students trace this path, so they do not need to use the labeling language. Recall that the top row—START—is row 0 and the left-most entry in any row is entry 0.)

   b. Three paths are possible from START to location C. For example, the frog can go right, right, and left. The representation for this path is 110. The other possible paths are 101 and 011.

    c. The remaining strings in row 3 are as follows: For entry 0, there is one string: 000. For entry 2 (location C), the three strings are 011, 101, and 110. For entry 3, the string is 111.

    d. All the binary strings in row 3 have exactly three digits because the frog takes three hops to get from START to row 3.

    e. Listed in order from the smallest to the largest binary number, the strings in row 3 are 000, 001, 010, 011, 100, 101, 110, and 111.

2. Just one string is in each "outside" location of the triangle because only one path is possible from START to those locations.

3. a. The numbers of strings in locations D and F are the same because they are located symmetrically in the triangle. To travel to location D rather than to location F, the frog just hops left instead of right and right instead of left in any path.

    b. The strings for all zigzag paths from START to location D are 1000, 0100, 0010, and 0001.

    c. Students may describe and explain some of the following similarities and differences.

- The strings for locations D and F are "opposites." That is, switching 1s for 0s and 0s for 1s turns a string for D into a string for F, or vice versa, by switching left and right in paths to D as compared with paths to F.

- The strings in D and F all have length 4 because the frog takes four hops to get to row 4.

- The strings for D have exactly one 1, and the strings for F have exactly one 0, because all paths to D must contain exactly one hop to the right and all paths to F must contain exactly one hop to the left.

4. a. Six strings code the zigzag paths to E: 1100, 1010, 1001, 0011, 0101, and 0110.

    b. With the exception of the outside right location, which contains the single string 1111, students have already found strings for all locations in row 4, or previous problems have given them. Patterns that students may notice in the strings in row 4 include the following:

- Each string has length 4.

- The strings for D and F and for the two outside locations are "opposites."

- The opposite of any string in E is also in E.

- The center location has the most strings.

- All possible binary strings of length 4 are in row 4.

- If students know about binary numbers, they may notice that all the binary strings in row 4 represent all the decimal numbers 0 through 15.

- The number of strings in row 4 is 16, which is 2^4.

5. a. The strings for location G are 11001, 10101, 10011, 00111, 01011, 01101, 01110, 10110, 11010, and 11100.

    b. Because every path to G must travel through E or F and be one more hop beyond E or F, the strings for G can be determined by adding a 1 to each string for E and a 0 to each string for F.

6. The numbers in row 10 of Pascal's triangle are 1, 10, 45, 120, 210, 252, 210, 120, 45, 10, and 1.

7. a. Each number in row 4 of Pascal's triangle is the number of binary strings in the corresponding location in row 4 of the lily-pad triangle.

    b. The three numbers that the students underline (6, 4, and 10) are the numbers of binary strings in locations E, F, and G, respectively. In problem 5, students described how each path to G must pass through E or F and be one additional hop beyond E or F. Thus, the number of paths to G must be the number of paths to E plus the number of paths to F.

c. Every zigzag path to a given location must pass through the locations directly above it to the left or the right. Thus, the sum of the numbers of paths to the locations just above to the left and the right must be the number of paths to the given location.

d. Each number in Pascal's triangle is the number of binary strings in the corresponding location of the lily-pad triangle.

8. *a.* The path represented by 0010011 goes left, left, right, left, left, right, right.

 b. A variety of paths are possible. Two such paths are 0000111 and 1110000.

 c. Each binary string that represents a path from S to the underlined 35 has length 7. The length of the string represents the number of hops needed to travel to the location, which is also the number of the row—in this example, row 7.

 d. Each string corresponding to the underlined 35 has three 1s and four 0s. Zigzag paths must consist of three hops to the right and four hops to the left to travel from S to the underlined 35.

 e. All zigzag paths of length 7 finish at row 7. The sum of all the numbers in row 7 is the number of paths of length 7. This sum is 128. If all paths are equally likely, the probability that a path of length 7 stops at the underlined 35 is 35/128.

9. *a.* Every path from S to the underlined 84 consists of nine hops, since the underlined 84 is in row 9. Also, every such path includes six hops to the right and three hops to the left.

 b. A path from S to any location in row 9 has length 9.

 c. A nine-step path stops at row 9. If the path includes four hops to the right, then it must stop at the location that is four steps to the right from the outside left location of row 9. This location is the leftmost 126. Therefore, a total of 126 nine-step paths include four downward steps to the right.

 d. Strings of length 9 that contain three 1s correspond to paths with nine hops that include three hops to the right. Such paths finish at the location in row 9 that is three steps to the right from the outside left edge. This location is the leftmost 84. Therefore, 84 strings of length 9 contain three 1s.

10. The fact that two numbers at symmetric locations in a given row are equal indicates left-right symmetry. In terms of zigzag paths, the reason is that any path that leads to one location can be converted to a path that goes to the symmetric location simply by changing left hops to right hops, and vice versa. Thus, the number of paths to the symmetric locations is the same, and therefore the numbers at those locations are equal.

Solutions for "Combinations and Subsets"

Paths, Strings, and Combinations in Pascal's Triangle—Part 3

1. Row 6 of the triangle contains the following entries: $C(6, 0)$, $C(6, 1)$, $C(6, 2)$, $C(6, 3)$, $C(6, 4)$, $C(6, 5)$, $C(6, 6)$.

2. In this problem, students learn about $C(n, k)$ in terms of zigzag paths.

 a. $C(3, 2)$ refers to zigzag paths that have length 3.

 b. $C(3, 2)$ refers to zigzag paths with two zigs to the right.

 c. $C(5, 1)$ refers to zigzag paths that are five hops long with one zig to the right.

 d. $C(n, k)$ is the number of zigzag paths of length n that include k zigs to the right.

3. In this problem, students learn about $C(n, k)$ in terms of binary strings.

 a. The strings at the location represented by $C(3, 2)$ have length 3.

 b. The strings at the location represented by $C(3, 2)$ contain two 1s.

 c. Five strings are at the location represented by $C(5, 1)$. Each string has length 5 and contains one 1 and four 0s.

 d. The number of binary strings of length 4 that contain exactly three 1s is $C(4, 3)$, which is entry 3 in row 4 of Pascal's triangle. That entry is 4.

e. $C(n, k)$ is the number of strings of length n that contain k 1s.

4. In this problem, students learn and practice the "choose" language.

   a. Students can simply list all the possibilities: 1110, 1101, 1011, and 0111. Therefore, there are four ways to choose three digits to be 1s in a string of four binary digits. In terms of the "string" triangle, these strings are at entry 3 in row 4. This number of strings is represented by $C(4, 3)$.

   b. The number of binary strings of length 6 that contain exactly four 1s is $C(6, 4)$, or 15.

   c. The value of "5 choose 2" is $C(5, 2)$, or 10. It is also the answer to the following questions: What is the number of zigzag paths of length 5 that contain two zigs to the right? What is the number of binary strings of length 5 that contain two 1s?

5. In this problem, students learn two fundamental patterns related to the numbers $C(n, k)$ and Pascal's triangle.

   a. $C(6, 2)$ is entry 2 in row 6 of Pascal's triangle, and $C(6, 4)$ is entry 4 in row 6. These entries are symmetrically located in row 6; therefore, they are equal. In terms of binary strings, $C(6, 2)$ is the number of binary strings of length 6 that contain two 1s and four 0s. When students think about switching 1s and 0s, they can see that this result is the same as the number of binary strings of length 6 that contain two 0s and four 1s—that is, $C(6, 4)$. Thus, $C(6, 2) = C(6, 4)$. In terms of zigzag paths, $C(6, 2)$ is the number of paths of length 6 that contain two hops to the right and four hops to the left. By thinking about switching right and left, students can see that this result is the same as the number of paths of length 6 that contain two hops to the left and four hops to the right—that is, $C(6, 4)$. Therefore, $C(6, 2) = C(6, 4)$.

   b. The general rule is $C(n, k) = C(n, n - k)$. For example, $C(10, 7) = C(10, 3)$.

   c. Students can compute $C(8, 5)$ by using the basic pattern in Pascal's triangle: a given number in the triangle is the sum of the two numbers above it to the left and the right. For $C(8, 5)$, the two numbers above to the left and the right are $C(7, 4)$ and $C(7, 5)$. Therefore, $C(8, 5) = C(7, 4) + C(7, 5) = 35 + 21 = 56$.

   d. The general rule is $C(n, k) = C(n - 1, k - 1) + C(n - 1, k)$. For example, $C(10, 8) = C(9, 7) + C(9, 8)$. This general rule reflects the basic construction rule for Pascal's triangle that a given number in the triangle is the sum of the two numbers above it to the left and the right, as follows: $C(n, k)$ is entry k in row n; the number above it to the left is entry $k - 1$ in row $n - 1$, or $C(n - 1, k - 1)$; and the number above it to the right is entry k in row $n - 1$, or $C(n - 1, k)$.

6. In this problem, students learn about $C(n, k)$ in terms of subsets.

   a. Answers will vary. Other subsets of L include, for example, $\{v\}$, $\{v, x, z\}$, and $\{x, y, z\}$.

   b. The binary string 01011 corresponds to $\{w, y, z\}$; 11111 corresponds to $\{v, w, x, y, z\}$.

   c. The binary string 01010 represents the subset $\{w, y\}$, and 00000 represents the empty set. For the sets given as examples in part (*a*), 10000 represents $\{v\}$, 10101 represents $\{v, x, z\}$, and 00111 represents $\{x, y, z\}$.

   d. Subsets of L that contain three elements correspond to binary strings of length 5 that contain three 1s. The number of such strings is $C(5, 3)$, or 10, which is entry 3 in row 5 of Pascal's triangle.

   e. When students list the elements of L alphabetically—v, w, x, y, z—they can assign a binary string of length 5 to each subset of L by letting the first digit represent whether v is (1) or is not (0) in the subset, the second digit represent whether w is (1) or is not (0) in the subset, and so on. In this representation, the number of subsets containing k elements from a set with n elements is the number of binary strings of length n that contain k 1s, which, as students learned in problem 3, is $C(n, k)$.

7. In this problem, students learn the term combinations and learn more about combinations.

   a. $C(3, 2)$ is the number of subsets containing two elements chosen from a set with three elements.

   b. The number of different pizzas containing three of these toppings is $C(5, 3)$, or 10.

8. In this problem, students solve an applied problem and relate the problem to strings, paths, and $C(n, k)$.

   a. The string 01101111 represents {Bobbi, Caitlin, Earl, Floricel, Guillermo, Hilary}.

b. The string 01111110 represents the team when Amy and Hilary are not playing.

c. The number of different teams of six

= the number of strings of length 8 that include six 1s

= the number of subsets containing six elements from a set with eight elements

= the number of zigzag paths with eight hops, six of which are to the right

= entry 6 in row 8 of Pascal's triangle

= $C(8, 6)$

= 28.

9. Entry k in row n of Pascal's triangle

= the number of binary strings of length n containing k 1s

= the number of zigzag paths of length n containing k zigs to the right

= the number of subsets containing k elements from a set with n elements

= $C(n, k)$.

Solutions for "Combinations, Pascal's Triangle, and the Binomial Theorem"

1. *a.*

n	$(a + b)^n$	Expansion of $(a + b)^n$	Coefficients
0	$(a + b)^0$	1	1
1	$(a + b)^1$	$a + b$	1, 1
2	$(a + b)^2$	$a^2 + 2ab + b^2$	1, 2, 1
3	$(a + b)^3$	$a^3 + 3a^2b + 3ab^2 + b^3$	1, 3, 3, 1
4	$(a + b)^4$	$a^4 + 4a^3b + 6a^2b^2 + 4ab^3 + b^4$	1, 4, 6, 4, 1
5	$(a + b)^5$	$a^5 + 5a^4b + 10a^3b^2 + 10a^2b^3 + 5ab^4 + b^5$	1, 5, 10, 10, 5, 1

b. Patterns that students might notice in the exponents include the following: the sum of the exponents in each term is n, the exponents of a are decreasing, the exponents of b are increasing, and a "hidden" b^0 and a^0 occur at the beginning and end, respectively, of each expansion.

c. Patterns that students might notice in the coefficients include the following: the first and last coefficients are 1, the second and next-to-last coefficients are n, the method of finding the "middle" coefficients is to add the coefficients just above to the left and to the right, and the sum of the coefficients is 2^n.

d. $(a + b)^5 = a^5 + 5a^4b + 10a^3b^2 + 10a^2b^3 + 5ab^4 + b^5$.

2. *a.* Students should construct or obtain a copy of Pascal's triangle, including at least rows 0 to 5.

b. The coefficients in the table are the rows of Pascal's triangle.

c. The coefficient of the ab^2 term in the expansion of $(a + b)^3$ is the same as entry 2 in row 3 of Pascal's triangle. (Note that this coefficient is also the same as entry 1 in row 3. However, for consistency and ease of seeing and describing the connections between coefficients and entries in Pascal's triangle, it is useful to focus on the power of b.)

d. The coefficient of the a^2b^3 term in $(a + b)^5$ is 10, which is entry 3 in row 5 of Pascal's triangle. (It is also entry 2 in row 5, but focusing on the power of b is useful for the sake of consistency.)

e. In general, the coefficient of the $a^{n-k}b^k$ term in $(a + b)^n$ is the same as entry k in row n of Pascal's triangle. (Note that it is also the same as entry $n - k$ in row n.)

f. $(a + b)^6 = a^6 + 6a^5b + 15a^4b^2 + 20a^3b^3 + 15a^2b^4 + 6ab^5 + b^6$.

3. a. The students should obtain the following results:

  • $C(2, 0) = 1$, $C(2, 1) = 2$, $C(2, 2) = 1$.

  • $C(3, 0) = 1$, $C(3, 1) = 3$, $C(3, 2) = 3$, $C(3, 3) = 1$.

  • For $n = 4$, the result is 1, 4, 6, 4, 1.

b. The coefficients of $(a + b)^n$ are the combination numbers, $C(n, k)$, for $k = 0$ to $k = n$.

c. The coefficient of the ab^2 term in $(a + b)^3$ is $C(3, 2)$—and also $C(3, 1)$. For consistency, it is useful to focus on the power of b.

d. $C(5, 3)$ equals the coefficient of the a^2b^3 term in $(a + b)^5$, as does $C(5, 2)$, which students explore in problem 3(e).

e. $C(5, 3) = 10$
$$= C(5, 2)$$
$$= \text{the coefficient of the } a^2b^3 \text{ term}$$
$$= \text{the coefficient of the } a^3b^2 \text{ term.}$$

Reasons that students might give for this relationship include the symmetry in Pascal's triangle, the symmetry in the expansion of $(a + b)^n$, the formula for computing $C(n, k)$, the idea that choosing 3 from 5 is the same as not choosing 2 from 5, and the idea of choosing a's and b's for each term (see problem 4).

f. The coefficient of the $a^{n-k}b^k$ term in $(a + b)^n$ is $C(n, k)$ (and also $C(n, n - k)$).

4. a. A student who focused on a^{87} instead of b^{13} to find the coefficient of the $a^{87}b^{13}$ term in $(a + b)^{100}$ would think about multiplying by a in 87 of the 100 sets of parentheses and would therefore choose 87 sets of parentheses from the 100 sets of parentheses, a choice that corresponds to $C(100, 87)$.

b. To find the coefficient of the $a^{13}b^{87}$ term in $(a + b)^{100}$, a student could focus on a^{13} or on b^{87}. A student who focused on a^{13} would obtain $C(100, 13)$ as the coefficient, and a student who focused on b^{87} would obtain $C(100, 87)$ as the coefficient.

c. $C(100, 13) = C(100, 87)$ because both are the coefficient of the $a^{87}b^{13}$ term in $(a + b)^{13}$ and because both are the coefficient of the $a^{13}b^{87}$ term in $(a + b)^{100}$.

d. The coefficient of the $a^{n-k}b^k$ term in $(a + b)^n = C(n, k) = C(n, n - k)$.

5. a. If $n = 5$ in the binomial theorem, then $(a + b)^5 = a^5 + 5a^4b + 10a^3b^2 + 10a^2b^3 + 5ab^4 + b^5$.

b. If $n = 5$ and $b = -b$ in the binomial theorem, then $(a - b)^5 = a^5 - 5a^4b + 10a^3b^2 - 10a^2b^3 + 5ab^4 - b^5$.

c. If $a = x$, $b = 4$, and $n = 3$ in the binomial theorem, then $(x + 4)^3 = x^3 + 12x^2 + 48x + 64$.

d. If $n = 4$, $a = 4x$, and $b = 2y$ in the binomial theorem, then $(4x + 2y)^4 = 256x^4 + 512x^3y + 384x^2y^2 + 128xy^3 + 16y^4$.

6. a. $C(4, 2) = 6$. It is entry 2 in row 4 of Pascal's triangle; $C(5, 3) = C(5, 2) = 10$, which is both entry 2 and entry 3 in row 5 of Pascal's triangle.

b. $C(n, k)$ is entry k in row n of Pascal's triangle, as well as entry $(n - k)$ in row n.

c. Students can see a vertical line of symmetry in the binomial theorem by noticing that the coefficients are symmetrically placed in the formula, since $C(n, k) = C(n, n - k)$, and this relationship also creates the symmetry in

Pascal's triangle. Another related instance of symmetry occurs in the exponents. Students can see it by comparing the $a^{n-k}b^k$ term with its counterpart, the $a^k b^{n-k}$ term, noting that the exponents are switched for a and b and that both terms have the same coefficient—that is, $C(n, k) = C(n, n - k)$.

7. Students can think of $C(n, k)$ as an entry in Pascal's triangle (it is entry k in row n). Then $C(n - 1, k - 1)$ is the entry in the row just above, because of the $n - 1$, and just to the left, because of the $k - 1$. Similarly, $C(n - 1, k)$ is the entry in the row just above and to the right. Thus, they can visualize this combination property as a statement of the construction rule for Pascal's triangle.

8. *a.* For example, if $n = 6$ and $k = 4$, then

$$C(n, k) = (6, 4)$$
$$= 15;$$
$$C(n - 1, k - 1) = C(5, 3)$$
$$= 10;$$
$$C(n - 1, k) = C(5, 4)$$
$$= 5.$$

Therefore,

$$C(n, k) = C(6, 4)$$
$$= 15$$
$$= 10 + 5$$
$$= C(5, 3) + C(5, 4)$$
$$= C(n - 1, k - 1) + C(n - 1, k).$$

b.

$$C(n - 1, k - 1) + C(n - 1, k) = \frac{(n-1)!}{(k-1)!(n-1-k+1)!} + \frac{(n-1)!}{k!(n-1-k)!}$$

$$= \frac{(n-1)!}{(k-1)!(n-k)!} + \frac{(n-1)!}{k!(n-k-1)!}$$

$$= \frac{k(n-1)! + (n-k)(n-1)!}{k!(n-k)!}$$

$$= \frac{(n-1)!(k+n-k)}{k!(n-k)!}$$

$$= \frac{n(n-1)!}{k!(n-k)!}$$

$$= \frac{n!}{k!(n-k)!}$$

$$= C(n, k)$$

c.

	Explanation
$C(n, k)$ = number of k-element subsets of the set $\{1, 2, 3, …, n\}$	By the subset definition of $C(n, k)$
= [number of k-element subsets that include n] + [number of k-element subsets that do not include n]	n either is or is not in a given subset.
= [number of $(k - 1)$-element subsets of the set $\{1, 2, 3, …, n - 1\}$ (and automatically include n in each of these subsets)] + [number of k-element subsets of $\{1, 2, 3, …, n - 1\}$]]	k-element subsets that include n consist of $(k - 1)$-element subsets of $\{1, 2, 3, …, n - 1\}$ with n added, and k-element subsets that do not include n consist of k-element subsets of $\{1, 2, 3, …, n - 1\}$.
= $C(n - 1, k - 1) + C(n - 1, k)$	By the subset definitions, $C(n - 1, k - 1)$ is the number of $(k - 1)$-element subsets of $\{1, 2, 3, …, n - 1\}$, and $C(n - 1, k)$ is the number of k-element subsets of $\{1, 2, 3, …, n - 1\}$.

d. The combinatorial proof seems to relate more directly to the counting process. By contrast, the factorial proof is more algebraic. Different students may prefer different proofs.

9. The number of combinations is $C(n, k)$. Pascal's triangle is a triangular array of numbers. Each row of Pascal's triangle begins and ends with 1, and each inner entry is the sum of the two entries in the row above it to the left and to the right. The binomial theorem states how to expand a binomial expression of the form $(a + b)^n$. The basic connections among these three topics are shown in the following:

$$C(n, k) = \text{entry } k \text{ in row } n \text{ of Pascal's triangle}$$
$$= \text{the coefficient of the } a^{n-k}b^k \text{ term in } (a + b)^n.$$

Solutions for "Paths at Camp Graffinstuff"

In many instances, several answers are possible. Representative solutions are given in such cases.

1. *a.* An Euler path for Bay View Cabins is 3 1 2 3 4 5 6 7 5, and a Hamilton path is 2 1 3 4 5 6 7.

   b. An Euler circuit for Hillside Cabins is 1 3 7 6 8 10 7 9 12 13 11 8 5 2 4 1; neither a Hamilton path nor a Hamilton circuit exists.

   c. An Euler path for the frog pond is *A B C A D B*, a Hamilton circuit is *A D B C A*, and a Hamilton path is *A D B C*.

   d. Neither an Euler path nor an Euler circuit exists for the duck pond; a Hamilton circuit is *A B D F E C A*, and a Hamilton path is *A B D F E C*.

   e. An Euler circuit for the east playing field is *A F G H I D C H E G B E C B A*, a Hamilton circuit is *A F G E H I D C B A,* and a Hamilton path is *A F G E H I D C B.*

   f. No Euler path, Euler circuit, Hamilton path, or Hamilton circuit exists for the west playing field.

   g. An Euler circuit for the camp flag is *A D E H D M N C B F G I L J K H J I F E B A*, and a Hamilton path is *A B F G I L J K H E D M N C.*

2. *a.* Using method 1, the minimum lift method, for the 2 × 2 grid requires two lifts; a possible path is 7 1 8 3 10 5 11 4 12 6 *lift* 2 9 *lift.*

   Using method 2, the minimum retracing method, for the 2 × 2 grid requires two retracings, indicated in bold type in the following possible path: 7 1 8 3 10 5 11 **8** 2 9 4 **11** 6 12.

b. Using method 1 for the 3 × 3 grid requires four lifts; a possible path is 6 5 4 13 1 14 18 22 10 21 17 *lift* 7 8 9 20 16 3 2 *lift* 15 19 23 11 *lift* 12 24 *lift.*

Using method 2 for the 3 × 3 grid requires three retracings, indicated in bold type in the following possible path: 6 5 4 13 1 14 18 22 10 21 17 **17** 7 8 9 20 16 3 2 **2** 15 19 23 11 **11** 12 24.

c. Both methods give six as the minimum number of lifts or retracings for a 4 × 4 grid, so the groups tie.

d. Using method 1 for the 2 × 3 grid requires three lifts; a possible path is 10 1 11 4 14 7 15 5 16 8 *lift* 2 12 6 13 3 *lift* 9 17 *lift.*

Using method 2 for the 2 × 3 grid requires two retracings, indicated in bold type in the following possible path: 4 5 6 13 3 2 1 10 14 7 15 11 **2** 12 16 8 **8** 9 17.

Using method 1 for the 2 × 4 grid requires four lifts; a possible path is 8 7 6 5 13 1 14 19 9 18 *lift* 2 15 20 10 *lift* 11 21 16 3 *lift* 4 17 22 12 *lift.*

Using method 2 for the 2 × 4 grid requires four retracings, shown in bold type in the following possible path: 8 7 6 5 13 1 14 19 9 18 **5 14** 2 15 20 10 **10** 11 21 16 3 **3** 4 17 22 12.

e. Method 1 gives five lifts as minimum for a 2 × 5 grid, and method 2 gives four retracings, so group 2 wins.

3. a. With each camper indicated by his first initial, a Hamilton circuit for this problem is B H A E G F D C B. A Hamilton circuit can help solve this problem because each person (or vertex), other than the start and end, occurs exactly once, and the starting person must be the ending person.

b. The corresponding circular seating arrangement is shown at the right.

4. The square medallion does not satisfy the criteria. It does not have an Euler circuit, but it does have a Hamilton circuit: 5 6 7 9 12 11 8 10 3 4 2 1 5. The pentagonal medallion does satisfy the criteria. It has neither an Euler circuit nor a Hamilton circuit, although it does have a Hamilton path that is not a circuit: 6 10 7 8 9 4 5 3 1 2. Students should reach this conclusion by applying a systematic trial-and-error strategy.

Solutions for "The Sports Director's Dilemma"

Decisions … Decisions … Decisions at Camp Graffinstuff–Part 1

In many instances, several answers are possible. Representative solutions are given in such cases.

1–3. The following information describes an algorithm that students might construct. Vertices in the figure represent the sports, and an edge connecting two vertices indicates that at least one camper is interested in both sports. Different shapes in the figure correspond to different colors.

Step 1: The vertices (degrees) are as follows: A (4); BB (4); SO (4); SW (4); T (4); H (3); SB (1).

Step 2: A, BB, SO, SW, and T each have a degree of 4, so students must decide which one of them to color first. This example assumes that students decide to use the color gray—corresponding to a pentagon in the figure—for the first vertex—the vertex labeled "A" for "archery."

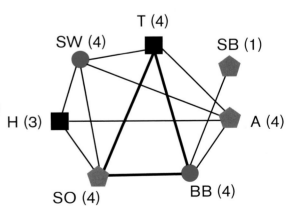

Step 3: Students should then use gray to color vertices that do not connect with A, but they should not color any vertex gray if an edge connects it to a vertex that they have previously colored gray. In the example, vertices SB and SO are gray.

Step 4: Students repeat the process from step 2, but they select a different color for vertices. In this example, BB, with degree 4, is turquoise (corresponding to the circle). SW does not connect to BB, so it is also turquoise. Although H does not connect to BB, students cannot color it turquoise because it connects to SW.

Step 5: Students again repeat the process from step 2. In this example, T, with degree 4, is black (corresponding to a square); and so is the remaining vertex, H, which does not connect to T.

This coloring plan uses three colors, but how can students determine that no other plan can use fewer colors? Students might recognize that they can form triangles in this graph (one triangle is shown with bold sides in the illustration), and a triangle requires three colors, since all three vertices are adjacent to one another.

4. *a.* Because the graph requires three colors, three time slots are necessary.

   b. The sports director can group the sports as follows:

   Time slot 1—A, SB, and SO; time slot 2—BB and SW; time slot 3—T and H.

   Because no edge connects SB to either T or H, the sports director can offer SB in time slot 3 rather than in time slot 1.

Solutions for "The Tour Director's Dilemma"

Decisions ... Decisions ... Decisions at Camp Graffinstuff—Part 2

1–3. The following information describes an algorithm that students might construct. Different shapes in the illustration correspond to different colors. Vertices correspond to the different tours, and the edges indicate that the connected tours have at least one stop in common.

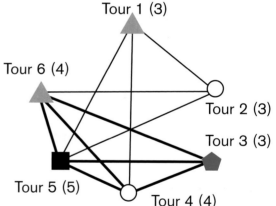

4. Step 1: The vertices (degrees) are as follows: tour 5 (5); tour 4 (4); tour 6 (4); tour 1 (3); tour 2 (3); tour 3 (3).

   Step 2: In this example, assume that students decide to use black (denoted by ■) to color the first vertex, tour 5, which has degree 5. Since edges connect tour 5 to all other vertices, no other vertex can be black.

   Step 3: Students repeat the process from step 2. Tour 4 and tour 6 each have a degree of 4. In the example, tour 4 (denoted by ○) is white. Because no edge connects tour 2 to tour 4, tour 2 can also be white. Because edges connect all other vertices to tour 4, no other vertex can be white.

   Step 4: Students again repeat the process from step 2. In this example, tour 6, with degree 4, is gray, denoted by the symbol ▲. Tour 1, which no edges connect to tour 6, is also gray. An edge connects tour 3 with tour 6, so tour 3 cannot be gray.

   Step 5: Since tour 3 is the last remaining uncolored vertex, it is turquoise, denoted by ⬠.

This coloring plan uses four colors. But students might use many other coloring strategies. How do they know for sure that no other coloring strategy can possibly use fewer than four colors? They might explain by noting that they need to use four colors because the graph contains a quadrilateral with both diagonals (shown in bold in the illustration). In such a configuration of vertices and edges, all four vertices are adjacent to all other vertices, and so four different colors are necessary.

5. a. Since the graph requires four colors, the minimum number of days needed to operate all tours is four days.

   b. The following tours can be on the same days: tours 1 and 6; tours 2 and 4. Tour 5 and tour 3 must operate on different days.

   c. In an alternative solution, the following tours can be on the same days: tours 1 and 3, and tours 2 and 4. Tour 5 and tour 6 must operate on different days.

Solutions for "The Bus Director's Dilemma"

Decisions … Decisions … Decisions at Camp Graffinstuff–Part 3

1. a. The minimum road count that meets the given conditions is seven.

   b. Three routes that have the minimum road count and start from TC are as follows:
   - TC-TS-MV-CG-WF-CW-MM-BB
   - TC-CG-WF-CW-MM-BB-MV-TS
   - TC-TS-MV-BB-MM-CW-WF-CG

   c. Three routes that have the minimum road count and start from CG are as follows:
   - CG-WF-CW-MM-BB-TS-TC-MV
   - CG-MV-TC-TS-BB-MM-CW-WF
   - CG-TC-MV-TS-BB-MM-CW-WF

   d. A route with the minimum road count of seven can start from any vertex. Students can visualize an eight-road count that connects all eight locations, beginning and ending at TC and visiting each location only once. Such a route is similar to a bracelet. If the route breaks at any point, it becomes a route that goes through every location once and has a road count of seven. Since the bus does not need to return to the initial location, it does not need to travel on the last road.

2. a. A route that starts at TC and ends at CG is TC-TS-MV-BB-MM-CW-WF-CG. It is a total of $3 + 4 + 9 + 5 + 9 + 8 + 4$, or 42, miles.

   b. A route that starts at CG and ends at WF is CG-TC-TS-MV-BB-MM-CW-WF. It is a total of $10 + 3 + 4 + 9 + 5 + 9 + 8$, or 48, miles.

   c. A route that starts at MM and ends at BB is MM-CW-WF-CG-MV-TC-TS-BB. It is a total of $9 + 8 + 4 + 7 + 6 + 3 + 7$, or 44, miles.

3. a. The total number of miles for all the roads on the map is 85 miles. The cost of painting a center stripe on all roads is $2125.

   $$10 + 9 + 9 + 8 + 7 + 7 + 6 + 6 + 5 + 4 + 4 + 4 + 3 + 3 = 85 \text{ miles}$$

   b. The path with the fewest miles is $3 + 3 + 4 + 4 + 4 + 5 + 7 = 30$ miles. The cost of painting a center stripe is $750.

   c and d. Step 1: Draw the eight vertices.

   Step 2: Arrange the road mileage from least to greatest: 3, 3, 4, 4, 4, 5, 6, 6, 7, 7, 8, 9, 9, 10.

   Step 3: Take a road with the fewest miles and draw the edge; it is three miles.

   Step 4: Continue taking roads and drawing edges with the fewest miles; remember that you do not want to form a circuit.

   Step 5: When drawing the seventh and last road, which is seven miles long, you can draw either of two possible edges. You can draw either the road between MV and CG or the road between TS and BB. Both sets of connected roads, shown in the following illustration, are minimum spanning trees.

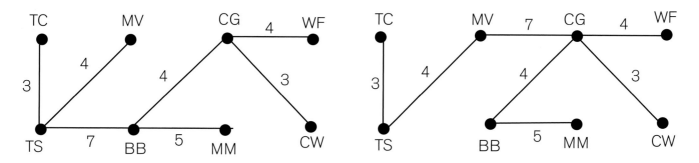

Solutions for "Planning a Festival"

Using Critical Paths to Schedule Large Projects–Part 1

1. Students' responses will vary. Possible tasks include choosing a date, finding a location, determining the main topics, finding speakers, choosing activities, designing a logo, and making arrangements for food.

2. *a.* An example of a task that is a prerequisite for another task is determining the main topics, which is a prerequisite for finding speakers.

   b. Two tasks that two different teams can work on at the same time are finding speakers and making arrangements for food.

3. *a.* Two different teams can work on tasks V and M at the same time.

   b. The earliest finish time (EFT) is 20 days.

   c. Rama has found the sum of all task times, Amy has found the length of the longest path through the graph, and Jocey has found the length of the shortest path. Amy's answer is correct.

   d. A critical path (longest path) is START-T-V-B-END.

   e. The length of the critical path is 20, which is also the EFT.

   f. The critical tasks are START, T, V, B, and END. If a critical task gets two days behind schedule, then the EFT increases by two days. If a noncritical task (for example, M) gets two days behind schedule, the EFT does not change. Note that a delay in a noncritical task can sometimes change the EFT, but not in this example.

   g. and *h.* In the following table, the times shown for the earliest start time (EST) and the latest start time (LST) can be read as "at the end of day *n*." The slack time is the "cushion" for each task, or the amount of "slack" in the schedule—that is, the amount of delay that is possible in starting the task while still finishing the whole project by the EFT. It makes sense to call (LST − EST) *slack time,* since it is the difference between the earliest possible time that the task can begin and the latest time that the task can begin and still keep the whole project on schedule.

Task	Earliest Start Time (EST)	Latest Start Time (LST)	Slack Time
T	0	0	0
V	3	3	0
M	3	7	4
B	11	11	0

Solutions for "Building a House"

Using Critical Paths to Schedule Large Projects–Part 2

1. *a.* A digraph for the house-building project follows:

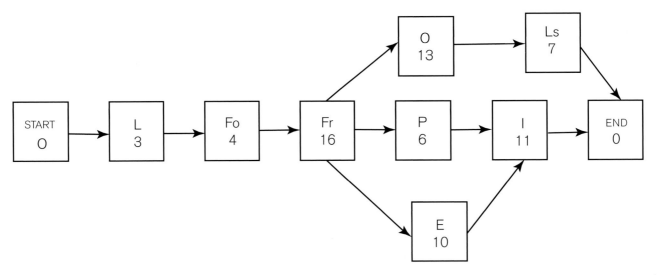

b. The three paths are as follows: START-L-Fo-Fr-O-Ls-END (length = 43), START-L-Fo-Fr-P-I-END (length = 40), START-L-Fo-Fr-E-I-END (length = 44).

c. A critical path is Start-L-Fo-Fr-E-I-END.

d. The EFT is 44 days.

2. a. A two-day foundation delay makes the EFT two days longer, but the critical path remains the same.

b. A two-day plumbing delay causes no change in the EFT or the critical path. (Note, however, that a five-day plumbing delay creates a new critical path and new EFT of forty-five days. The important factor in this situation is that plumbing has a slack time of four days.)

c. A one-day landscaping delay causes no change in the EFT, but two critical paths then exist—the original path and START-L-Fo-Fr-O-Ls-END.

d. A two-day landscaping delay makes the EFT one day longer, and the only critical path is then START-L-Fo-Fr-O-Ls-END.

e. Students should summarize what they have learned in problems 2(a) to 2(d). Delays on a critical path increase the EFT and the length of the critical path, but the vertices that compose the critical path remain the same. A delay off a critical path may or may not affect the EFT and critical path, depending on how the length of the delay compares with the task's slack time. There may be no change in either the EFT or the critical path (delay is less than slack time; see problem 2[b]). The EFT may not change, but there could be a critical-path change (delay is equal to slack time; see problem 2[c]). Or both the EFT and critical path may change (delay is greater than slack time; see problem 2[d]).

3. The following table shows the EST and LST for each task. Students should recognize that the times for EST and LST refer to the end of day n. They should describe how they determined the EST and the LST. They may describe the procedures given on pages 68–69. The most complicated procedure is finding the LST for noncritical tasks. However, in this relatively simple example, students will probably just describe their method for each individual task. For example, the length of the path from task O to END is 20. Since the EFT at the END is 44, task O cannot start any later than $44 - 20 = 24$. Thus, the LST for task O is 24.

Task	Earliest Start Time (EST)	Latest Start Time (LST)	Slack Time
L	0	0	0
Fo	3	3	0
Fr	7	7	0
E	23	23	0
P	23	27	4
O	23	24	1
I	33	33	0
Ls	36	37	1

Solutions for "Who Is the Winner?"

1. A round-robin tournament with four players has six matches. Students' explanations may vary. One explanation is that each of the four players plays the other three, which results in 4 × 3 = 12 matches. Since this process counts each match twice, division by 2 is necessary, so the number of matches played is six.

2. The following vertex-edge graphs represent the information in the matrices.

3. With the players indicated by their first initials, the Hamilton path in the boys' graph is F-S-C-B. The girls' graph has the following Hamilton paths: C-A-M-N, A-M-N-C, A-N-C-M, N-C-A-M, M-N-C-A.

4. The single Hamilton path in the boys' graph yields a clear ranking: F-S-C-B. In the girls' graph, there are five Hamilton paths, so the ranking is unclear. One resolution is to use the matrix method in problem 5. An alternative is to consider that A and C each won two matches and C beat A, and that N and M each won one match and M beat N. Thus, a possible ranking is C-A-M-N.

5. *a.* The row sums for the boys are as follows: C-1, S-2, F-3, B-0. These sums give a ranking of F-S-C-B, which is the same ranking obtained by using Hamilton paths. Again, no ambiguity occurs in the boys' rankings. The row sums for the girls are as follows: C-2, A-2, N-1, M-1. These sums do not yield a clear ranking, since C and A, both with 2, appear to be tied; and N and M, both with 1, also appear to be tied. However, these results do indicate that C and A should be ranked above N and M.

   b. The square of the girls' matrix is as follows:

   $$G^2 = \begin{bmatrix} 0 & 0 & 2 & 1 \\ 1 & 0 & 1 & 0 \\ 0 & 1 & 0 & 1 \\ 1 & 0 & 0 & 0 \end{bmatrix}.$$

   The entries are the numbers of paths of length 2, or "two-stage wins." The row sums are as follows: C-3, A-2, N-2, M-1. Comparing the row sums of the square of the girls' matrix with the original row sums can resolve the ties between C and A and between N and M. Using both sets of row sums results in a ranking of C-A-N-M.

   c. The ranking in problem 5 differs from the possible ranking given in problem 4 because it reverses M and N. One justification for this reversal is that N beat C, who is the tournament winner, so perhaps N deserves to be ranked above M. Students may have other comments. For example, they may argue for ranking M above N, since M beat N in a head-to-head match. See the discussion on pages 72–73 for more information about this ranking problem.

6. (Extension) Solutions depend on the students' reasoning and the latest ATP Masters Cup results.

Solutions for "The Traveling Salesman Problem (TSP)"

1. The vertex-edge graph on the right represents the information in a matrix.

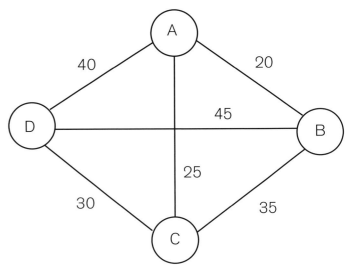

2. The six possible circuits are ABCDA, ABDCA, ACBDA, ACDBA, ADBCA, and ADCBA. Some pairs—for example, ABCDA and ADCBA—are simply the reverse of each other; there are only three circuits with different edges. Students explicitly confront this issue in problem 3.

3. ABCDA and ADCBA are two circuits that use the same edges but in reverse order.

4. The lengths of the three Hamilton circuits that use different edges are as follows: ABCDA is 125 miles, ABDCA is 120 miles, and ACBDA is 145 miles.

5. The shortest route, and thus the solution to this example of the TSP, is ABDCA, which is 120 miles. The reverse circuit, ACDBA, is also correct.

6. *a.* Students' answers will vary. They may think that a computer could check all possible Hamilton circuits and solve the problem quickly.

   b. The number of four-city routes is $24 \times 23 \times 22$, or 12,144. The number of 25-city circuits is 24!.

   c. A computer that can check 70 trillion circuits each second would need about 281 years to check all the circuits. This example indicates the limitations of computers and brute-force methods. Some students may relate this problem to previous problems in this investigation and suggest that the number of circuits is 24!/2, which yields half the time. That answer is also acceptable.

Solutions for "Looking at Square Tiles from All Angles"

Targeting Squares—Part 1

1. Each new design consists of the design preceding it with a new row added at the bottom. The next two designs in the sequence are as follows:

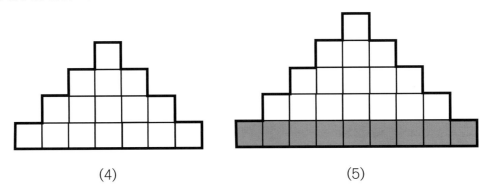

(4)   (5)

2. *a.*

Design *n*	1	2	3	4	5	6	7	8	9	10
Area a_n	1	4	9	16	25	36	49	64	81	100

b. $a_1 = 1$;

$a_2 = 4 = 1 + 3 = a_1 + (2 \cdot 2 - 1)$;

$a_3 = 9 = 4 + 5 = a_2 + (2 \cdot 3 - 1)$.

The recursive formula for the nth area is $a_1 = 1$, $a_n = a_{n-1} + (2 \cdot n - 1)$, for $n \geq 2$.

c. The explicit formula for the nth area is $a_n = n^2$, for $n \geq 1$. To use the tiles to justify this answer, students can begin by partitioning the tile designs as shown in the following diagram. Then they can rotate the left-hand section of the design, demonstrating that it fits next to the right-hand section so that the two parts of the design form a square.

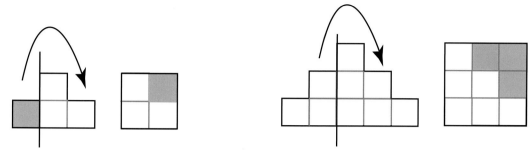

3. a.

Design n	1	2	3	4	5	6	7	8	9	10
Perimeter p_n	4	10	16	22	28	34	40	46	52	58

b. The recursive formula for the nth perimeter is $p_1 = 4$, $p_n = p_{n-1} + 6$, for $n \geq 2$.

c.

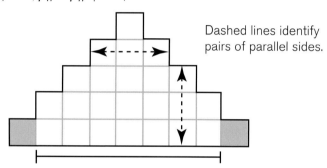

Dashed lines identify pairs of parallel sides.

$$p_1 = 4;$$
$$p_2 = 10 = 4 + 6 = (4 + 0 \cdot 6) + 6 = 4 + 1 \cdot 6;$$
$$p_3 = 16 = 10 + 6 = (4 + 1 \cdot 6) + 6 = 4 + 2 \cdot 6;$$
$$p_4 = 22 = 16 + 6 = (4 + 2 \cdot 6) + 6 = 4 + 3 \cdot 6;$$
$$p_n = 4 + (n - 1)6 = 6n - 2, \text{ for } n \geq 1.$$

In these designs, the perimeter of each new design is $3 + 3$, or 6, units longer than the one preceding it. Alternatively, the $(3n - 1)$ pairs of parallel sides (see the illustration above) each have a length of 1. The perimeter p_n therefore equals $2(3n - 1) = 6n - 2$.

4. a.

Design n	1	2	3	4	5	6	7	8	9	10
Right-angle count r_n	4	6	8	10	12	14	16	18	20	22

b. Each new tile design consists of the preceding design with a row of tiles added at the bottom. There is a loss of two right angles from the preceding design and a gain of four right angles in the new row, for a net gain of two right angles. A recursive formula for the right-angle count is $r_1 = 4$, $r_n = r_{n-1} + 2$, for $n \geq 2$.

c. An explicit formula for the nth right-angle count is $r_n = 2n + 2$, for $n \geq 1$. Two right angles occur in the end squares at each level (or step), and the number of levels is n. In addition to these right angles, two right angles occur at the base of the end squares on the longest level (base step). The right-angle count is therefore $2n + 2$.

5. *a.*

Design n	1		3	4	5	6	7	8	9	10
1×2 rectangle count t_n	0	1	4	9	16	25	36	49	64	81

b. 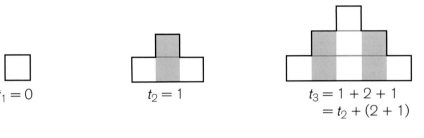 is a 1×2 rectangle. The numbers in the following sums represent the number of 1×2 rectangles in the corresponding column of the design.

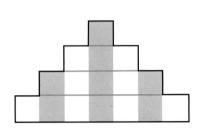

$t_1 = 0$ $t_2 = 1$ $t_3 = 1 + 2 + 1$
$= t_2 + (2 + 1)$

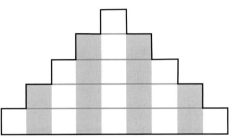

$$t_4 = 1 + 2 + 3 + 2 + 1 \qquad\qquad t_5 = 1 + 2 + 3 + 4 + 3 + 2 + 1$$
$$= t_3 + (3 + 2) \qquad\qquad\qquad = t_4 + (4 + 3)$$

The recursive formula is $t_n = t_{n-1} + (n - 1) + (n - 2) = t_{n-1} + (2n - 3)$, for $n \geq 2$, with $t_1 = 0$.

c. The data from part 5(*b*) indicate the following:

$t_1 = 0$;

$t_2 = 1$;

$$t_3 = 1 + 2 + 1 \qquad\qquad = (1 + 1) + 2 \qquad\qquad = 2 \cdot 2 \quad = 4;$$
$$t_4 = 1 + 2 + 3 + 2 + 1 \qquad = (1 + 2) + (2 + 1) + 3 \qquad = 3 \cdot 3 \quad = 9;$$
$$t_5 = 1 + 2 + 3 + 4 + 3 + 2 + 1 \quad = (1 + 3) + (2 + 2) + (3 + 1) + 4 \quad = 4 \cdot 4 \quad = 16;$$

The explicit formula is $t_n = (n - 1)^2$, for $n \geq 1$.

6. Students' answers will vary.

Solutions for "Squares around the Triangle?"

Targeting Squares–Part 2

1. The next two designs in the sequence are as shown:

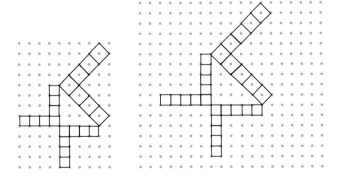

2. a.

Design n	1	2	3	4	5	6	7	8	9	10
Small-square count s_n	2	6	10	14	18	22	26	30	34	38

b. Each new design adds one small square to each end of the two **L** shapes, for a total of four additional small squares. The recursive formula for the small-square count is $s_1 = 2$, $s_n = s_{n-1} + 4$, for $n \geq 2$.

c. The explicit formula for the small-square count is $s_n = 4n - 2$, for $n \geq 1$. In the nth design, n small squares are in a strip along each leg of the right triangle. In addition, n small squares are in a strip perpendicular to each of these two strips, overlapping on one of the small squares. In all, the number of small squares is $(2)(2n - 1)$, or $4n - 2$. Other reasoning is possible. For example, in the nth design, the four strips each have n small squares. Since this method counts the two corner squares twice, the total is $4n - 2$.

3. a.

Design n	1	2	3	4	5	6	7	8	9	10
Large-square count S_n	1	3	5	7	9	11	13	15	17	19

b. Each new design adds one large square to each end of the **L** shape, for a total of two more large squares. A recursive formula for the large-square count S_n is $S_1 = 1$, $S_n = S_{n-1} + 2$, for $n \geq 2$.

c. An explicit formula for the large-square count S_n is $S_n = 2n - 1$, for $n \geq 1$. In the nth design, n large squares are in a strip along the hypotenuse of the right triangle. That same number of large squares is on the strip perpendicular to this strip and overlapping one of the large squares. In all, the number of large squares is $2n - 1$.

4. a.

Design n	1	2	3	4	5	6	7	8	9	10
Area t_n	$\frac{1}{2}$	$\frac{4}{2}$	$\frac{9}{2}$	$\frac{16}{2}$	$\frac{25}{2}$	$\frac{36}{2}$	$\frac{49}{2}$	$\frac{64}{2}$	$\frac{81}{2}$	$\frac{100}{2}$

b. The following figures can help explain how to express the area of each new right triangle in terms of the one preceding it:

The recursive formula is $t_1 = \dfrac{1}{2}, t_n = t_{n-1} + (2n - 1)\dfrac{1}{2},$ for $n \geq 2$.

$$t_1 = \frac{1}{2} \qquad t_2 = t_1 + 3 \cdot \frac{1}{2} \qquad t_3 = t_2 + 5 \cdot \frac{1}{2} \qquad t_4 = t_3 + 7 \cdot \frac{1}{2}$$

c. The pattern in the table in question 4(a) implies that the explicit formula is $t_n = n^2/2$, for $n \geq 1$; t_n is one-half the area of the square whose side is n.

5. a.

Each large square region has an area of two square units, which equals four triangular regions, each with an area of $1/2$.

b.

Design n	1	2	3	4	5	6	7	8	9	10
Area A_n	2	6	10	14	18	22	26	30	34	38

c. Each new design has two more large squares than the one preceding it. Therefore, each new design has an area that is 4 square units larger than the one preceding it. The recursive formula is $A_1 = 2$, $A_n = A_{n-1} + 4$, for $n \geq 2$.

d. $A_1 = 2$;
$A_2 = 6 = A_1 + 4 = 2 + 1 \cdot 4$;
$A_3 = 10 = A_2 + 4 = (2 + 1 \cdot 4) + 4 = 2 + 2 \cdot 4$;
$A_4 = 14 = A_3 + 4 = (2 + 2 \cdot 4) + 4 = 2 + 3 \cdot 4$;

The explicit formula is $A_n = 2 + (n - 1)4 = 4n - 2$, for $n \geq 1$.

Also, note the following:

$A_1 = 2 = 2 \cdot 1$;
$A_2 = 6 = 2 \cdot 3$;
$A_3 = 10 = 2 \cdot 5$;
$A_4 = 14 = 2 \cdot 7$, with $A_n = 2 \cdot (2n - 1) = 4n - 2$, for $n \geq 1$.

e. The number of small squares is twice the number of large squares. But two small squares equal one large square in area. The two sums are therefore the same. The sum of the areas of the shapes on the legs of the right triangle equals the area of the shape on the hypotenuse of the right triangle. Students may note the similarity to the Pythagorean theorem.

Solutions for "Investing with Lotta Cash"

The computations below ignore leap years. Students' solutions may vary slightly, depending on their computations and rounding.

1. a.

End of year n	1	2	3	4	5	6	7	8
Lotta's age	13	14	15	16	17	18	19	20
Amount in account	2080.00	2163.20	2249.73	2339.72	2433.31	2530.64	2631.86	2737.14

b. The account balance on Lotta's seventeenth birthday is $2433.31.

c. The account balance on Lotta's twentieth birthday is $2737.14.

d. At the end of the first year, the balance in the account is ($2000)(1.04). To find the balance at the end of the second year, students can multiply that product by 1.04. They can continue multiplying each product by 1.04 for each subsequent year. The account balance on Lotta's twentieth birthday is $2737.14.

e. The initial balance, b_0, is $2000.

$b_0 = 2000$;
$b_1 = (2000)(1.04) = (b_0)(1.04)$;
$b_2 = (b_1)(1.04)$;
$b_3 = (b_2)(1.04)$;
$b_4 = (b_3)(1.04)$.

The recursive formula is $b_n = (b_{n-1})(1.04)$, for $n \geq 1$, with $b_0 = 2000$.

2. Students might use any of the following methods for solving problem 1 with a graphing calculator.

- *First method:* Compute ($2000)(1.04) for the balance at the end of the first year. Multiply that result, $2080, by 1.04 again for the following year. Pressing the **ENTER** key on the graphing calculator then gives the balance for each subsequent year.

- *Second method:* Set the calculator to the **SEQUENCE** mode. In the **y=** window, set **nMin = 0; u(n) = u(n − 1)(1.04); u(nMin) = {2000}**. In the **TBLSET** window, set **TblStart=0, ΔTbl = 1**, and press the **TABLE** key to see the results.

- *Third method:* Use the **FUNCTION** mode with $y_1 = (2000)(1.04)^x$ to find each year's balance.

3.

First Year Quarters	First Quarter	Second Quarter	Third Quarter	Fourth Quarter
Amount in account at end of each quarter	2020.00 = $(2000)(1.01)$	2040.20 = $(2000)(1.01)^2$	2060.60 = $(2000)(1.01)^3$	2081.21 = $(2000)(1.01)^4$

The following table shows data for problems 1, 4, and 5.

Year	Lotta's Age	(1) Balance with 4% Interest Compounded Yearly $P(1.04)^n$	(4) Balance with 4% Interest Compounded Quarterly $P((1 + 0.04/4)^4)^n = P(1.01)^{4n}$	(5) Balance with 4% Interest Compounded Daily $P((1 + 0.04/365)^{365})^n = P(1.00010958)^{365n}$
0	12	2000.00	2000.00	2000.00
1	13	2080.00	2081.21	2081.62
2	14	2163.20	2165.71	2166.56
3	15	2249.73	2253.65	2254.98
4	16	2339.72	2345.16	2347.00
5	17	2433.31	2440.38	2442.78
6	18	2530.64	2539.47	2542.46
7	19	2631.86	2642.58	2646.22
8	20	2737.14	2749.88	2754.21

4. *b.* With quarterly compounding, the balance in Lotta's account on her seventeenth birthday is $2440.38.

  c. With quarterly compounding, the balance in Lotta's account on her twentieth birthday is $2749.88.

  d. Students can use any of several strategies to complete the table. One strategy is to start with 2000, then multiply that result by 1.01 to find the balance after one quarter, then multiply that result by 1.01 to get the balance after two quarters. Students can carry out this strategy quickly by using the **ENTER** or **ANS** keys on a graphing calculator. Every four such computations give the balance at the end of the following year. Another strategy is to start with $(2000)(1.01)^4$ for the end of the first year. For the end of the second year, students multiply that product by $(1.01)^4$, which equals 1.040604, for the end of year 2. They continue multiplying each product by 1.040604 for each subsequent year.

  e. The recursive formula for the bank balance at the end of year n is
  $$B_0 = 2000, B_n = B_{n-1} \cdot (1.01)^4 = B_{n-1} \cdot 1.040604, \text{ for } n \ge 1.$$

5. *b.* With daily compounding, the balance in Lotta's account on her seventeenth birthday is $2442.78.

  c. With daily compounding, the balance in Lotta's account on her twentieth birthday is $2754.21.

  d. Students should start with $(2000)(1 + 0.04/365)^{365}$ for the end of the first year. They then multiply that product by $(1 + 0.04/365)^{365}$, which equals 1.0408084, for the end of the second year. They continue multiplying each product by 1.0408084 for each subsequent year.

  e. An explicit expression for the bank balance at the end of year n is $B_n = 2000((1 + 0.04/365)^{365})^n$, for $n \ge 1$.

6. Lotta's money will double in the eighteenth year. Students can use trial and error to answer this question. The following shows a more formal method of arriving at the result:

$P(1.04)^n = 2P$, where P is the initial amount;

$(1.04)^n = 2$;

$n \log 1.04 = \log 2$;

$n = (\log 2)/(\log 1.04) \approx 18$.

7. *a.* The following table shows the bank balances when Lotta receives an additional $1000 gift for her sixteenth birthday.

Year n	Lotta's Age	Balance with 4% Interest Compounded Yearly $P(1.04)^n$	Balance with 4% Interest Compounded Quarterly $P((1 + 0.04/4)^4)^n$ $= P(1.01)^{4n}$	Balance with 4% Interest Compounded Daily $P((1 + 0.04/365)^{365})^n$ $= P(1.00010958)^{365n}$
0	16	$1000 + 2339.72$ $= 3339.72^*$	3345.16^*	3347.00^*
1	17	3473.31	3480.98	3483.59
2	18	3612.24	3622.33	3625.75
3	19	3756.73	3769.41	3773.71
4	20	3907.00	3922.46	3927.71

* The starting amounts for year 0 are the result of adding $1000 to the amount on the line for year 4 (age 16) in the tables for problems 1, 4, and 5.

b. None of the three interest options results in Lotta's having $4000 on her twentieth birthday.

Solutions for "A Constant Rate of Change"

A Recursive View of Some Common Functions—Part 1

1. Students' answers will vary; they might observe that the numbers in the *x*-column increase by 1 or that the numbers in the *y*-column increase by 3, or they might describe the *x*-*y*-pattern as $y = 3x + 4$.

2. The NEXT-NOW equation that describes the pattern in the *y*-values is NEXT = NOW + 3.

3. The $y = \ldots$ equation that shows the relationship between *x* and the corresponding *y* is $y = 3x + 4$.

4. The table and equations represent a linear function. The following are characteristics of linear functions: their graphs are straight lines, they have a constant slope, they have a constant rate of change, they have no powers (other than 1) of *x* in the $y = \ldots$ equation, and they have an added constant in the NEXT-NOW equation.

5. The graph is a straight line with a slope of 3. It crosses the *y*-axis at $y = 4$, as shown.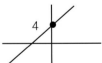

6. The table shows the constant rate of change of *y* with respect to *x* in the following way: As the *x*-values increase by 1, the *y*-values increase by 3.

7. In the equation NEXT = NOW + 3, the added constant, 3, is the slope and constant rate of change. In the equation $y = 3x + 4$, the coefficient of *x*, or 3, is the slope and constant rate of change. Students should circle the number 3 in each equation. Students will probably believe that the slope and constant rate of change are more directly and meaningfully shown in the NEXT-NOW equation.

8. Students should look back, summarize, and explain their work. You might ask your students to use their summaries and explanations as the basis for class discussion or reports.

Solutions for "A Constant Multiplier"

A Recursive View of Some Common Functions—Part 2

1. Students' answers will vary. Students might notice that the numbers in the *x*-column increase by adding 1 each

time or that the numbers in the *y*-column increase by multiplying by 3 each time, or they might describe the *x-y*-pattern as $y = 4 \cdot 3^x$.

2. The NEXT-NOW equation that describes the pattern in the *y*-values is NEXT = NOW • 3.

3. The $y = \ldots$ equation that shows the relationship between *x* and the corresponding *y* is $y = 4 \cdot 3^x$.

4. The table and equations represent an exponential function. The characteristics of this function include a non-constant rate of change, a nonlinear graph, a constant multiplier in the NEXT-NOW equation, and *x* as an exponent in the $y = \ldots$ equation.

5. The graph is not linear, so it does not have constant slope, and the rate of change of *y* with respect to *x* is not constant, as shown in the sketch.

In their explanations, students might refer to the nonlinear shape of the graph by noting that for a constant horizontal increment of *x* at different locations along the *x*-axis, the corresponding vertical increment of *y* is not constant.

6. The table depicts the constant multiplier in the following way: As the *x*-values increase by 1, the *y*-values are sequentially multiplied by 3.

7. The NEXT-NOW equation clearly shows the constant multiplier. In the $y = \ldots$ equation, it is the base of the exponential expression. Students should circle the number 3 in each equation. They will probably believe that the NEXT-NOW equation more clearly and meaningfully shows the constant multiplier.

8. Students should look back, summarize, and explain their work. You might ask your students to use their summaries and explanations as the basis for class discussions or reports.

9. *a.* A similarity is the constant 3 in each equation. The important difference that the students should note is that in the NEXT-NOW equation in "A Constant Rate of Change," they add 3, but in the NEXT-NOW equation in "A Constant Multiplier," they multiply by 3.

   b. Students should recognize that in the equation NEXT = NOW + 3, they add 3 each time. Since repeated addition is actually multiplication, this process yields 3*x* in the $y = \ldots$ equation. In the equation NEXT = NOW × 3, they multiply by 3 each time. Since repeated multiplication is actually exponentiation, this process yields 3^x in the $y = \ldots$ equation.

   c. Students should understand that in the graph associated with the equation NEXT = NOW + 3, adding 3 each time leads to a graph that is a straight line; by contrast, the graph associated with the equation NEXT = NOW × 3 is nonlinear.

   d. Students should understand that the tables clearly show the difference. In the table for the equation NEXT = NOW + 3, they add 3 each time to find the sequence of *y*-values; in the table for the equation NEXT = NOW × 3, they multiply by 3 each time.

10. *a.* The word *combined* indicates that this process is a combination of addition and multiplication by a constant.

   b. (Optional) The applet-based activity on the CD-ROM guides students in investigating a combined recursive formula.

Solutions for "A Recursive View of Skydiving"

1 and 2. Instantaneous Speed

   Acceleration caused by gravity is 32 ft/sec², and students are ignoring all other factors for the sake of simplicity. Thus, they assume that a skydiver's instantaneous speed increases by 32 ft/sec each second. At time $n = 1$ sec, the speed is 32 ft/sec; and at time $n = 2$ sec, the speed is 64 ft/sec.

   Average Speed

   Speed is a linear function of time, and instantaneous speed $= 32t$ ft/sec, which is a linear function of time, so the average speed between any two times is the average of the instantaneous speeds at the two times. Thus, the average speed during the first second is the average of the speeds at time $n = 0$ sec and at time $n = 1$

sec, which is the average of 0 ft/sec and 32 ft/sec, or 16 ft/sec. Likewise, the average speed during the second second is the average of the speeds at time $n = 1$ sec and at time $n = 2$ sec, which is the average of 32 ft/sec and 64 ft/sec, or 48 ft/sec.

Distance Fallen
The distance that the skydiver falls during each second is simply the average speed for that second multiplied by 1 (the number of seconds). The distance that the skydiver falls during the first second is 16 ft/sec × 1 sec, or 16 ft; and the distance that the skydiver falls during the second second is 48 ft/sec × 1 sec, or 48 ft.

Total Distance Fallen
The total distance that the skydiver has fallen after 1 second is the same as the distance that the skydiver fell during the first second, which is 16 ft. The total distance that the skydiver has fallen after two seconds is the distance that the skydiver fell during the first second plus the distance that the skydiver fell during the second second, which is 16 ft + 48 ft, or 64 ft.

3. The completed table through time $n = 4$ sec is as follows:

Time n in Seconds	Instantaneous Speed at Time n	Average Speed during Each Second	Distance Fallen during Each Second $D(n)$	Total Distance Fallen after n Seconds $T(n)$
0	0	0	0	0
1 sec	32 ft/sec	16 ft/sec	16 ft	16 ft
2 sec	64 ft/sec	48 ft/sec	48 ft	64 ft
3 sec	96 ft/sec	80 ft/sec	80 ft	144 ft
4 sec	128 ft/sec	112 ft/sec	112 ft	256 ft

4. *a.* The equation for NEXT in terms of NOW is NEXT = NOW + 32.

   b. The equation for $D(n)$ in terms of $D(n - 1)$ is
   $$D(n) = D(n - 1) + 32.$$

   c. The equation for $D(n)$ in terms of n is
   $$D(n) = 16 + 32(n - 1) = 32n - 16.$$

5. *a.* Students might say that $T(3)$, the total distance that the skydiver has fallen after three seconds, is the distance that the skydiver has fallen after two seconds plus the distance that the skydiver fell during the third second, or 64 ft + 80 ft, or 144 ft.

   b. Students' answers will vary. They might say that $T(n)$ is the distance that the skydiver has fallen after $n - 1$ seconds plus the distance that the skydiver fell during the nth second or that $T(n)$ is the sum of the distances that the skydiver has fallen during each second through the nth second.

   c. A formula for $T(n)$ in terms of $T(n) - 1$ and $D(n)$ is
   $$T(n) = T(n - 1) + D(n).$$
   Combining this equation with the formula for $D(n)$ in question 4(*c*) gives the following result:
   $$T(n) = T(n - 1) + D(n) = T(n - 1) + 32n - 16.$$
   Students revisit this formula in problem 8(*a*).

6. *a.* Students should examine and explain this method of computing $T(n)$ if they did not do so in their answer to question 5(*b*).

   b.
   $$T(n) = \text{sum of the arithmetic sequence}$$
   $$= D(1) + D(2) + \ldots + D(n)$$
   $$= 16 + 48 + \ldots (32n - 16)$$
   $$= \frac{\left(16 + (32n - 16)\right)(n)}{2}$$
   $$= 16n^2 \text{ ft}$$

7. *a.* The completed table is as follows:

Navigating through Discrete Mathematics in Grades 6–12

n	$T(n)$	First Differences	Second Differences
1	16	–	–
2	64	$64 - 16 = 48$	–
3	144	$144 - 64 = 80$	$80 - 48 = 32$
4	256	$256 - 144 = 112$	$112 - 80 = 32$
5	400	$400 - 256 = 144$	$144 - 112 = 32$

b. The pattern in the second-differences column is that all entries are the same constant, 32.

c. For $n = 1$, the original skydiver table indicates that $T(1) = 16$. The general form for $T(n)$ indicates that $T(1) = a(1^2) + b(1) + c$, so $16 = a + b + c$.

For $n = 2$, the original skydiver table indicates that $T(2) = 64$. The general form for $T(n)$ indicates that $T(2) = a(2^2) + b(2) + c$, so $64 = 4a + 2b + c$. Similar reasoning yields the equation for $n = 3$.

d. The entries in the leftmost matrix are the coefficients of the three expressions on the right side of the three equations in part (*c*) of this problem. The entries in the middle matrix are the variables from the equations in part (*c*). The entries in the rightmost matrix are the three constants on the left side of the three equations in part (*c*). This matrix equation is equivalent to the system of three equations in part (*c*) because the result of the indicated matrix multiplication is the three equations.

e. Using a calculator to find the inverse matrix and carry out the multiplication yields the following:

$$\begin{bmatrix} a \\ b \\ c \end{bmatrix} = \begin{bmatrix} .5 & -1 & .5 \\ -2.5 & 4 & 1.5 \\ 3 & -3 & 1 \end{bmatrix} \begin{bmatrix} 16 \\ 64 \\ 144 \end{bmatrix} = \begin{bmatrix} 16 \\ 0 \\ 0 \end{bmatrix}.$$

Therefore, $a = 16$ and $b = c = 0$.

f. The formula for $T(n)$ is

$$\begin{aligned} T(n) &= an^2 + bn + c \\ &= 16n^2 + 0 + 0 \\ &= 16n^2. \end{aligned}$$

g. Evaluating $T(n) = 16n^2$ for $n = 1, 2, 3, 4,$ and 5 yields the same values as those in the tables.

h. Students should obtain the same solution that they found in part (*f*).

8. *a.* The recursive formula for $A(n)$ has a corresponding explicit formula that is an exponential function. A linear function corresponds to $B(n)$, and a quadratic function corresponds to $C(n)$.

b. (Optional) The applet-based activity on the CD-ROM guides students in investigating a combined recursive formula.

Solutions for "A Recursive View of Proof by Mathematical Induction"

1. This statement is designed to stimulate discussion about whether statements are true and how to tell whether they are true.

a. The statement is true for $n = 0$, $n = 1$, and $n = 2$.

b. Students should try several other values of n. They will probably try small values and find that $n^2 - n + 41$ generates prime numbers.

c. Students' responses will vary. If students found a value of n that does not yield a prime number, then they can conclude that the statement is false. If all values of n that they tried yielded prime numbers, then they should explain whether and why they believe that the statement is true for all nonnegative integers.

d. The equation $n = 41$ yields $(41)^2$, which clearly is not prime, since it factors as 41×41.

2. When students use any positive integral power of 41 or any positive multiples of 41 for n, $n^2 - n + 41$ is not prime.

3. Students should carefully explain the domino analogy in this problem.

   a. Setting up the dominoes so that whenever a given domino falls over, its fall makes the next domino fall over is analogous to stating that whenever $S(n - 1)$ is true, $S(n)$ is true.

   b. Knocking over the first domino is analogous to saying that $S(n)$ is true for the first value of n, which is n_0.

   c. In the domino analogy, the conclusion is that all the dominoes fall. In the principle of mathematical induction, the conclusion is that $S(n)$ is true for all $n \geq n_0$.

4. Students should systematically record their results. This skill is an important one to develop, so let them build and organize their own tables. (You can create a blank table for them to fill in if you think that they need this assistance.) A recursive formula is $E(n) = E(n - 1) + (n - 1)$. Students might justify this recursive formula by explaining that to obtain a complete graph on n vertices, they can start with a complete graph on $(n - 1)$ vertices, then add one more vertex and connect that new vertex to the $(n - 1)$ existing vertices, thereby creating $(n - 1)$ new edges. Thus, $E(n) = E(n - 1) + (n - 1)$.

5. This problem guides students through the induction step.

   a. The explicit formula for $E(n - 1)$ is

   $$E(n - 1) = \frac{(n - 1)(n - 2)}{2}.$$

   b. Possible responses to the questions are displayed below. Each response is paired with the mathematical expression that the students must explain.

$E(n - 1) = \dfrac{(n - 1)(n - 2)}{2}$

Students may assume that

$$E(n - 1) = \frac{(n - 1)(n - 2)}{2}$$

because this is the assumption that the statement that they must prove is true for $n - 1$.

$E(n) = E(n - 1) + (n - 1)$

This statement uses the recursive formula from problem 4.

$E(n) = \dfrac{(n - 1)(n - 2)}{2} + (n - 1)$

This statement again uses the assumption that

$$E(n - 1) = \frac{(n - 1)(n - 2)}{2}$$

and substitutes into the preceding equation.

$E(n) = \dfrac{n^2 - 3n + 2}{2} + (n - 1)$

The result of multiplying $(n - 1)(n - 2)$ is $n^2 - 3n + 2$. Of course, students might use other ways to simplify. For example, they might choose to factor out $(n - 1)$ from the previous step, which yields

$$(n - 1)\left(\frac{n - 2}{2} + 1\right).$$

For the remainder of the proof, students carry out the algebraic simplification and explain their work.

6. To prove that the statement is true for the initial value of n, students must prove that it is true for $n = 1$. That is, students must prove that the number of edges in a complete graph on one vertex is

$$\frac{1(1-1)}{2}.$$

They must therefore determine the number of edges in a complete graph on one vertex and then verify that the preceding formula computation yields this number.

a. A complete graph on one vertex clearly has zero edges, which is indeed the result of evaluating

$$\frac{n(n-1)}{2}$$

for $n = 1$.

b. This step is analogous to knocking over the first domino.

7. In this problem, students must first make a conjecture for the explicit formula and then prove it.
   a. $S_1 = 1$, $S_2 = 1 + 3 = 4$, $S_3 = 1 + 3 + 5 = 9$, $S_4 = 1 + 3 + 5 + 7 = 16$. From examining this pattern, students can conjecture that $S_n = n^2$.

   b. As previously indicated, a typical situation involves using a recursive formula to help prove a conjecture about an explicit formula. Specifically, the students use the recursive formula in the induction step of the proof.

Induction Step:
Students must prove that $S_n = n^2$, assuming that $S_{n-1} = (n-1)^2$. To use this assumption, they need to step back to the $(n-1)$ case, so they need a recursive relationship. When they know the recursive relationship, they can lay out the proof as follows:

$$S_n = (\text{expression using } S_{n-1}), \text{ as determined by the recursive relationship}$$
$$= (\text{expression using } (n-1)^2), \text{ because they can assume that } S_{n-1} = (n-1)^2$$
$$= \ldots (\text{as a result of using some algebra}) \ldots$$
$$= n^2.$$

To fill in the details of this proof, students must determine the recursive relationship. Examining the sum indicates that to compute a given sum, they can take the previous sum and add the next odd number. Therefore, the recursive formula is

$$S_n = S_{n-1} + \text{the next odd number}$$
$$= S_{n-1} + (2n - 1).$$

The induction step of the proof follows:

$$S_n = S_{n-1} + (2n - 1)$$
$$= (n-1)^2 + (2n - 1)$$
$$= n^2 - 2n + 1 + 2n - 1$$
$$= n^2.$$

Base Step:
Students must prove that the statement is true for the initial value of n, or $n = 1$. That is, they must prove that the sum of the first n odd numbers, for $n = 1$, is 1^2, so they determine the sum when it includes only the first odd number and then verify that the formula yields this value. The formula clearly yields this value: the sum of the first odd number is 1, and $1^2 = 1$.

Students have then completed the two steps of a proof by mathematical induction, and they can conclude that $S_n = n^2$, for all integers $n \geq 1$.

8. This problem provides a conjecture for the explicit formula, in contrast to the situation in problem 7, so students do not need to make their own conjecture. They do need to determine a recursive formula for the perimeter, since they need that formula in the induction proof. Students may use various methods for determining a recursive formula. One method is the following:

$P_n = $ the perimeter at stage n
$= (\text{number of small dark triangles at stage } n) \times (\text{perimeter of a small triangle at stage } n)$
$= (3 \times \text{number of dark triangles at stage } (n-1)) \times (1/2 \times \text{perimeter of a triangle at stage } (n-1))$
$= 3 \times 1/2 \times (\text{number of dark triangles at stage } (n-1)) \times (\text{perimeter of a triangle at stage } (n-1))$

$= 3/2 \times$ (perimeter at stage $(n-1)$)

$= 3/2 \times P_{n-1}$.

The recursive formula is therefore

$$P_n = \frac{3}{2}P_{n-1}.$$

Induction Step:

$P_n = \frac{3}{2}P_{n-1}$ By using the previously obtained recursive formula

$= \frac{3}{2} \cdot \frac{3^{(n-1)+1}}{2^{n-1}}$ By using the assumption that the statement is true for $n-1$

$= \frac{3}{2} \cdot \frac{3^n}{2^{n-1}}$ By using algebraic simplification

$= \frac{3^{n+1}}{2^n}$ By multiplying by 3/2

Base Step:
Students must show that the perimeter at stage 0 is

$$\frac{3^{0+1}}{2^0} = 3.$$

This statement is clearly true, since computing the perimeter of the figure at stage 0 yields an answer of 3. Thus, students have completed the two steps of a proof by mathematical induction, and they can conclude that

$$P_n = \frac{3^{n+1}}{2^n},$$

for all integers $n \geq 0$.

References

Alper, Lynne, Dan Fendel, Sherry Fraser, and Diane Resek. *Interactive Mathematics Program.* Emeryville, Calif.: Key Curriculum Press, 2003.

Bezuszka, Stanley J., S.J. "Figurate Numbers." *NCTM Student Math Notes.* May 1984.

Burke, Maurice J., Ted Hodgson, Paul Kehle, Pat Mara, and Diane Resek. *Navigating through Mathematical Connections in Grades 9–12. Principles and Standards for School Mathematics* Navigations Series. Reston, Va.: National Council of Teachers of Mathematics, 2006.

Camp, Dane R. "Benoit Mandelbrot: The Euclid of Fractal Geometry." *Mathematics Teacher* 93 (November 2000): 708–12.

Consortium for Mathematics and Its Applications (COMAP). *Mathematics: Modeling Our World.* New York: W. H. Freeman & Co., 1999.

———. *For All Practical Purposes.* 7th ed. New York: W. H. Freeman & Co., 2006.

Coxford, Arthur F., James T. Fey, Christian R. Hirsch, Harold L. Schoen, Gail Burrill, Eric W. Hart, and Ann E. Watkins. *Contemporary Mathematics in Context.* Course 4: Part A, Unit 4. New York: Glencoe McGraw-Hill, 2003.

Crisler, Nancy, and Gary Froelich. *Discrete Mathematics through Applications.* 3rd ed. New York: W. H. Freeman & Co., 2006.

DeBellis, Valerie A., and Joseph G. Rosenstein. *Making Math Engaging: Discrete Mathematics for K–8 Teachers.* Greenville, N.C.: Javelando Publications, 2008.

DeBellis, Valerie A., Joseph G. Rosenstein, Eric W. Hart, and Margaret J. Kenney. *Navigating through Discrete Mathematics in Prekindergarten–Grade 5. Principles and Standards for School Mathematics* Navigations Series. Reston, Va.: NCTM, forthcoming.

Dick, Thomas. "Coloring Maps." *NCTM Student Math Notes.* November 1990.

Dossey, John A. "Discrete Mathematics: The Math for Our Time." In *Discrete Mathematics across the Curriculum K–12*, 1990 Yearbook of the National Council of Teachers of Mathematics (NCTM), edited by Margaret J. Kenney, pp. 1–9. Reston, Va.: NCTM, 1990.

Guillotte, Henry P. "The Method of Finite Differences: Some Applications." *Mathematics Teacher* 79 (September 1986): 466–70.

Hart, Eric W. "Discrete Mathematical Modeling in the Secondary Curriculum: Rationale and Examples from the Core-Plus Mathematics Project." In *Discrete Mathematics in the Schools*, edited by Joseph G. Rosenstein, Deborah S. Franzblau, and Fred S. Roberts, pp. 265–80. Vol. 36, DIMACS Series in Discrete Mathematics and Theoretical Computer Science. Providence, R.I.: American Mathematical Society; Reston, Va.: National Council of Teachers of Mathematics, 1997.

———. "Algorithmic Problem Solving in Discrete Mathematics." In *The Teaching and Learning of Algorithms in School Mathematics*, 1998 Yearbook of the National Council of Teachers of Mathematics (NCTM), edited by Lorna J. Morrow, pp. 251–67. Reston, Va.: NCTM, 1998.

Hirsch, Christian R., James T. Fey, Eric W. Hart, Harold L. Schoen, and Ann E. Watkins, with Beth Ritsema, Rebecca Walker, Sabrina Keller, Robin Marcus, Arthur F. Coxford, and Gail Burrill. *Core-Plus Mathematics.* 2nd ed. Columbus, Ohio: Glencoe McGraw-Hill, 2008.

House, Peggy A., and Roger P. Day, eds. *Mission Mathematics II: Grades 9–12.* Reston, Va.: National Council of Teachers of Mathematics, 2005.

Kenney, Margaret J., ed. *Discrete Mathematics across the Curriculum, K–12.* 1991 Yearbook of the National Council of Teachers of Mathematics (NCTM). Reston, Va.: NCTM, 1991.

Lemon, Patricia. "Pascal's Triangle—Patterns, Paths, and Plinko." *Mathematics Teacher* 90 (April 1997): 270–73.

Mathematical Association of America (MAA). *Report of the Committee on Discrete Mathematics in the First Two Years.* Washington, D.C.: MAA, 1986.

Maurer, Stephen B. "What Is Discrete Mathematics? The Many Answers." In *Discrete Mathematics in the Schools,* edited by Joseph G. Rosenstein, Deborah S. Franzblau, and Fred S. Roberts, pp. 121–32. Vol. 36, DIMACS Series in Discrete Mathematics and Theoretical Computer Science. Providence, R.I.: American Mathematical Society; Reston, Va.: National Council of Teachers of Mathematics, 1997.

National Council of Teachers of Mathematics (NCTM). *Curriculum and Evaluation Standards for School Mathematics.* Reston, Va.: NCTM, 1989.

———. *Discrete Mathematics and the Secondary Mathematics Curriculum.* Reston, Va.: NCTM, 1990.

———. *Principles and Standards for School Mathematics.* Reston, Va.: NCTM, 2000.

———. *Curriculum Focal Points for Prekindergarten through Grade 8 Mathematics: A Quest for Coherence.* Reston, Va.: NCTM, 2006.

National Research Council. *High School Mathematics at Work: Essays and Examples for the Education of All Students.* Washington, D.C.: National Academy Press, 1998.

Peitgen, Heinz-Otto, Hartmut Jürgens, Dietmar Saupe, Evan Maletsky, Terry Perciante, and Lee Yunker. *Fractals for the Classroom: Strategic Activities,* Vol. 1. New York: Springer-Verlag; Reston, Va.: National Council of Teachers of Mathematics, 1991.

———. *Fractals for the Classroom: Strategic Activities,* Vol. 2. New York: Springer-Verlag; Reston, Va.: National Council of Teachers of Mathematics, 1992.

Roberts, Fred S., and Barry Tesman. *Applied Combinatorics.* 2nd ed. Englewood, N.J.: Prentice Hall, 2004.

Rosenstein, Joseph G. "Discrete Mathematics in 21st Century Education: An Opportunity to Retreat from the Rush to Calculus." In *Foundations for the Future in Mathematics Education,* edited by Richard A. Lesh, Eric Hamilton, and James J. Kaput, pp. 214–24. Hillsdale, N.J.: Lawrence Erlbaum Associates, 2007.

Rosenstein, Joseph G., Deborah S. Franzblau, and Fred S. Roberts, eds. *Discrete Mathematics in the Schools,* Vol. 36, DIMACS Series in Discrete Mathematics and Theoretical Computer Science. Providence, R.I.: American Mathematical Society; Reston, Va.: National Council of Teachers of Mathematics, 1997.

Sandefur, James T. *Discrete Dynamical Systems: A Pattern-Discovery Approach to Problem Solving.* New York: Oxford University Press, 1990.

Seymour, Dale, and Margaret Shedd. *Finite Differences: A Pattern-Discovery Approach to Problem Solving.* Palo Alto, Calif.: Dale Seymour Publications, 1973.

Systemic Initiative for Montana Mathematics and Science (SIMMS). *SIMMS Integrated Mathematics: A Modeling Approach Using Technology.* Dubuque, Iowa: Kendall/Hunt Publishing Co., 2006.

Szetela, Walter. "Triangular Numbers in Problem Solving." *Mathematics Teacher* 92 (December 1999): 820–24.

Szydlik, Jennifer Earles. "Photographs and Committees: Activities That Help Students Discover Permutations and Combinations." *Mathematics Teacher* 93 (February 2000): 93–95.

Tannenbaum, Peter. *Excursions in Modern Mathematics.* 6th ed. Upper Saddle River, N.J.: Pearson Prentice Hall, 2007.

Wilson, Robin. *Four Colors Suffice: How the Map Problem Was Solved.* Princeton, N.J.: Princeton University Press, 2002.

Wilson, Robin J., and John J. Watkins. *Graphs: An Introductory Approach—A First Course in Discrete Mathematics.* New York: John Wiley & Sons, 1990.

Suggested Reading

The following three articles appear on the CD-ROM but are not cited in the text:

Biehl, L. Charles. "Massive Graphs, Power Laws, and the World Wide Web." *Mathematics Teacher* 96 (September 2003): 434–39.

Kenney, Margaret J., and Stanley J. Bezuszka. "Implementing the Discrete Mathematics Standard: Focusing on Recursion." *Mathematics Teacher* 86 (November 1993): 676–80.

Nord, Gail, Eric J. Malm, and John Nord. "Counting Pizzas: A Discovery Lesson Using Combinatorics." *Mathematics Teacher* 95 (January 2002): 8–14.

Many sources provide useful discussions of discrete mathematics in the school curriculum. The CD-ROM that accompanies this volume includes "A Bibliography of Print Resources for Discrete Mathematics," which identifies topics and grade levels for all materials.